SOLAR TRILLIONS

SOLAR TRILLIONS

7 MARKET AND INVESTMENT OPPORTUNITIES IN THE EMERGING CLEAN-ENERGY ECONOMY

TONY SEBA

FIRST BETA EDITION V.1.0
(0.99.01.18.10)

TABLE OF CONTENTS

ACKNOWLEDGEMENTS

"Success has many fathers. Failure is an orphan."
—President John F. Kennedy

First I want to thank the founders of Utility Scale Solar, Inc, Peter Childers and Jonathan Blitz. When they first asked me to help them build their solar startup company, none of us knew that it would start this journey. Entrepreneurship and innovation are the cornerstone of economic growth and the USS team has plenty of both. In the end they changed my life as much as I changed theirs. Next, I want to thank all the entrepreneurs, executives, educators, investors, scientists, engineers, and analysts who had the patience to sit with me and share their knowledge, passion, and wisdom. Here is a partial list: Santiago Seage, Valerio Fernandez, Isabel De Haro, Rainer Aringhoff, Ben Shyman, Ari Sargent, Margaret Cooney, Margot Gerritsen, Marco DeMiroz, Gary Zieff, Rajan Kasetty, Janice Cooper, David Arfin, Alexis Ringwald, Jose Luis Cordeiro, Matt LeCar, Andres Wydler, Richard Gill, Marie Hattar, John O'Donnel, Mark Fowler, and Zen Kishimoto.

I stand on the shoulders of numerous giants who have worked to understand energy and make clean energy a reality: Nathan Lewis, Franz Trieb, Daniel Nocera, Mark Jacobson, and many others who did the hardcore energy-science research that underlies this book and paved the way for the analysis it presents. I thank them on my own behalf and on behalf of the world.

I want to thank the students in my Stanford course "Clean Energy—Market and Investment Opportunities," which is based on this book (and vice versa.) I am blessed to be able to teach the innovators and entrepreneurs who are changing the world in a positive direction. I do my best to educate and inspire them, but many times they end up inspiring me: Pete Childers, cofounder of Utility Scale Solar, Inc, is a former student of mine at Stanford. I am hoping that the entrepreneurs taking my new "Clean Energy" course will start many companies like USS and help create wealth, grow the economy, and save the world. I also want to thank Hal Louchheim for giving me the opportunity to teach at Stanford— and therefore to write this book. I have created and taught four different courses at Stanford, and Hal has always been supportive of my efforts.

I want to thank my editor, Adam Cornford. Early reviewers of this book unanimously said two things: 1) it is urgent that the world sees this book; and 2) please find yourself a good editor. Well, I found myself a great editor. Adam poured his heart and soul into the work, he understood my vision and my voice, he had knowledge of the subject matter, and where he didn't have it, he did his research. More than anything, he was deeply committed to the success of the book. I hugely appreciate his help.

I want to thank the staffs at Java Beach Cafe and South Beach Cafe in San Francisco. Their cool and friendly ambiance, great food and (lots of) coffee, and of course free wireless Internet access, provided me with my second (some would say first) office to write this book.

Finally, I wish to thank my friends who have supported me through this rocky year.

"The amount of sunlight that reaches the earth's
surface in an hour contains enough energy
to meet the world's energy needs for a year."
—Susan Hockfield, President, MIT

"I'd put my money on the sun and solar energy.
What a source of power! I hope we don't have
to run out of oil and coal before we tackle that."
—Thomas Edison, 1931

"We live in a society exquisitely dependent
on science and technology, in which hardly anyone
knows anything about science and technology."
—Carl Sagan

CHAPTER 1
MYTHS, SECRETS, AND THE SOLAR INFRASTRUCTURE BOOM

One of the best-kept little secrets in the energy world lies near Kremer Junction, California. Under the searing Mojave desert sun are nine power plants that have been quietly generating solar electricity for more than twenty years. Owned and operated by Florida Power and Light (FPL) and Goldman Sachs, these plants, collectively known as Solar Energy Generating Systems (SEGS), have a capacity of 354 megawatts (MW) and have generated more than 14 terawatt-hour (TWh) of electricity[1], nearly ten times what all San Francisco homes needed during 2007[2].

The SEGS plants produce electricity at a cost of 9-12 cents per kilowatt-hour (¢/kWh), which is about what most Americans pay for electricity, and about the same cost as for power plants that run on natural gas—and much cheaper than those that use diesel or nuclear fuels. When the sun shines, SEGS have plant availability of better than 93%: a figure that "rivals utility-scale power plants of any type."[3] In operation since the mid-1980s, FPL has been improving plant efficiency ever since. According to the US Department of Energy's National Renewable Energy Labs (NREL), the cost of solar energy has gone down about 90% since 1980 will continue to drop for the foreseeable future.

How Can Solar Electricity Be Cheaper than Oil, Natural Gas, or Coal?

Financing a power plant is very much like financing a house: you pay a percentage of the total cost as equity down payment and borrow the rest from banks. When an electricity producer finances the construction costs of a power plant with debt (which is most of the time in market-based economies) a large portion of the cost of producing electricity goes to paying down the capital and interest expenses of building it. The other main components of electricity cost are *fuel* and *operations and maintenance* (O&M).

The energy cost of natural gas fuel varies by the minute, but it was recently around 8 ¢/kWh. The energy cost of coal fuel during the same period was about 5-6 ¢/kWh. Whatever the fuel cost, it is there for the life of the plant—and if it rises, so will the cost to the end user, because the plant operator will pass that cost through.

The sun is a free source of fuel, so the actual cost of producing solar electricity amounts to just O&M. Once the capital investment (the "mortgage" in our analogy) is paid off, the cost of producing solar electricity drops dramatically—and remains low for as long as the plant stays in operation. The total operating costs of a solar plant are about 1 ¢/kWh. This is about 1/10 the cost of the average electricity price in America. It's less than 1/8 the cost of natural gas-generated electricity and less than 1/6 of electricity generated with coal-fired plants. What could this difference in price mean to you?

- The average US household consumes 936 kWh per month. At 1 ¢/kWh, that monthly electricity bill would be $9.36 instead of $99.70.

- A battery-powered car like the Tesla would go 200 miles on about 53 kWh (the equivalent of 8 gallons of gasoline) for about 53 cents.[4]

- Yahoo's data-center power bill could be closer to $10 million than to $100 million.

Both households and businesses, in other words, are looking at savings of a whole order of magnitude—a factor of ten—with solar power.

Furthermore, much of the world pays more for energy than we do in the continental United States. In Europe, the price of residential electricity averaged about 15 ¢/kWh in 2007, compared with about 10.7 ¢/kWh on average in the U.S. (Hawaiians pay more than 30 ¢/kWh.) In the developing world, more than 2 billion people rely on kerosene lamps or on diesel-fuel generators, which can cost $1-$2 per kWh.

Solar electricity cost, reliability, and availability are as good as or better than those of fossil fuel electricity today. This is not what we hear in the media. At the same time, the cost of electricity has gone up and continues to go up. According to the United States Energy Information Agency (EIA), the cost of electricity in America has increased 446% over five decades—from 1.8 ¢/kWh in 1960 to 9.82 ¢/kWh in 2008.

I smell an opportunity.

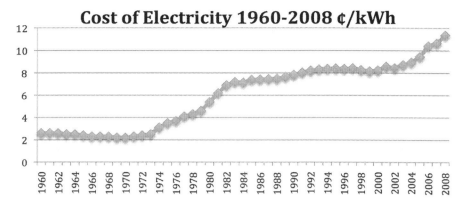

Figure 1.1—Cost of Electricity in the United States (Source: EIA[5])

The Solar Rush Has Already Begun

SEGS plants have generated more than $2.5 billion in revenues for their investors—twice the original investment.

Wall Street investment bank Goldman Sachs recently acquired two of these SEGS plants through its energy subsidiary Cogentrix[6]. Goldman Sachs is not known for its environmentally green investments. It's known for its financially green investments. Goldman is one of the few large investment banks to have survived and even thrived in the recent Wall Street meltdown. In 2008, Goldman was also said to be buying up prime solar-plant land in the Mojave desert in Southern California.

The savviest venture capital funds in Silicon Valley have been quietly shifting their investments away from information technology towards clean energy or "cleantech." During 2008 the cleantech sector became the second largest recipient of VC investments, clocking at $8.4 billion and trailing only health care (biotech and medical devices). Within the cleantech sector, solar attracted 40%—the largest slice of that investment pie.[7] Just seven years earlier, during 2001, VCs invested a grand total of only $5 million in solar companies.

After the Wall Street slump that started in September 2008, project financing for solar plants dried up. Even companies like Brightsource and eSolar, which had raised hundreds of millions of venture funding, were well connected in Wall Street and Washington, and had multibillion-dollar contracts with large utilities to build or provide solar electricity, had trouble finding the capital to build power plants. But while many companies were caught in the credit crunch, Spain's Abengoa Solar quietly broke ground on the largest single solar thermal plant under construction in the United States: a 280-MW plant called Solana. This plant, located in Gila Bend, 60 miles south of Phoenix, AZ, will supply enough power for 70,000 homes. Solana is expected to generate $4 billion dollars in revenues for Abengoa Solar during the life of its 30-year contract with Arizona Public Services APS)[8].

And the revenue isn't the only upside, of course. An equivalent natural gas plant would spew 400,000 tons of carbon dioxide into the air every year. An equivalent coal-fired plant would generate 2 million tons of carbon dioxide, 70,000 tons of ash, 108,000 tons of sludge, 95 pounds of mercury, and 125 pounds of arsenic every year[9]. Year after year after year.

Figure 1.2. Tony Seba with Parabolic Trough solar collector in Seville, Spain
(Photo: Tony Seba)

The technology that SEGS plants have used for two decades and Solana will use to generate all that solar electricity in Arizona is called "parabolic trough." It was developed and first used commercially by American inventor Frank Shuman in 1912. (That's right, 1912!) *This technology has been around for almost a century.* At a time when Egypt was the largest producer of cotton in the world, Shuman engineered, raised financing for, and built a solar power plant in Maadi that pumped 6,000 gallons of Nile river water per minute to irrigate the cotton fields. A quick glance at Shuman's original parabolic trough solar collectors (Fig 1.3) and you realize that they don't look much different from the technology built at SEGS in 1989—or by Abengoa Solar in Seville in 2009 (Fig. 1.2).

Fig 1.3. Shuman's parabolic trough solar plant in Maadi, Egypt ca. 1912.
(Source: *Egyptian Gazette*[10])

Before Shuman went to Egypt, he also considered Florida and California as sites for his first industrial scale solar plant. But he couldn't find the investors to finance the plant or buyers to purchase the power output. In North Africa, he found British investors and power buyers, so he built the plant in Maadi. World War I and the advent of "cheap" coal and oil delayed Shuman's dreams of a solar-powered world. Notice the quotes around "cheap." Fossil fuel is "cheap" on the books only because a lot of its most important costs are left off conventional balance sheets. We'll talk more about those a little later.

The Fossil-Fuel Century

The twentieth century was powered by fossil fuels—mainly oil and coal. Fossil fuels still generate more than 80% of the energy consumed in the United States and 97% of the energy used in transportation. Fossil-fuel sources supply 86% of the world's energy.

Entrepreneurs and investors in fossil-fuel-related industries—extraction, conversion, distribution, services, technology, and applications—made fortunes that were once unimaginable. Fourteen of the 30 companies that made up the blue-chip Dow Jones Industrial Average in 1959 were fossil-fuel-related—companies like Standard Oil, General Motors, General Electric, and Goodyear[11]. Industries that used fossil fuels to power their products, like the auto industry, reaped trillions of dollars in revenues and market capitalization. They were the industrial foundation of the "American Century" of global economic dominance.

As the world shifted from agricultural to industrial economies, the countries that led and won the technology race in fossil fuel-related industries (mainly the United States, Germany, and Japan) built an infrastructure that still permits them to be the most affluent nations in the world. The agricultural sector employed 43.5% of the American population in the year 1900, but by 2000 it generated only 2.5% of total employment.[12] Yet American food production is higher today than it ever was. Countries where most of the population remained agricultural lagged economically in the twentieth century.

For purpose of comparison, the global retail food retail industry is estimated to be worth $3.2 trillion. The world spent about half the money on food that it spent on energy.

2008: The Year the Rules Changed

But the rules of the game are changing. The world is at a new crossroads.

When economic historians look back at 2008 forty years from now, they will probably agree that it was the year that changed global consciousness about energy. Russia held Europe hostage to exports of natural gas (twice), oil prices rose to all-time record levels ($147 per barrel), and war in the Middle East cost America and other net fossil-fuel importing countries trillions of dollars. As energy prices doubled and then tripled, some countries ran out of currency to purchase oil or even basic food staples for their people. The world saw food riots for the first time in a generation.

In a way, this year of change started in December 2007, when former U.S. Vice-President Al Gore received a Nobel Peace Prize for his tireless advocacy of the dangers of global warming. His film *An Inconvenient Truth* received an Oscar for Best Documentary, and the audio version would later win an Emmy award.

The year 2008 ended with the election of Barack Obama to the presidency of the United States. President Obama moved quickly and decisively to support clean energy. He talked about the dangers of global warming in his inaugural address in January 2009 and made clean energy one of his top agenda issues during his first State of the Union address a month later.

The new President announced a goal of 25% of the nation's electricity from renewable energy by 2025 and allocated tens of billions of dollars in his first stimulus package for clean-energy grants and research and development. The Department of Energy alone received a budget in excess of $20 billion to invest in research and development of energy storage, solar, wind, geothermal, and the smart grid. President Obama also signaled that the United States would lead a new round of the Kyoto protocol to cut back on global-warming inducing greenhouse gases to levels below those of 1990. (The Kyoto Agreement had been repudiated by his predecessor in the White House.)

One of the biggest roadblocks to the adoption of solar energy is the bureaucratic process for building a solar power plant in the desert. This can take years of working through the requirements of various Federal and State agencies—or in the case of the

U.S. Bureau of Land Management (BLM), which manages millions of acres of prime desert lands in the Southwest, there had been no process to speak of. New Interior Secretary Ken Salazar promptly announced that the BLM would give high priority to the development of solar energy and would invest money to help do that. He said that the BLM would spend $22 million evaluating about 1,000 square miles of land in the Southwest to find solar-plant-appropriate sites. Generally, "solar-plant-appropriate" means that the sites have high direct normal incidence (DNI) radiation, gentle slopes, nearby transmission lines and roads, and minimal environmental impact. "Salazar estimated that the areas could generate nearly 100,000 MW.[13]"

Meanwhile, the once proud Big Three American auto makers (General Motors, Ford, and Chrysler) teetered on the edge of bankruptcy. During the winter of 2008-9, their share prices sank to penny-stock levels. GM was worth $1 billion, Ford $3.77 billion. Following its sale by Daimler Benz, Chrysler was privately held by an investment group, so no figures were available, but the company was probably worth less than GM. These companies stayed alive only because of tens of billions of taxpayer dollars the U.S. handed them as part of the bailout in early 2009. At that same time, solar photovoltaic market leader First Solar had a valuation of more than $10 billion—equal to or greater than the combined market valuation of the former Big Three.

This perfect storm of events, ideas, and technological progress also showed us that there was a high price to pay to use "cheap" fossil fuel energy sources. When someone says, for example, that coal is cheap, they are not including all the costs that society and taxpayers bear.

On Monday December 22, 2008, an ash dike ruptured at an 84-acre (0.34 km2) solid waste containment area at the Tennessee Valley Authority's Kingston Fossil Plant and spilled 5 million tons of waste coal in the "worst environmental disaster of its kind in American history."[14] The damage to the health of the citizenry in the area, to local and downstream water supplies and the rest of the environment will cost conservatively $1.2 billion.

Yet under the economic rules we have today, these huge cleanup costs are borne by you and me—not by the coal industry. (I'll talk more about this gigantic mess and its implications in the next chapter when we discuss "clean coal.")

Recently the *New York Times* reported that "when government scientists went looking for mercury contamination in fish in 291 streams around the nation, they found it in every fish they tested[15]." Coal-fired power plants are the largest emitters of mercury in the United States. Who pays for that contamination? Who pays for the physical and mental ailments that mercury poisoning causes thousands of people every year, including neurological and developmental damage to infants and young children that will affect their entire future lives? Who pays for the loss of fresh water? *You do.*

I began this chapter by saying that four decades from now, economists will likely look back at 2008 as the moment of change: the symbolic end of the fossil fuel era in America. In a hundred years they and everyone else will also wonder how we ever lived with energy that was so dirty, low-tech, wasteful, and expensive.

We are now paying attention to clean energy sources like solar and wind that are actually cheaper in the long term. The shift to clean energy sources like solar, as suggested by the recent solar investments of Goldman Sachs, is not just smart as an environmentally green move—it's also a financially green one.

The International Energy Agency (IEA) calculates that $45 trillion will need to be invested in alternative energy technology and deployment worldwide over the next 40 years[16]. This is an average of more than $1 trillion per year.

These trillions are up for grabs. American billionaires Ted Turner and T. Boone Pickens wrote that "the global transformation to a clean-energy economy may be the greatest economic opportunity of the twenty-first century."[17] The entrepre-

> *"$45 trillion will need to be invested in alternative energy over the next 40 years."*

neurs, companies, and industries that win this race will gain massive new wealth. The countries that enable these entrepreneurs to lead the new clean energy race will be the winners of the twenty-first century.

Who will take the lion's share of these trillions? Everyone wants into the act—although much of it is just an act in the sense of a pretense—greenwashing. Many companies will redefine their products as "green," "alternative," or "clean" energy. Industry incumbents will work through their lobbies to influence government regulations, budgets, and tax breaks in their direction. Even oil and coal companies say they are "clean" now. But we don't have to believe them—or to act and invest as if we did.

When the rules of the game change, as they did in the early twentieth century, and as they are changing again in the early twenty-first, massive economic, political, and social dislocations are sure to follow. Fossil-fuel incumbents will point to these dislocations as "proof" that solar or other clean energy sources are too expensive. Fear, uncertainty and doubt (FUD) has been successfully used by narrow interest groups to profit from society for generations. But FUD sooner or later loses the argument to reality and material rewards. There's only so long that the past can go on alternately trying to pretend to be the future and trying to scare us about it.

New Energy Rules

The cost of solar energy is expected to be as low as 3.5 ¢/kWh in 2020. That is, the cost of unsubsidized and clean solar power will be lower than the cost of power generated by dirty and subsidized fossil fuels like coal and oil. The economics of solar are undeniably superior.

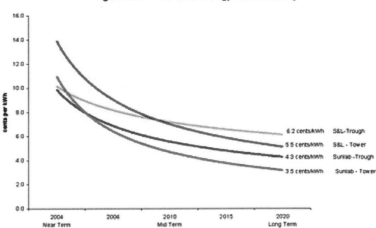

Figure ES-1 — Levelized Energy Cost Summary

Figure 1.4. Cost of Electricity produced by concentrating solar power
CSP methods, parabolic trough and power tower, to 2020.
(Source: Sargent and Lundy[18])

The cost of solar and wind fuel sources is zero. If the world
switches to these sources we won't need to pay for coal, oil, or
gas. We won't need to pay for mining, extracting, transporting,
storing, burning, and then cleaning up the pollution from fossil
fuels.

By switching to clean sources like solar and wind, the
world as a whole will save more than $5 trillion per year in fossil
fuel costs. By switching these sources, the United States would
save more than $1 trillion per year in fuel costs alone. By 2050
this savings could balloon to $2-3
trillion.

The countries that make
the transition to clean energy will
be the powers of the twenty-first
century. They will be able to run
their industry, agriculture, transportation, commerce, and homes
on fuel sources that are essential-

*"By switching to clean
energy sources like
solar and wind the
U.S. would save more
than $1 trillion per
year in fuel costs alone.
By 2050 these savings
could be $2 to $3
trillion per year."*

ly free. As a result, they will have more money in their pockets to invest in their futures.

What could America do with an extra $1 to $3 trillion per year? What could the world do with an extra $3-$6 trillion per year? In America, we could finance universal free health care, social security, education, research, new technology investments, and generally a higher standard of living than we have today. We can also pay down the trillions in debt that is accumulating as we borrow from the international markets to pay for oil imports.

This book guides the reader through some of the big-picture opportunities that could open up as we build the clean energy and solar infrastructure over the next 40 years.

The Present and Future of Energy

The world has an energy infrastructure capacity of about 14 TW (terawatts or trillions of watts) today.

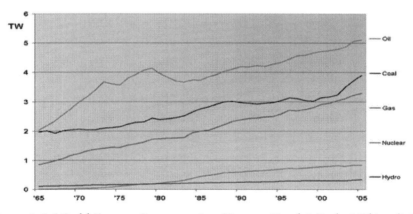

Figure 1.5. World Energy Consumption (Source: Frank Mierlo, Wikipedia[19])

A huge proportion of the existing global energy infrastructure is in need of replacement. According to the United Nations: "…40 percent of the world's power generating capacity has to be replaced in the next 5 to 10 years.[20]" Much of the rest of that capacity will have to be replaced over the next 40 years.

If the world demands energy in 2050 at the rate Americans use energy today, we may need a 102-TW infrastructure. If we use energy at Europe's rate then we will need about 45 TW[21]. Both American and European consumption will rise by 2050, as will much of the world's.

Assuming that all sensible energy and conservation measures are applied—retrofitting older buildings and plants, making all new buildings and plant as efficient as feasible, doing the same with appliances and transportation, fixing obsolete power grids, and so forth—the world is going to conservatively need around 28 to 35 TW by 2050[22]. Note that scientists use ranges rather than specific figures for their forecasts. For simplification purposes, I will use 30 TW as the capacity that the world is going to need in 2050.

This means that the world will need to build more than 14 TW of *replacement* energy capacity *and* 14-16 TW of new energy capacity over the next four decades. Much of this infrastructure will necessarily be based on clean energy sources.

Note: We should not confuse energy and electricity. The United States has a capacity of about 1 TW of electricity today. The world's electrical generating capacity is about 3 TW. The other 11 TW of energy are used mostly for transportation (petroleum for engines) and heating and cooling (oil, natural gas, and biomass for residential, commercial and industrial.)

According to Professor Robert Burgelman, Andrew Grove, and Debra Schiffer of the Stanford Graduate School of Business, the world energy industry had 2007 revenues in excess of $6 trillion[23]. About half that number, $3 trillion, went to the oil industry. That was before oil prices doubled in 2008.

> "*Energy industry revenues in 2007 were $6.3 trillion. That was before oil prices doubled in 2008.*"

Energy Industry Revenue, 2007

Oil:	$3 trillion
Gas and Consumable Fuels:	$2.57 trillion
Coal:	$249 billion
Nuclear:	$200 billion
Total "Renewable": Biofuels/Wind/Solar/ Fuel Cells/Hydroelectric:	$246 billion
Total:	**$6.27 trillion**

Figure 1.6. World Energy Industry Revenues[24]

Energy demand is projected to at least double by 2050. Assuming 1.725% annual growth in energy demand from 2009 to 2050 and assuming 2007 prices, total energy-industry revenues over those four decades add up to a staggering $382 trillion. This is a simple calculation, but it shows the magnitude of what is essentially the largest industry in the world.

> *"Energy industry revenues from 2009 to 2050 add up to $382 trillion."*

Additionally, seven of the top 10 best-paid CEOs in America in 2008 were oil executives, according to the *Corporate Library*. Their average yearly compensation was $127 million[25]. Not bad for a crisis year. It's highly unlikely that they are going to let go of this cash flow easily. The coal, oil, and natural gas lobbies are too wealthy and politically powerful for political leaders and media influencers to resist—though as the financial clout and promise of the cleantech industry grows, that grip will loosen. The fossil-fuel giants will not just go quietly into the sunset.

It is also true that even if it were politically possible, a switch could not take place overnight. The fossil-fuel infrastructure is massive: refineries all over the world, pipelines across all continents, thousands of coal plants, tens of thousands of gas stations. Just as the computer mainframe industry didn't die when the PC stormed into the world, the fossil-fuel energy industry will not disappear. In fact, as energy demand grows, the industry is spending trillions to grow this infrastructure.

For these reasons and others, planning for a clean energy future is still not a clean conversation. So far it has been shaped more by special interest and partisan groups than science and technology data. Substantial scientific and technical research has been done in the area. The United Nations Development Programme, Stanford University, the California Institute of Technology (Caltech), the Massachusetts Institute of Technology MIT), the German Aerospace Institute (DLR), and many other organizations have researched the science and technology of energy and the future of energy for years. However, agricultural and oil lobbies as well as Wall Street have so far had a bigger say on "renewables" than has the scientific community.

So let's assume that the lobbies are too powerful, that the status quo is hard to change, and that the current infrastructure is hard to replace. Let's assume that fossil fuels and nuclear will still generate 14 TW four decades from now. That is, their existing capacity won't increase or decrease. It will remain flat. We will still need to build about 16 TW of new energy capacity by 2050.

More than one source will be needed to build that 16 TW capacity. But what percentage will each source produce? What percentage nuclear? What percentage wind? What percentage geothermal? And what percentage solar?

The scientific research points in a clear direction: solar energy is the biggest hope for a clean energy future. Nothing else even comes close.

But before we get into the choices, let's look at some of the myths about solar.

"The scientific research points to a simple direction: solar energy is the biggest hope for a clean energy future. Nothing else even comes close."

Myths about Solar Energy

Fossil-fuel lobbies and politics aside, the main impediments to solar and clean energy adoption may well be lack of understanding. There are many myths about energy and about new, clean energy technology that need to be dispelled. (The fossil-fuel lobbies are not helping here.)

Let's start with the United States of America, the largest consumer of electricity in the world. In 2007 the U.S. consumed nearly 4 trillion kilowatt-hours (kWh) of electricity.[26] This does *not* include the energy we use to power our cars (oil), cook, or heat our houses in the winter (natural gas).

Yet the deserts in Arizona, Nevada, New Mexico, Southern California, and Texas receive some of the highest levels of direct sunlight radiation (insolation) in the world. According to Caltech Professor David Rutledge, it would take 11,600 square miles of remote desert land to satisfy all the electricity requirements of the United States. This is a square with 108-mile (174 Km) sides. Prof. Rutledge based his calculation on the actual power output of Nevada Solar One, a CSP plant built and operated by Acciona 35 miles Southwest of Las Vegas.

That 108-by-108-mile square of desert land could generate all the electricity the United States needs all year. It would generate electricity to light every single light bulb and air conditioner and microwave oven from Maine to San Diego. Every single refrigerator and television set and laptop computer from Seattle to Miami in use today could be powered *day and night* with solar thermal power produced in 0.1%—one tenth of one per cent—of the desert land in the U.S. Southwest.

Got your attention?

We have literally one of the most important energy resources anywhere and we are not taking advantage of it.

Solar Energy: Some Q&A

As I go around the country on speaking engagements I get many interesting questions, but a few comments and queries seem to recur. These comments and queries reflect both continuing myths about solar power, and also very understandable and reasonable concerns. Here they are.

Question: But isn't that a lot of land?

Answer: Well, yes. But not in relative terms. And there are also the questions of where the land is, what it's good for, and what the environmental issues at stake are. According to the United States House of Representatives, the oil and gas industries lease 47.5 million acres (74,219 square miles) of land from the Bureau of Land Management for extraction purposes. They also lease a further 44 million acres (68,750 mi^2) of offshore space[27]. So the oil and gas industries lease 143,000 square miles from the U.S. government. This is land next to downtown Los Angeles, off the coast of Santa Barbara, and in pristine and ecologically fragile areas of Alaska. (This does not include the land that they own themselves or lease from third parties.) All this public land and water space—143,000 square miles—is used to generate about one third of U.S. oil consumption. Despite the massive land giveaway, we're more dependent on oil imports today than we were three decades ago—and we're paying much more for each barrel.

> *"To generate all of America's electricity needs Solar would need less than one-tenth of the land space requirement that the oil and gas industries use today."*

Solar power, by contrast, would need less than one-tenth (8.1% to be exact) of the land space requirement of the oil and gas industries to generate all our electricity needs. *Solar* would have no need to drill off the coast of Santa Barbara or the pristine lands of Alaska. Furthermore, these figures are based on existing technology. *Solar* is improving its cost/performance by 20% per year and is expected to continue to do so for the foreseeable future.

Question: What do we do in the evening?

Answer: A simple thermal energy-storage technology is used to store energy generated by solar plants during the day and then release it as electricity later in the evening—when electricity demand peaks. This technology is called "molten-salt energy storage" and uses naturally occurring sodium and potassium nitrate salts to store the heat energy in the evening. (More on energy storage in Chapter 8.)

Molten-salt storage has the opposite battery cycle to that of your cell phone. You charge your phone battery during the evening so you can use it during the day. The sun charges the salt battery during the day and the plant releases the energy at night—so you can charge your cell phone.

The 50 MW Andasol-1 solar plant near Granada, Spain has a 7.5 hour "battery" so it can store the heat from the afternoon sun and generate the electricity right when folks get back home and switch on those air conditioners at 7 pm., watch TV at 9 pm., or email at 11 pm. The 280 MW Solana plant in Arizona will also have a 7-hour salt battery. The Gemasolar plant in Spain will have a 15-hour salt battery.

Solar round the clock. Gemasolar will probably be the first solar plant in the world able to generate electricity 24/7.

Question: What do we do in New York? It's a long way from Phoenix—won't all that electricity be lost in the transmission lines?

Answer: Our existing transmission infrastructure is crumbling. It was built nearly a century ago to power Edison's light bulbs, and now it has to power Google's Wal-Mart-size computer data centers. We need to build a new transmission grid if we are to remain a world-class industrial and economic power. How?

There is new transmission technology called High Voltage Direct Current (HVDC) that loses just 3% of power every 620 miles (1,000 km.) This type of transmission line already operates between China's Three Gorges Dam and the industrial centers of Shanghai and Guangdong. The Guangdong link runs a distance of 975 Km (606 miles) and was built in 32 months[28]. (More on the transmission grid in Chapter 9.)

The distance from Phoenix to NYC is 3,500 km. (2,200 miles), which would mean a transmission loss of just about 11% from a solar plant in Arizona to a consumer in New York City.

Question: But aren't solar panels expensive?

Answer: There is a set of technologies for collecting and harvesting solar energy that does not use PV panels to generate power. These technologies are collectively called Solar Thermal or Concentrating Solar Power (CSP). CSP collectors are made of mirrors, steel, cement, and aluminum—not very high-tech—though the twenty-first century versions of the technology add sophisticated computer software to make the collectors track the sun for maximum energy yield throughout the day. CSP generators use basically the same steam turbines that are found in gas or coal plants today. No technology breakthroughs needed there.

By the early 1990s, about 90% of all the solar electricity generated in the world came from concentrating solar power in the desert rather than from photovoltaic panels. Though this percentage has dropped and will continue to change as the distributed nature of solar energy adoption plays out, it is likely that a large portion of the generation of solar energy will continue to come from utility-scale CSP plants.

According to the Solar Electric Power Association (SEPA), the top utilities in the United States had announced 7,521 megawatts-worth of solar projects as of mid-2009. Concentrating Solar Power (CSP) represented 5,042 MW (67%), while solar photovoltaics amounted to 2,379 MW (33%)[29]. Granted, these numbers apply only to the largest utilities in the country and don't include the many independent residential and commercial PV installations. The point is that the media conversation about solar has been about photovoltaics, not about the whole of solar. Concentrating Solar Power has been largely ignored in the public conversation so far, but is actually the leading mechanism in solar energy, especially on a large scale that can move the needle relatively quickly.

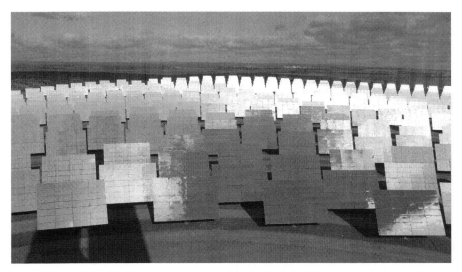

Figure 1.7. The PS10 heliostat field has nearly 75,000 m² (800,000 ft²) of mirrors. Not one solar photovoltaic panel. (Photo: Tony Seba)

Question: *How about other sources of clean energy? How about wind, geothermal, ocean waves, and others?*

Answer: Glad you asked, because we have choices to make right now. Just as there are myths, lies, and misunderstandings about solar, there are even more about the whole "renewable," "sustainable," or "clean" energy space.

Let's look at the real choices.

"There is nothing more difficult to take in hand,
more perilous to conduct, or more uncertain
in its success than to take the lead in the
introduction of a new order of things"
—Jean-Jacques Rousseau

"We choose to go to the moon. Not because it's easy
but because it's hard. Because that challenge is one
that we are willing to accept, one we are unwilling
to postpone, and one which we intend to win"
—John F. Kennedy

"An age is called dark, not because the light fails
to shine but because people refuse to see it."
—James Michener

CHAPTER 2
MAKING THE ENERGY CHOICE: RENEWABLE AND CLEAN ENERGY ALTERNATIVES

The July 8, 2009 issue of the *Wall Street Journal* had the usual *Sturm und Drang* about the financial markets and the recession. While this newspaper generally complains about Democratic government spending, an opinion piece complained about cost-cutting measures—specifically questioning why the Obama administration was pulling the government's $1.9 billion subsidy to oil and gas drilling. I suppose subsidies are OK as long as they're for your favorite industries. Nothing new there.

A 6-column article on page 4 caught my attention: "Wood Pellets Catch Fire as Renewable Energy Source."[30] Wood pellets?

To make wood pellets, trees are "cut up in a wood chipper, dried, and hammered into a powder, which is formed into pellets under very high pressure." Countries like Vietnam, South Africa, and Argentina are exporting pellets—which are now a global commodity traded on an Amsterdam energy exchange[31].

Since when does deforestation qualify as "renewable"? What would happen if we totally clear-cut rainforests in Brazil, Indonesia, and Malaysia? Would they "renew" themselves? Is the Amazon renewable? Is the Pacific Northwest renewable? What is "renewable energy" anyway? This term gets bandied about as if there were an accepted meaning. In fact, sometimes you feel like it comes from the marketing departments of lobbies and interest groups who are looking for yet another government handout or tax break and advantageous laws, rules, and regulations for their industrial clients.

Some sources of energy that generate more carbon dioxide and consume far more resources than "dirty" oil get "renewable" subsidies. It also seems that dirty fossil-fuel industries will get billions if they promise to maybe, kind of, sort of say they will be a tiny bit cleaner ten or twenty years from now. Wink, wink.

But, as Nobel-prize-winning physicist Richard Feynman said: "You can fool yourself, but you can't fool Nature."

The life of a coal or nuclear plant is about 40 years. Every coal and nuclear plant that we build today will be with us for 40 years. Maybe more. Our children and their children will live with the consequences of our choices. And energy is a global industry with global impact. Children in San Francisco and Sydney will live with the consequences of coal plants opening in China today. Children in Texas and Brazil will live with the choices we make when we grow millions of acres of corn to produce ethanol in the American Midwest or the Amazon Basin.

So to make the kinds of decisions we need to make as a society, we should take a look at the world energy picture in 40 years: 2050. This chapter is a beginning.

To start the scenario process, I looked at the best and most up-to-date scientific information. I built on the models, data, and studies that our top universities and research institutions have provided, including:

- decision frameworks created by world-renowned energy scientists Prof. Nathan Lewis at the California Institute of Technology (Caltech) and Prof. Daniel Nocera at the Massachusetts Institute of Technology (MIT);

- the work of Stanford's Prof. Mark Jacobson;

- models developed by Dr. Franz Trieb and others at the German Aerospace Center (DLR) as well as by Dr. Gerhard Knies and others at Desertec;

- the copious data accumulated by the U.S. Department of Energy over the last few decades.

I have also created a simple decision model to look at clean energy choices, starting with one straightforward Big Question and then establishing three criteria for a checklist for each potential source.

The Big Question

The Big Question in this chapter is this: what clean energy sources can realistically add up to 16 terawatts (TW) by 2050? Let's talk about units of electric power for a moment. One watt is the amount of power generated by one ampere of current flowing with a potential of one volt. Now we scale up:

Unit	Quantity	Abbreviation
kilowatt	one thousand (10^3) watts	kW
megawatt	one million (10^6) watts	MW
gigawatt	one billion (10^9) watts	GW
terawatt	one trillion (10^{12}) watts	TW

In 2050 the world will need from 28 TW to 35 TW of energy—up from 14 TW today. That's between 28 and 35 *trillion watts*.

This forecast range, what's more, assumes that the world is going to invest in energy efficiency. As in any prediction, there is not one figure but a range of figures that will depend on our choices: how we eat, what we buy, how efficiently we use power, and so on. If we *don't* increase our energy efficiency, the number in 2050 might well rise to 102 TW—an unsustainably large number given any mix of energy sources now known.

I have gone through a very simple exercise to find out what our clean energy choices are. Precision to the nth degree was not the goal. It was rather to use available scientific data and technological information to build a simple framework that approximates reality and can help us make better choices.

For the purposes of this exercise I assume the following:

- The world will need 30 TW energy capacity—a midrange figure between 28 and 35 TW. I assume that we're not going to substantially run out of oil, gas, or coal in 40 years.

- Today's $6-$7 trillion energy industry, composed mostly of fossil fuels like oil, coal, and gas—with some nuclear and hydro thrown in—is not going away.

- Therefore the first 14 TW of energy are going to come from a mix similar to what we have today: oil, coal, gas, nuclear, and hydro.

- The net increase in energy from now on will be clean energy. That is, new oil, coal, or gas plants are only built to replace similar-sized oil, coal and gas plants.

- That means the additional 16 TW of energy capacity that the planet needs to develop over the next 40 year will be from clean energy.

None of this should be understood as advocacy or even signify that I like this scenario. This is just a starting point for a thought exercise to help us make better decisions. We can develop finer approximations later.

Calculating Real Cost: Freeloading and "Externalities"

A key issue that must be considered in cost calculations is that of freeloading.

Our society has not been very good at pricing or protecting some of our most precious resources—such as air and water. As a result, many companies and industries have assumed that air and water are "free" resources and have exploited it accordingly. Our air has been a "free" sink. Therefore whole industries spew toxic waste like CO_2 and NO_x into our air as if they can do it forever without paying the cost. Economists call these environmental costs "externalities" and leave it at that.

Our forests have been essentially "free." Need pellets? Just take the bulldozer to the Amazon forest and chop up the trees. Need billions of cubic meters of water to produce ethanol? The Ogallala Aquifer is "free"—buy the land above this vast freshwater ocean and you get the water for free. The River Amazon is "free." Just pump the water. Need to get rid of mercury pollution? Just dump it in the river. While the costs of the forest, water, air and other such resources are material to society, they barely figure when calculating the cost of producing energy.

As we run out of water, this calculus is changing. Witness South Australia, where they have been in a water crisis for years, or Texas, which is going through one as I write. Water suddenly becomes the precious resource that it is. (See Chapter 8.)

However you feel about water, what is crystal clear is that the practice of freeloading on society's resources is not sustainable. The overuse of water for bioenergy, for instance, will ultimately lead us into a water crisis. *It's a matter of when, not if.* The practice of dumping air-bound toxic waste has been thoroughly covered in the pollution control and climate change literature, so I won't go over it again here. What that literature tells us is that overuse of our atmosphere as a dumping ground for carbon dioxide, methane, nitrogen oxides, sulfur oxides, and other pollutants is already coming back to bite us.

These practices are just not sustainable. Unsustainable means they can't last forever. You may take short-term shortcuts. But in the long term, you just can't fool Mother Nature.

Three Criteria for Clean, Sustainable Energy: The Checklist

To help me think about what would be adequate sources of clean energy, I examined each potential source with an eye to three key criteria:

1. Is this source of energy clean and sustainable?

Clean means that the source produces no significant airborne waste by-products like carbon dioxide, sulfur dioxide, nitrous oxide or the like; no solid toxic waste like coal ash, mercury, plutonium, or thorium to pollute our lands and rivers—or to bury for future generations to clean up. In economist-speak, it produces no significant pollution externalities. Sustainable means that you can do what you're doing for hundreds of years—pick a number: 500 years or 1,000 years. Can we keep pumping oil or mining coal and polluting the environment the way we've been doing for 500 more years? Can we pump all the water we want to grow biofuels for 500 years? If the answer is no, then it's *not sustainable*. Will the sun be shining and the wind blowing in 500 years? You'd better believe it!

2. Is this source of energy scalable?

The energy source should *scale to terawatts of capacity and multi-terawatt-hours of yearly production.* And, as Criterion 1, indicates, it should do so cleanly and sustainably—without consuming excessive resources, without producing "externalities," without freeloading on society's resources like water, air, or forests or agricultural land.

3. Is this source of energy financially viable?

If you were to start building a new power plant this year using this source, *would it be financially viable?* For mature industries (like nuclear), is this energy financially viable today? If it's an earlier-stage industry (wind, solar), will it be financially viable when it matures? This assumes both that "externalities" are priced into the cost and that neither one receives massive government subsidies, favorable laws, rules and regulations, or accounting preferences. Externalities here include the full human costs, pollution costs, and other societal and environmental costs that the industry has not been paying for. The key index for financial viability in the electric power industry today, however, is the levelized cost of electricity (LCOE). LCOE is the accounting cost of producing the electricity. It includes the cost of equipment and services (including operations and maintenance), but also the cost of the capital and interest payments. And, of course, the cost of *fuel*.

Given these criteria, the answers to nearly every other energy question would follow right out of the answer to the Big Question. For instance,

- How do we allocate clean energy research and development money today?

- Which clean energy industry should we encourage?

- What kind of clean energy career should I (or my kids in college) pursue?

- Should the country invest in biofuels or wind? Geothermal or solar?

- Where should I focus *my* entrepreneurial efforts? Where should I invest?

I looked at the following choices:

1. *Wind*
2. *Geothermal*
3. *Hydroelectric*
4. *Biofuels*
5. *"Green" Nuclear*
6. *"Clean" Coal*
7. *Solar*

If the 16 TW clean energy total were a pie, which slices would go to each one of these choices? Let's do the numbers.

Choice 1: Wind Energy

Wind is cheap, abundant, and clean.

In 2007, Denmark's energy capacity was almost 20% wind-based, with Spain coming in at 10% and Germany at 7%.[32] Wind-power capacity clocked in at 121 GW worldwide and was growing at about 25% per year[33].

All the elements to make wind a "world power" are there: it is a clean source, it is getting cheaper, it is well understood, and most importantly, it has wide institutional support. Governments, NGOs, educational and research institutions, banks, and utilities understand wind and have adopted the idea of wind as an important energy source.

The cost of wind capacity has been steadily dropping since European countries committed to developing this technology and deploying it widely in the early 1990s.

Wind - World Total Installed Capacity (MW)

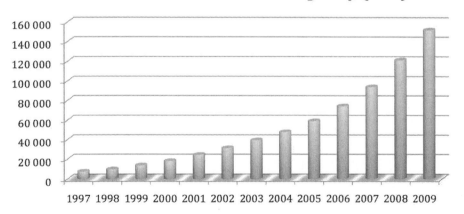

Figure 2.1. World wind energy capacity and projected growth.
(Source: World Wind Energy Association.)

Checklist: Is Wind Clean?

Wind is as clean, literally, as a whistle. No one disputes that. Wind energy produces no carbon dioxide, nuclear radiation, coal ash, or any other form of toxic waste. Nor does it use water in the production of energy.

Some of the main complaints about wind have centered on the noise that blades make, the killing of birds by the blades, and the "unsightly" visual aspect of wind farms, especially on the highly visible ridges and hills where they are best sited for energy generation.

But look again. Wind would in fact save not just birds but also human lives. According to Stanford Professor Mark Jacobson: "If the world were powered on wind, bird loss would be less than 15 percent of the 50 million lost annually from U.S. communication towers alone and would be offset by 800,000 human lives saved by eliminating fossil fuels."[34]

Checklist: Is Wind financially viable?

Wind electricity is one of the cheapest forms of electricity today.

Clocking in at just under 5 ¢/kWh, wind is already cheaper than natural gas and is near parity with coal-produced electricity. Certainly the cost depends on several factors like the size of the wind turbine, the wind speed, and the capacity factor (number of hours of operation.) But it's doing well in these areas. Wind is one of the biggest financial success stories in the clean energy world.

Checklist: Can Wind Scale?

The World Wind Energy Association forecasts an installed capacity of 1.5 TW by 2020[35]. Can wind achieve that even by 2050? Data suggest that there is an upper limit to what we can get out of wind. But first, a basic wind turbine primer.

How do you decide whether to invest in a wind turbine or a wind farm? You bring in an expert to look at the "Wind Power Class" and "Wind Power Density" in your area. Wind is divided into 7 classes, depending on how fast it blows at a certain height. You need that to calculate its power density, which is measured in Watts per square meter (W/m^2).

Today class 4 winds (and higher) are preferred for large-scale grid-connected wind turbines. Class 4 winds blow at an annual average of 5.6 to 6.0 meters per second (12.5 to 13.4 miles per hour) at a height of at least 10 meters (about 30 feet) and generate 400 to 500 W/m^2. However, to get sustainable wind energy production you can erect that wind turbine even at a class 3 site, with wind blowing at 5.1 meters per second (12 miles per hour) or more at a height of 10 meters or greater[36].

If every site on the globe with class 3 winds or greater were occupied with wind turbines (regardless of transmission lines) they would help the world generate about 2.1 TW of energy, according to Caltech Prof. Nathan Lewis and MIT Prof. Daniel Nocera. So wind can grow to terawatt-scale, which means it can make a major contribution to the world's clean energy infrastructure.

However, the sky is *not* the limit for wind. The theoretical limit is about 2.1 TW; and the realistic limit is likely much less than that, since the estimate doesn't take into account transmission lines to all those spread-out, remotely located wind turbines.

What if we improve technology? Wind blows harder at higher altitudes. What if we made taller wind turbines that took advantage of the stronger winds?

In fact, larger wind turbines are being manufactured to do exactly this. A modern 2.5-MW wind power plant stands at 80 meters (240 feet), which is 50% taller than the Statue of Liberty; the blades are 48.7 meters (150 feet) long and have a wingspan larger than that of a Boeing 747-400; and the interior is so roomy that it can hold a 2-person elevator with plenty of room to spare[37].

The problem is that the larger the wingspan of the wind blades, the wider the area that they sweep. The blades on a 2.5

MW plant like the one described above can sweep an area of 7,845 m² (1.94 acres), so you need a larger area to site it in. The maximum energy capacity per area covered (the wind density) does not increase.

Wind power is cheap. Wind power is clean. Wind is scalable—to a *theoretical* maximum of 2.1 TW. I like wind energy. We should invest accordingly.

Choice 2: Geothermal

Geothermal energy comes from water superheated to steam underground by the heat from volcanism (upthrusts of molten or semi-molten rock) in the earth's interior. It has become an essential source of energy in "hotspots" around the world, like Iceland, New Zealand, and California.

In 2006, geothermal energy generated 26% of Iceland's electricity needs and met the heating and hot water requirements of 87% of that nation's buildings.[38] The largest geothermal power plant complex in the world, however, is located about 72 miles north of San Francisco. Owned and operated by Calpine, The Geysers is a 30-square-mile, 22-power-plant complex with a capacity of 725 MW—enough to power a city the size of San Francisco.[39]

Geothermal is one of the great hopes of the "renewable" energy community. As such it has received much support from the government and investors. As we embark on the quest to build a clean energy future, geothermal has a seat at the table. How large is that seat?

Checklist: Is Geothermal clean?

The Geysers started operating commercially with 11 MW in 1960 and has grown by a factor of more than 60 since then.

The electric utilities like this form of energy in part because it can generate "baseload" electricity. Baseload is utility-speak for a "controllable," always-on type of energy source. Power from the Geysers is available 97% of the time.

In a way, geothermal is not "sustainable." Just like oil, underground sources of water are not infinite. The Geysers actually started running out of water and had to develop new technology to literally "pump up the volume." They borrowed technology from the oil industry and started drilling holes to pump water into the earth. This water would be superheated and come out of another pipe in the form of steam—which would run a turbine and generate electricity. In a stroke of smarts, The Geysers management used "recycled" water from the nearby town of Sonoma instead of fresh water. But the water for geothermal power still did not come from the original underground locations.

Another potential problem with geothermal is that the steam may bring toxic metals such as mercury from underground. If these metals are not properly cleaned up, they can also pollute the environment. However, "there is practically no chance for contamination of surface facilities or the surrounding area by the discharge of solids per se from the geofluid" according to the MIT "Future of Geothermal" report[40].

Steam may also bring up some carbon dioxide, but not much. "Geothermal fields can produce about one-sixth of the carbon dioxide that a relatively clean natural-gas-fueled power plant produces, and very little if any, of the nitrous oxide or sulfur-bearing gases.[41]" However, binary plants, which are "closed cycle" operations, release essentially no emissions.

So geothermal is indeed clean.

Checklist: Is Geothermal financially viable?

According to the U.S. Department of Energy's Geothermal Energy Program, The Geysers sells electricity at 3 to 5 ¢/kWh[42]. According to the Alameda Municipal Power Company, geothermal electricity costs 5-8 ¢/kWh[43]. This is in the same range as coal and natural gas.

The capital costs of installing a new geo plant depend on the size, but it's likely between $2.50 and $5 per watt (compared to $4-$6 for solar thermal and $8-$12 for nuclear.)

Checklist: Can Geothermal scale?

A 2006 MIT study called "The Future of Geothermal" found that the U.S. could generate 0.1 TW through geothermal by 2050[44].

That figure sure looks low. Our planet is a boiling cauldron surrounded by a thin layer of earth-crust and water and an even thinner layer of oxygen and nitrogen. Can't we develop new sources of geothermal energy to tap into that cauldron?

There is research in an area called Enhanced Geothermal Systems (EGS) that again borrows technology from the oil industry to dig several miles deep into the earth's crust. The difference between EGS and conventional geothermal is that EGS locates hot rocks in order to cause fractures in those rocks. It then injects water into the fractures to be superheated and come back up as steam. This steam could be used to run a turbine and generate electricity—just like The Geysers.

Some advocates hope that EGS could make geothermal as big as wind is. However, fracturing deep-underground hot rocks is essentially the same thing as purposely causing earthquakes—which makes many of us who live in seismically unstable areas like the San Francisco Bay Area a little nervous.

According to Prof. Nathan Lewis, if we were to use every single square foot of landmass in the world just for Geothermal production and we were to sink a 15-km (9-mile) geothermal pipe on all the landmass in the world we would get about 11 TW. That assumes we had 100% efficient heat engines and left no room for houses, farms, industry, schools or anything other than geothermal plants[45].

There are, however, simple ways to use geothermal energy to heat buildings in the winter and keep them cooler in the summer: heat pumps. This could be a tremendous energy-saving device.

Knowing what we know, we can say that geothermal is not scalable. America could reach 0.1 TW and the world 0.15 TW by 2050. Will new technologies like EGS help scale to terawatts in the future? Probably not, but it may be too early to tell.

Choice 3: Hydro

Water and energy have had a long history together—one that I come back to in Chapter 7. The Egyptians and the Greeks built wheels to turn flowing water into energy to grind grain into flour. The Romans used paddle wheels to lift water far above the river flow so that it could be transported kilometers away[46].

Modern hydroelectric power started in 1896. When electric-power genius Nikola Tesla first harnessed the mechanical energy of falling water at Niagara Falls, he completed one of history's greatest engineering achievements—and kicked off a rush to build dams.

By 2006, hydro represented about 7% of US electricity generation.

Checklist: Is Hydro power clean?

When hydro dams are first built, they can cause serious damage that many of us may not be aware of. As an article in *New Scientist*[47] explains: "This is because large amounts of carbon tied up in trees and other plants are released when the reservoir is initially flooded and the plants rot. Then after this first pulse of decay, plant matter settling on the reservoir's bottom decomposes without oxygen, resulting in a build-up of dissolved methane. This is released into the atmosphere when water passes through the dam's turbines." Certainly, though, this is nothing like the hundreds of millions of tons of greenhouse gases that coal produces.

A hydro plant also changes the downstream environment permanently. For instance, sediment becomes trapped behind the dam and thus cannot bring nutrition to animal and plant life downstream. This trapping of sediment also means that agricultural production that may have used the river's own nutrition has to purchase fertilizers. This increases energy demand and fossil fuel demand (like natural gas) to produce the fertilizers. The buildup of silt behind dams also causes them to lose efficiency as flow through the dam is more and more impeded by the sediment.

So hydro electric power generation is relatively clean, but not without environmental consequences—or human-rights ones, as we shall see.

Checklist: Is Hydro financially viable?

The cost of hydro electricity depends on the size of the plant and the assumptions that go into the calculations. A study of 6 relatively small hydro plants in Hawaii, for example, found a LOC of 5.8 ¢/kWh to 8.6 ¢/kWh[48].

According to the Energy Information Administration (EIA), the levelized cost of electricity from a new hydroelectric plant entering service in 2016, including transmission, would be on the order of 11.4 ¢/kWh[49]. This figure is probably higher than you would expect for hydro. However, as the next point implies, the era of "cheap" hydro may be over.

A major issue with hydro is that of human resettlements. It is estimated that 40 to 80 million people were displaced in the process of building hydro plants in the twentieth century. It is also believed that "most of these people never regained their former livelihoods."[50]

"40 to 80 million people were displaced in the process of building hydro plants in the twentieth century."

A *negative externality* is a real cost that is not reflected in the product offered—mostly because that cost is born by society (or at least a segment of society.) As sad at it sounds, human resettlement has been considered an "externality" when building hydro plants. When accountants at these dams calculate the cost of electricity, they use the investment that went into the dam and the plant. But how do you calculate the cost of displacing and relocating millions of people? How do you calculate the human loss? How do you calculate the loss of history and artifacts? The human cost of resettling millions of people to build a hydro dam is one that most societies will not be willing to bear in the twenty-first century.

To be fair, hydro dams may provide a benefit to society that is not accounted for in the levelized cost of electricity. Dams can act as water storage systems. This water can be used for irrigation, urban, or industrial water distribution. Dams also act as flood control mechanisms.

Checklist: Can Hydro scale?

According to the United States Geological Services (USGS) "most of the good spots to locate hydro plants have already been taken."[51]

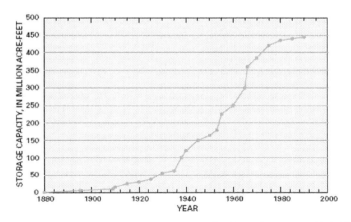

Figure 2.3. Reservoir construction in the U.S. (Source: USGS[52])

During the twentieth century hydroelectric power had many enablers:

- Relatively "easy" rivers to tap.

- Massive political encouragement from both governments and NGOs like the World Bank.

- Relatively easy financing from governments and NGOs.

- Easy regulatory framework to take over the lands, water, and build the dams.

- Smaller populations to be displaced, industry, and property around these prime hydro sites.

- Tolerance for removing and "resettling" millions of people.

- Little knowledge of (or care about) the environmental effects.

- Fewer perceived gigawatt-size generation alternatives.

After a century of furious construction in the "easy" rivers, with all possible enablers, the world built a capacity of 0.7 TW.

How much can the world build with none of the above enablers to hydro power? What can we possibly build in less energy-efficient rivers, with a higher cost of displacing populations, industry, and ecosystems; without the encouragement and easy financing provided by the World Bank and other international development agencies? Can we build in four decades under less-than-ideal conditions what took a century under "ideal" conditions?

According to Caltech Professor Nathan Lewis, the total capacity of all the rivers in all the world is about 3 TW. This includes the Charles River in Boston and the Seine in Paris. The world may have about 1.5 TW of "technically feasible" hydro power left.

But none of the hydro enablers in the twentieth century is there anymore. There are very few "easy" rivers left. Society won't tolerate the resettlement of millions of people to build a hydro dam any time governments feel like it. Even when they do, the costs of doing so may make hydro financially infeasible.

Can we even develop half the capacity that we built in the twentieth century? For scenario planning let's say we will build that: 0.35 TW. But I seriously doubt it. Easy hydro is over.

Choice 4: Bio Energy

As we run out of energy to power our cars, commerce, and industry, some have advocated the use of bio energy on an industrial scale to produce fuels. Biofuels like ethanol and biomass like wood pellets have been supported by governments around the world as forms of "renewable" energy and as way to substitute for oil and coal and achieve energy independence.

Bio energy is a form of solar power. Just as solar photovoltaic panels convert solar energy into electricity, green plants convert solar energy into biomass that releases the energy.

But is bio energy clean? And can it scale?

Checklist: Are biofuels and biomass clean?

Biomass and biofuels are inefficient and dirty ways to convert sunlight into power. Corn ethanol, to take America's favorite biofuel, pollutes more than gasoline.

Science magazine reports that when taking into account land use change, not only does ethanol not save on the CO_2 emissions—it almost doubles them.[53] Biofuels may emit 90% more carbon dioxide than gasoline on a per-mile basis!

According to *Scientific American*, biofuels use up to 20 times the water that gasoline production does per car mile when taking into account the production lifecycle—from irrigating crops to pumping at the biogas station.[54] Biofuel production also contributes to soil erosion, deforestation, and other types of pollution like pesticide and fertilizer runoff.

What about development of cellulosic ethanol as a way to increase the efficiency of biofuels? Proponents of biofuels point to switchgrass as a better plant to produce ethanol. Switchgrass is in fact more efficient than corn but still a poor energy production mechanism—and still emits 50% more CO_2 than gasoline when taking into account the production lifecycle[55]. The production of switchgrass ethanol produces climate-altering pollutants like sulfur dioxide (SO_2) and nitrogen oxides (NO_x). Plus, of course, switchgrass plantations still consume massive amounts of water, fertilizers, and pesticide and need gasoline throughout the whole production process.

The problem with trying to use biofuels is that biology is inherently inefficient at energy production. Green plants convert solar energy into biomass with a yearly efficiency average of less than 0.3%. Furthermore, to convert this little sunlight into energy, plants need to consume other resources like water, land, and fertilizer nutrients. By contrast, solar photovoltaic panels convert about 14-15% of the sunlight (50 times better than bio) without the need for water, fertilizers, pesticides, or the prime agricultural land! And it's improving fast. Solar CSP can convert around 30% and up to 80% if we combine heat and power.

> *"Green plants convert solar energy with a 0.3% efficiency. Solar PV panels convert 14%—without the need for water, fertilizers, and pesticides.*
> *Solar CSP can convert up to 80%."*

Biology is designed for fuel consumption, not fuel production. It's that simple.

Can we engineer plants and algae for fuel production? Sure. But if the history of genetically modified foods is any indication, bioengineered life will require orders of magnitude more resources like water, fertilizers, and pesticides in the production process. So we'll just be creating even more pollution.

Checklist: Is bio energy financially viable?

Given how inefficient green plants are at producing energy, it should not come as a surprise that biofuels are not financially viable. What may be surprising is that biofuels are energy-negative—that is, it takes more energy to produce biofuels than the energy you can get out of them.

Professors David Pimentel of Cornell University and Tad W. Patzek of the University of California at Berkeley studied the economics of bio energy and concluded: "Energy outputs from ethanol produced using corn, switchgrass, and wood biomass were each less than the respective fossil energy inputs. The same was true for producing biodiesel using soybeans and sunfower."[56] "There is just no energy benefit to using plant biomass for liquid fuel," says David Pimentel. "These strategies are not sustainable."

In terms of energy output compared with energy input for ethanol production, the Cornell/Berkeley study found that:

- Corn requires 29% more fossil energy than the fuel produced,

- Switchgrass requires 45% more fossil energy than the fuel produced; and

- Wood biomass requires 57% more fossil energy than the fuel produced.

Is this a reason why oil companies have been investing in biofuel companies? It's a nice, large protected market for fossil fuels!

So biofuels from biomass are making us more (not less) dependent on imported fossil fuels; they are producing more (not less) CO_2 and other pollutants; they consume more (not less) water in the production process than gasoline does; and they consume some of our best agricultural land making our food more expensive.

Checklist: Can biofuels and biomass scale?

Biofuels lose energy (and money) with every gallon produced. Can they make it up in volume?

It would take up to 35% of the United States landmass growing switchgrass to produce just enough E85 ethanol to cover all U.S. on-road vehicles, according to Stanford Professor Mark Jacobson[57]. That's about three times the size of California.

The water needed to run this vast agricultural empire would probably double the current consumption in the U.S. How long will our great Ogallala freshwater ocean last under this water consumption pressure? According to *Water Footprint*, it takes 13,676 gallons of water to produce a single gallon of biodiesel from soybean.[58] Switch to Jatropha, a favorite biodiesel plant in countries like Brazil and the Philippines, and it takes 19,924 gallons of water to produce one gallon of biodiesel.

> "It takes 13,676 gallons of water to produce 1 gallon of biodiesel from soybean."

Pretending that biology is going to solve a significant portion of the world's energy problem is to deny basic physics. "Some of the claims from the venture capitalists and government officials violate the laws of thermodynamics," says Stanford Professor Margot Gerritsen, a world-renowned energy systems expert.

How about making biofuels from municipal waste? This is a worthy pursuit that has the potential to solve two problems at once: generating energy while cleaning up waste. A company called Fulcrum Energy has announced a technology that would turn 90,000 tons of waste into 10.5 million gallons of ethanol. If extrapolated over the whole United States, this process could generate 1 billion gallons of ethanol per year[59]. That sounds like a lot until you consider that the U.S. consumes 378 million gallons per day[60]. So while processing every municipal waste site in the nation (and the world) might be a worthy pursuit from both economic and environmental reasons, it would cover less than 3 days worth of American gasoline consumption.

Choice 5: "Green" Nuclear

In 1958, Ford Motor Company unveiled the Ford Nucleon, a concept car powered by a small nuclear reactor in the back. The car would go about 5,000 miles (8,000 km) before coming back to the shop for the little nuclear core to be easily swapped for a new one[61]. The history of nuclear power in America is littered with promises of "new" nuclear that never came true.

The United States has 105 nuclear plants that generate about 20% of America's electricity. The last one came on line in 1986. Construction stopped. The nuclear industry blames environmentalists this.

Are environmentalists that powerful? Over the past twenty years, environmentalists in America haven't stopped the coal industry from record expansion of power plants or the oil industry from reaping record sales and profits. Greenpeace hasn't stopped the buildup of the nuclear industry in France or China. Could they really stop the nuclear industry in America? There's another reason for the stalling of nuclear plant development, one that the industry and its supporters in government don't like to talk about.

Checklist: Is nuclear financially viable?

The fact is that nuclear is not financially viable—and never has been.

According to the *Wall Street Journal*, the 75 nuclear plants built between 1966 and 1986 were three times more expensive than originally estimated. "The existing Vogtle plant, put into service in the late 1980s, cost more than 10 times its original estimate."[62] Every nuclear plant built in the United States has been late and over budget.

A 2003 MIT report entitled "The Future of Nuclear" states: "Nuclear power is not an economically competitive choice.[63]" Nuclear power finances are treated like a state secret, but capital costs are believed to be around $8-$12 per Watt[64]. This is almost twice the capital cost of Concentrating Solar Power (CSP) plants today.

Furthermore, the cost curve for nuclear power has gone steadily up since its inception in the 1950s—while the cost curves for clean sources like solar and wind have gone steadily down and will likely continue to do so for many years if not decades. Wind, for instance, has gone from about 80 ¢/kWh in 1979 to about 5 ¢/kWh in 2009.

Construction time is another issue. Nuclear plants take at least ten years to build. The aforementioned Vogtle plant took 14 years to build. Many plants, like the planned second Seabrook reactor in New Hampshire, have been cancelled due to "construction delays, cost overruns and troubles obtaining financing."[65]

The main reason the 105 nuclear plants in the United States are profitable is that "they were sold to current operators for less than their actual cost,"[66] according to the *Wall Street Journal*.

The world's governments have bestowed hundreds of billions in subsidies on the nuclear industry. But governments influence energy markets through laws, rules, and regulations that escape many of us. This is true for both the fossil-fuel and nuclear industries.

A major reason utilities that like nuclear plants has to do with an obscure accounting concept called "Early Cost Recovery" or "Construction Work in Progress" (CWIP) which allows utilities to charge ratepayers for the costs of building nuclear plants while they're building them. That is, ratepayers pay for the costs of building the nuclear plants a decade or more before the plant powers the first residential light bulb. CWIP can account for up to 1/3 of the capital costs of building a nuclear plant[67]. This is another case of socializing the risks and privatizing the profits.

Progress Energy, for instance, requested a 31% rate increase from Floridians in 2009 in large part to finance the construction of a nuclear plant[68]. The $8-12 bn. cost of building such a plant would be too much for a utility to bear. It could wreck their balance sheet. They know the risks involved. Why not outsource the risks?

Yet utilities are not allowed to do CWIP with solar plants. Solar plant builders have to bear the whole investment cost and can't recover capital costs until they start delivering the power. In fact until recently the utilities could not even use the Investment Tax Credit (ITC) to build solar plants. This meant that utilities had to pay full cash from their balance sheet for solar investments but were allowed to use the ratepayer's cash to build nuclear plants.

Sixty years after the first nuclear plant came on line in America, this is a mature industry that generates almost 20% of America's electricity. After more than $100 billion in known government subsidies[69] it still demands newer and larger subsidies from the American ratepayer and the U.S. government. Call it "nuclear double dipping": the utility's capital costs are subsidized by the ratepayer on one end and by the taxpayer (the U.S. government) on the other end. Nice subsidy! You have to love that kind of accounting!

According to Eric Severance: "generation costs for 'new' nuclear (including fuel and O&M but not distribution to customers) are likely to be from 25-30 cents per kWh." This is much more expensive than wind or solar thermal are today—and in the same ballpark as solar photovoltaics. The average American pays about 10 c/kWh.

Furthermore, an expansion of the nuclear industry would require the government to spend tens of billions of dollars to store the spent nuclear waste in Yucca Mountain or equivalent storage facilities.

This is billions of dollars in subsidies to a mature industry. It's much too expensive to build and run nuclear plants. Only with really massive government subsidies and favorable legal and accounting treatment can nukes be built and run.

Checklist: Is Nuclear clean?

A Ukrainian student of mine at Stanford shared with me that his mother was killed by radiation from the Chernobyl nuclear plant. An area larger than 6,000 km² (2,300 square miles) is now a wasteland, more than 400 settlements were literally buried and removed from the map, and tens of thousands of people had to be evacuated[70]. Uranium and plutonium are the most dangerous forms of waste in the world.

Yet because nuclear power does not produce climate-changing carbon dioxide, it has been adopted by some as a "green" source of energy. Advocates make claims like "we have the technology to make it safe," "next-generation nuclear is clean," or "Russian technology wasn't up to standards." Their clever use of language implies but can't actually say that nuclear is clean. What it does say is: "we can contain the radiation."

The spent nuclear fuel will pose nuclear radiation risks for the next forty thousand years or more. Even France, which relies on nuclear power for 80% of its electricity needs, has not resolved the waste storage problem.

National security is also a real concern. Anyone following in the media the ongoing tussle between the governments of Iran and the United States can read that nuclear can be converted into weapons capable of inflicting civilization-ending destruction. There are of course grave national security concerns over the theft of nuclear material by terrorists or the conversion of nuclear material and technology from civilian to military use.

Proponents of nuclear energy argue that it is a non-carbon source of energy and that in this time of crisis we should set aside security, military, environmental, financial, and health concerns. They say we need to save the planet from carbon sources and nuclear is there to help.

But none of these arguments makes nuclear clean.

Checklist: Can nuclear scale?

To figure whether nuclear can scale, let's do a stretch-scenario mental exercise. Let's assume that money is not an object and the nuclear industry continues to receive the massive government financial subsidies to which it has become accustomed. Let's also assume we're not worried about military or environmental consequences, nuclear proliferation, plant decomissioning, or nuclear-waste storage.

Let's assume even further that instead of the 10-14 years that it takes to build a nuclear plant, we somehow figure out a way to build one every two weeks. (Bear with me if you have recently done kitchen remodeling.) In this scenario the industry would build about 1,000 nuclear plants over the next 40 years. One thousand nuclear plants, each generating about 1 GW, would provide 1 TW of capacity under these stretch assumptions. We don't even know if there is enough uranium or plutonium to power 1 TW. And even then, nuclear could generate just 1 TW out of the 30 TW we need over the next forty years. So sure, with a juiced-up total fantasy scenario and lots of lobbying it can scale to 1 TW.

So far, we aren't even close to bridging that 16-terawatt gap.

Interjection: So Can Clean Energy Scale, Period?

I have surveyed all the obvious "alternative" or "renewable" energy sources except one.

For purposes of the above exercise I included "stretch" scenarios with assumptions worthy of a Wall Street hedge-fund spreadsheet. Despite these scenarios, the "renewable" energy sources I have examined can only generate at best 5 or 6 TW of the clean energy that the world will need by 2050.

There are other energy sources discussed in the literature. Ocean wave and tidal energy seem to be promising ways to generate power. However, we just don't know enough about tidal's potential. Some of the advocates place its at about the size of hydro power—which would place it at 0.5 TW. Others equate it to geothermal, which would place it in the 0.15 TW neighborhood. We also won't know the economically feasible potential until we deploy more and learn more.

Energy Source	Clean?	Financially Viable?	Scalable?	"Stretch" Energy Contribution (in TW)
Wind	Yes	Yes	Yes	2
Geothermal	Yes	Yes	No	0.15
Hydro-electric	Yes	Yes	No	0.35
Bio Energy	No	No	No	1
Nuclear	No	No	No	1
Tidal/Ocean	Yes	?	?	0.5
Total				5 TW

Figure 2.4. Comparative Summary of "Clean Alternative" Energy Sources

Fusion has also gotten some press lately. The problem is that fusion has been the energy source of the future for the last forty years—and it will likely still be the next big hope for the next forty.

So are we doomed to our addiction to fossil fuels?

Energy is one of the most important issues on the planet right now. Our industrial economy depends on abundant and inexpensive energy. Transporting and cleaning our water take massive quantities of energy. The environment (and the whole planet) lives and dies with our energy choices. Solutions to problems like war and terrorism, population growth and economic growth, poverty and disease, all depend on our energy choices. Dirty choices lead to dirty outcomes.

There's another source of energy that can probably scale. But is it clean? Can we afford it?

Choice 6: "Clean" Coal

Christmas Eve is usually a happy but uneventful day in the small town of Kingston, Tennessee, population 5,250. December 24, 2008, however, brought a dark surprise: What was originally estimated to be about 1.8 million cubic yards of "coal ash" were released in the town and the river when a retention wall holding the coal byproduct broke. Homes were destroyed, rivers irreversibly polluted, and lives ruined. It was later shown that the spill was in fact triple the original estimate: 5.4 million cubic yards, or enough to cover 30,000 acres (121 km^2) one foot deep.[71] Cleaning up that disaster would cost $1.2 billion.

But this was no freak accident. "United States coal plants produce 129 million tons of post-combustion byproducts a year, the second-largest waste stream in the country, after municipal solid waste. That is enough to fill more than a million railroad coal cars,"[72] according to the National Research Council. According to the Union of Concerned Scientists the "typical" 500-MW coal plant would generate 193,000 tons of sludge and 125,000 tons of ash, and 10,500 tons of nitrous dioxide every year—the equivalent of half a million old cars on the road.[73]

According to *Scientific American*: "Coal ash is more radioactive than nuclear waste."[74] The problem is that coal contains trace amounts of uranium and thorium, both of which are highly radioactive elements. "When coal is burned into fly ash, uranium and thorium are concentrated at up to 10 times their original levels. Fly ash uranium sometimes leaches into the soil and water surrounding a coal plant, affecting cropland and, in turn, food."

The coal industry, in the face of these facts, is cleverly promoting "clean coal." They have promoted the concept of "Carbon Capture and Sequestration" (CCS) by which coal plants would take the CO_2 emissions and toxic waste and bury them underground.

Last summer I helped my brother move into a new place. We had some extra boxes that needed to be disposed of. We drove them to the city dump and paid for disposal. The price? About $100 per ton of garbage. That is only fair. Cities and counties have learned to price waste collection and management. Households that produce more garbage pay more; households that produce little pay less. No government in its right mind would allow for households to dump garbage in the middle of the street (or, heaven forbid, bury it!) and expect the government to collect it, transport it, process it, and store it—for free. Fairness requires that garbage producers and polluters pay their fair share.

It is quite important that coal pay for its garbage, because assuming that CCS were to actually work as advertised, some day the industry would need an additional 25% more coal *just to capture and sequester the waste from the coal.* (That is, it takes a lot of extra coal to generate energy to clean up the mess generated by the coal.) Then we'd be adding another 30 million tons or so to America's waste stream.

Is the coal industry going to pay our cities, counties, and states $100 per ton to dispose of their billions of tons of garbage? (Notice that I have only talked about solid waste. Air-bound CO_2 pollution is a whole other waste stream!) Not likely.

The U.S. government has actually allocated $3.4 billion for the coal industry to develop CCS. I'm wondering why a 200-year old, trillion-dollar industry can't clean up its act on its own. The Australian government has also handed their coal industry more than A$1 billion.

So coal plants must be rushing to implement CCS, right?

Nope. No major American coal plant is even testing this supposed coal industry savior. There are a few demonstration pilot projects and nothing much else. According to *The Economist*: "CCS is not just a potential waste of money. It might also create a false sense of security about climate change, while depriving potentially cheaper methods of cutting emissions of cash and attention—all for the sake of placating the coal lobby."[75] The fact that the coal industry even got into the clean energy conversation is a feat of advertising and lobbying. Mad Men indeed.

I said at the beginning of this chapter that I didn't think coal, oil, natural gas, or nuclear were going away any time soon. In this exercise, I have them keep the same collective energy capacity in 2050 as they have today: 14 TW. Coal falls into that camp. Coal should battle it out with oil, natural gas, and nuclear to see who can pollute less.

However, there's still a 10-TW gap in energy production in this exercise—about 33% of all the energy demand in the world in 2050. Let's look at the solar choice.

Choice 7: Solar

The sun drenches the world with about 120,000 terawatts of energy each year[76]. In other words, the sun showers us with 4,000 times the energy that humanity is expected to consume in 2050.

To put that figure another way: we would have to convert about 0.025%—*one quarter of one percent*—of the energy the sun freely and cleanly sends us to cover *all 30 TW* of power that the world will need in 2050. That's not just 16 TW of clean energy needs. Converting just 0.025% of the energy that the sun cleanly and freely gives us every day can power the whole world—and then some. How hard is that?

As I explained in the introductory chapter, with existing (2009) technology, we would need to build solar plants in the equivalent of a square of 108 miles on each side in a desert of the U.S. Southwest to generate all the electricity the United States consumes today. I repeat, *a little over 10,000 square miles of America's deserts can generate all the electricity the U.S. needs.* That's less than 1% of America's deserts.

Another square with 100-mile sides of solar plants in the Sahara desert would quench all of Europe's and Africa's electricity thirst. A few more square miles of deserts in Mexico, China, India, Australia, Chile, and Saudi Arabia and... well, you know where this is going.

This feat can be achieved using today's technology.

A consortium of some of the largest European industrial companies is raising $555 billion to develop solar plants across the Sahara and feed electricity to Europe and Africa as well as to desalinate water for the Middle East and North Africa.

> *"A European consortium is raising half trillion dollars to develop solar in the Sahara."*

$555 billion. *Half a trillion dollars.* No other alternative comes remotely close to solar. Whereas every other energy scenario shown above has low ceilings and wild assumptions (let's all go hungry, place wind turbines in the middle of the Pacific Ocean, or build a nuke every two weeks) solar energy can fulfill all our needs with tiny conversion rates of the massive energy we get from the sun.

Solar energy is more land-efficient, more resource-efficient, and more scalable than any other energy source, clean or dirty. "From each km² of desert land, about 250 GWh of electricity can be harvested each year using concentrating solar thermal power technology. This is over 200 times more than what can be produced per square kilometer by biomass, or 5 times more than what can

> *"For each square mile, solar can harvest over 200 times more than biomass or 5 times more than wind and hydro"*

be generated by the best available wind and hydropower sites."[77]

The land needs for solar plants are puny when compared with oil drilling or even coal. Oil companies lease 74,219 square miles (47.5 million acres) of land just in the United States to drill oil. They also lease a further 44 million acres (68,750 mi²) of offshore space[78].

So the oil and gas industries lease 143,000 square miles from the U.S. government—to meet just about a third of America's transportation needs. That's *more than 10 times* the land that solar would need to generate all of America's electricity.

When you include the vast land area that coal mining uses, it is on a par with solar plants on a per-square mile basis. And of course, solar does not require the removal of entire mountaintops in what used to be beautiful countryside. Solar produces no billions of tons of pollution like what coal spews into the air and onto the land—which destroys even more territory. No need to sequester any coal ash or thorium with solar!

The only other genuinely clean energy source that can realistically scale to produce more than a terawatt of energy is wind. However, as I have shown, even wind can probably not grow beyond 1TW to 2 TW. The additional energy we need to build by 2050 is simply not attainable from bio, hydro, geothermal, or other known clean or dirty alternatives.

So here's the thesis of this book: *Given what we know today, the only realistic, scalable, financially viable clean energy alternative to fossil fuel energy production is* **solar energy**.

Humanity will have to build the multi-terawatt energy infrastructure using mainly (but not exclusively) solar energy. The buildout of this clean energy infrastructure will generate business opportunities for entrepreneurs, companies, industries and countries unlike anything we have seen. The market opportunities will add up to trillions of dollars of new wealth. They will also save our societies trillions of dollars in fuel expenses every year, and more trillions in pollution-related costs—waste disposal, public health, environmental cleanup, and climate change.

The rest of the book highlights seven large opportunities that I have identified. Once again, in defining these opportunities, I have prepared big-picture, long-term scenarios and calculations that highlight big-picture opportunities. I didn't intend this to be a business plan with nth-degree pinpoint accuracy.

What Are the Market Opportunities?

I believe that solar is the only source of energy that is scalable to multi-terawatts, clean, and economically viable. I think only solar can scale to the 10TW level that the world is going to need in 2050. However, even if you only believe a fraction of this scenario, you're still looking at trillions of dollars of revenue opportunity.

What are the market opportunities unfolding as we build the solar infrastructure? What other complementary markets can develop? Where are the entrepreneurial opportunities?

Over the last year and a half I've visited deserts in Dubai, Mexico, and the United States. I've worked with solar-technology startups in Silicon Valley that are bringing innovative technologies to push the cost curves further down than anyone thought possible just a few years ago. I've talked to dozens of venture capital investors, scientists, engineers, and executives from my backyard in Silicon Valley to Seville, from Munich to Abu Dhabi. I have seen innovations from my alma maters at MIT and Stanford, from NASA and Caltech.

As I wrote this book over the last year and a half I kept surprising myself at the size of the market opportunities I was uncovering. The map is not the territory—but what a territory clean energy could be!

1. Utility-Scale Solar:	$9.0 trillion
2. Industrial-Scale Solar:	$7.1 trillion
3. Island/Village-Scale Solar	$2.6 trillion
4. Home/Commercial-Scale Solar	$8.7 trillion
5. Solar Clean Water	$1.5 trillion
6. Clean Energy Storage	$5 trillion
7. Transmission & Smart Grid	$6.5 trillion
Total Market Opportunities:	**$35.4 trillion**

This is truly an insane-looking number—until you put it in its proper context.

The energy industry today generates revenues of $6-$7 trillion per year. Energy demand is going to at least double by 2050. Assuming fuel prices remain stable, the global energy industry is going to make $382 trillion in revenues over the next 40 years. Which is to say: I'm only showing *less than a tenth* of the really astounding revenue opportunities that are going to flow through this industry.

I wish I were running an early-stage venture fund. I wish I could invest in the early-stage entrepreneurial opportunities that are just opening up. In the meantime I'll be uncovering more clean energy market opportunities.

This moment may be like 1981 at the dawn of the PC era. That year started one of the most important "paradigm shifts" in technology and business history. The clean energy "paradigm" that we're entering is financially bigger. Maybe ten times bigger. So put your sunglasses on and accompany me on this journey. I'll show you more than $35 trillion in market opportunities.

We can save the planet and make serious money at the same time. We can be green and make some green. We can create wealth, grow the economy, and save the world.

"Solving big problems is easier than solving little problems."
—Larry Page, cofounder, Google

"There is nothing more frightful than ignorance in action"
—Johann Wolfgang von Goethe

"It's better to light a candle than curse the darkness."
—Carl Sagan

CHAPTER 3
OPPORTUNITY I— DESERT POWER: UTILITY-SCALE SOLAR

The Archivo General de Indias is located next to the Seville Cathedral, the largest Gothic church in the world. Although it is a UNESCO World Heritage Site, I missed the Archivo the first time I visited the city; the soaring, lavishly decorated cathedral caught my eye instead. As an American and a Silicon Valley technology entrepreneur I enjoy, indeed thrive on, the shock of the new: innovations and discoveries that change the world. The Archivo, which contains a library within its austere architecture, quietly imposes the kind of awe that can only be felt when one is in presence of world-changing history. Within its 6 miles of shelving lie more than 43,000 volumes and manuscripts: 80 million pages that document how, during tough economic times and amidst brutal religious wars, an unlikely entrepreneur financed by an unlikely venture capitalist embarked on a journey that changed the arc of world history forever[79].

This entrepreneur and many others after him turned Seville into Europe's main center of trade and industry and Spain into the Old World's wealthiest country for the following three centuries. The Spanish translated his Italian name as Cristóbal Colón. We call him Christopher Columbus.

In 2009, Seville is going through another unlikely boom. After a century of economic angst, Seville has set forth on a new journey. This time it is not conquering lands or peoples, nor is it looking for gold mines. This time there is not yet a single entrepreneur like Christopher Columbus or a colorful venture capitalist like Queen Isabella to personify the era. This time Spain is conquering something bigger than the Americas. The city that was the entrepreneurial center of the sixteenth and seventeenth centuries is refashioning itself as a world center for solar power development and solar thermal technology entrepreneurship. Seville is the epicenter of the Spanish conquest of the sun.

In 2008 the electricity generation capacity in Spain grew by 4,243 MW, of which 1,739 MW was wind energy and 1,416 MW was new solar energy. Solar grew by 212% over 2007 levels and represented a third of all new power generation in the country.[80]

Spain is well on its way to meeting the goal of generating 20% of its electricity by renewable forms of energy by 2020[81], and the Andalucia region (of which Seville is the capital) generates 40% of that. "We are taking risks to make it happen. We have the sun, the financial commitment of the Spanish and Andalucia governments, and the commitment from the transmission grid operator. We are bringing together the companies and the people who are the catalysts." So says Isabel de Haro, President of the Andalucia Energy Agency.

In Southern Spain hundreds of companies, employing thousands of engineers, are building two dozen CSP plant projects. These plants will have a combined capacity of more than 1 GW of capacity by 2010—enough to meet all of Seville's 700,000 inhabitants" energy needs.[82] There are 6 more GW of solar CSP plants in the pipeline and a goal of 25 GW by 2020[83]. These numbers do not include photovoltaic-panel solar plants.

"There are massive investments that only clear leadership and a coordinated plan can turn into reality," explains Ms de Haro. "You need a robust energy infrastructure that includes generation, transport, and distribution systems as well as standards, processes, and policies that guarantee energy quality and security. You have to modernize the whole energy system, not just bits and pieces. Ultimately the market has to work, but right now we're germinating the field so the market can flourish."

The U.S. too provides examples of what such government commitment can achieve. The U.S. government nurtured the Internet for more than two decades before the Net engendered industries worth trillions of dollars and companies like Google, Cisco, and Amazon. Two to three decades earlier, the same U.S. government built the Interstate highway system that created trillions of dollars in new wealth and millions of American jobs for half a century, and not just in the auto industry. The Interstates made possible the whole suburban economy of the second half of the twentieth century including affordable single-family tract housing, planned developments, shopping malls, Wal-Mart and McDonalds and their ilk, and the rest of the modern real-estate business.

But in 2008, not a single utility-scale solar thermal power plant saw the light of day in the United States. To see the latest shining example of the future of energy I had to travel to the Old World: Abengoa Solar's PS10 solar plant outside Seville.

Solar Power Tower

I visited the Solúcar Solar Park on a crisp February morning. Located about 16 miles (25 km) northwest of Seville in the municipality of Sanlúcar La Mayor, the Solúcar complex is as ambitious a solar project as exists anywhere in the world. By the time Abengoa Solar is finished building this complex in late 2012, it will have a capacity of 300 MW and generate enough electricity to power a city the size of Seville. But this is not just miles of solar generating equipment.

Figure 3.1. The PS10 Solar Power Tower plant in Sanlúcar, near Seville, Spain. (Photo: Tony Seba)

From far off I could see the 330-foot (110-m) PS10 tower and the triangular solar-ray silhouette, a solar tutu if you will, converging at an imaginary point on top of the tower. PS10 (Plataforma Solar 10), which has a generating capacity of 11MW, is the first commercial solar plant in Europe that uses the "Solar Power Tower" concept to generate electricity. Launched in the fall of 2006, it generates 24.3 GWh of electricity per year—about enough to fully power 5,500 homes.

It's time to get more technical about the two forms of solar power.

Two Ways to Harness the Sun: PV and CSP

We can capture the sun's energy in two ways: by converting its light directly into electricity or using it to heat a fluid (a liquid or a gas).

When most people think about solar energy generation, they think of photovoltaic (PV) panels on the roof of a house or building. PV converts photons directly into electricity, using the photoelectric effect discovered by Albert Einstein over a century ago. Photons—tiny packets of light energy—strike atoms of a conducting element like copper and raise them to a higher energy state. That causes the atoms to shed electrons, because the electrons are negatively charged while the nucleus is positively charged. With this additional energy from the photon, the electrons in orbits or "shells" closest to the atom's nucleus are pushed away from it, knocking the outermost ones loose as they displace them. These high-energy electrons strike other atoms and knock electrons off their outer shells too. This becomes a cascade of electrons through the conducting substance—*electric current.*

The photoelectric effect has been used for things like remote garage door openers and TV controls for decades, operating on the weak current from AA-size batteries to send a weak beam of infra-red light. The light in turn generates an equally weak current in a photoelectric cell that triggers switches inside the appliance. But the sun puts out a *lot* of photons that carry a lot more energy, so the current generated in a good-sized array of PV cells is measured in hundreds of volts and thousands of watts.

PS10 and other CSP plants use the sun's energy to generate power in a different way. It uses the sun's heat to generate steam which then drives a turbine to generate electricity. The idea is to concentrate the sunlight to heat a fluid, which is then used to drive a turbine that generates electricity. Instead of knocking electrons loose from the atoms of a conducting film and generating a current directly (PV), the photons from the sun excite the atoms in the fluid and make them move around more quickly. If the fluid is a liquid—say, water—the molecules unhook from each other and start flying about as a vapor, in this case steam. If the fluid is already a gas, the already separate molecules zip around even faster with the additional energy, literally bouncing off the walls of whatever container they're inside. In both cases the result is increased pressure with increased temperature.

Channel that pressure down narrow insulated pipes (increasing the temperature still further by compression) and you have force to work with—that is, to turn into other forms of energy.

If you've ever used a magnifying glass or better yet a concave mirror to focus sunlight and burn a hole in a piece of paper, you get the idea. Use thousands (or millions) of square meters of mirrors (not PV panels!) to reflect that same sunlight on a single point, and you can heat a fluid flowing past it up to several hundred degrees Celsius and use that superheated fluid to drive an industrial-scale turbine. The mirrors are called *heliostats*—and I'll have a lot more to say about them elsewhere in the book. As I mentioned earlier, this is called Concentrating Solar Power or CSP. In the literature, the term "solar thermal" is generally used interchangeably with CSP.

About a mile from PS10 there was a larger tower (PS20) and a smaller one in between, neither of which was lit yet. PS20, with a 20-MW tower about 50% taller (165 meters or 540 feet) and with twice as many heliostats as its cousin PS10, was set to open in the spring of 2009. Sure enough, less than three months later, PS20's 1,255 new heliostats were switched on and sunshine was reflected to the receiver atop the tower. The power light went on as they had told me it would. Construction is well underway on Abengoa's Solnova 1 and Solnova 2, each with 50 MW capacities, which will use "parabolic trough" technology not unlike Frank Shuman's original 1912 plant in Maadi, Egypt or the 1980s SEGS plants in California that I described in Chapter 1.

Between the PS10 and PS20, the company has built a third smaller, 2-MW "high-temperature" tower dubbed "Eureka" to test the next generation of solar technologies it is hoping to release in its future plant developments. In June 2009, Abengoa announced that Eureka was open for business. High-temperature research is a key development effort in solar thermal power. The higher the temperature you can manage, the more electricity you can generate and the more energy you can store for later use.

But despite its focus—no pun intended—on power-tower CSP, Abengoa is by no means neglecting other approaches. As I drove around the plant I saw a dozen "Stirling dish" units—mirrors arranged into a single parabolic reflector that concentrates light on a receiver, much as a satellite dish concentrates a TV signal—and about 1 MW worth of concentrating photovoltaics, all tracking the sun. Within the Solúcar complex, Abengoa has evidently been researching, developing, building, and operating solar plants using a variety of technologies. Having R&D labs right next to its commercial operations gives this company an edge that many competitors lack. Solúcar as a whole can be seen as one enormous, full-scale solar-energy research and development lab.

"In just over two years of operating PS10 we have learned efficiencies at all levels," says Valerio Fernández, director of operations at the Solúcar complex and one of the first three engineers on staff when PS10 first broke ground in 1999. "We are already developing receivers that are 20% more efficient. We generate solar electricity up to one hour after sundown and are working on improving energy s torage technologies that will help generate solar energy around the clock. We test these technologies right here and then incorporate them into our future plant developments."

When I walked into the control room I saw computer screens that tracked every single heliostat in the field as well as other metrics like solar radiation, temperature, and power generation. That afternoon the plant was working at higher than 97% efficiency.

Then I saw the dot icons representing heliostats go from "on" to "off" and got worried. I asked what was happening, and the technicians explained that the heliostats had gone into "stow" mode due to high winds. I looked outside and saw all but one heliostat in horizontal position (fig 3.2). This reminded me of the other component in CSP installations: the two-axis (horizontal and vertical) alignment systems of the heliostats. Each heliostat is constantly being adjusted on these two axes so that it is always at the best possible angle to catch the sun's light as it moves across the sky from dawn to dusk—while always directing that light at the concentration point on the tower.

Figure 3.2. PS10 heliostat field in stowed position—due to high winds. (Photo: Tony Seba)

Perhaps needless to say, these incredibly precise control systems, involving thousands upon thousands of independently moving mirrors, could never have existed before the computer revolution. But the gear-works that move a heliostat at PS-10 on its mounts to follow the sun's rays and direct them back at the concentration point are its most expensive component to produce —much more than the computers and software. In Chapter 10, I'll talk about the surprising opportunity being seized by a new company that is revolutionizing the design of the heliostat tracking mount and thereby drastically shrinking the cost of making these artificial sunflowers.

Beauty and Wealth: Hidden in Plain Sight

In 1540, when the Spanish conquistador García López de Cárdenas traveled north across what is now Arizona and came to the edge of the Grand Canyon, he regarded it as a "useless freak of nature." Tired, thirsty, and hungry, he and his small band of soldiers and explorers had found no easy treasures in the desert, no El Dorado gold mines—only a vast crevasse thousands of feet deep and miles across, with nothing at the bottom but a meandering river. Spain proceeded to mostly ignore this amazing terrestrial feature and the high desert around it for the following three hundred years[84]. It took a cultural shift in the nineteenth century for our society to truly recognize the Grand Canyon's stunning beauty and extraordinary scientific interest.

It is easy to disparage the untrained eyes or lacking cultural sophistication of civilizations past; yet one of the most astonishing treasures in the world lies in plain view in those deserts of the U.S. Southwest and most of us still cannot see it. We see the beauty, but we still have a hard time seeing the wealth. We still import oil to the tune of hundreds of billions of dollars every year and pollute the air we breathe when burning it. We still use coal to generate half our electricity while the sludge and fly ash it generates pollutes our rivers, acidifies our oceans, and shortens our lives. We still cannot see that a relatively small patch of desert can solve nearly all our energy problems. Our grandchildren will wonder how we could drive through the Nevada or Arizona deserts to admire the Grand Canyon without noticing the wealth before us.

Abengoa Solar knows what lies in the Arizona desert—and the company is not waiting before applying this knowledge. While the U.S. solar industry was caught up in the credit crunch in 2009 and unable to finance projects, Abengoa quietly broke ground on the largest single concentrating solar thermal power (CSP) plant in the United States: a 280 MW plant called Solana. This plant, located in Gila Bend, 60 miles south of Phoenix, AZ, will supply enough power for 70,000 homes and use the technologies that Abengoa has developed in its Solúcar plant outside Seville. (The alternative natural gas plant would have spewed 400,000 tons of carbon dioxide each year.)

Like its Spanish forebears centuries ago, Abengoa has already fanned out into the rest of the world and is building or planning solar power plants in the Americas, Africa, and Asia. It is also developing hybrid solar/gas plants in Algeria and Morocco. With 2008 revenues of $100 million, Abengoa Solar has billions of dollars of solar power plant development in its pipeline and is planning on at least doubling in size each year for the foreseeable future.

What is Utility-Scale Solar?

Energy can be produced at several scales: if you produce it in your home, it's residential scale, probably in the order of 2 to 10 kilowatts (kW). At the other end of the scale ladder, if a utility like Pacific Gas & Electric produces it for a city like San Francisco or Los Angeles, then we are talking about utility scale—several hundred or even several thousand megawatts (MW). A "standard" coal or nuclear plant in the United States has a capacity of about 1,000 MW (1 GW.)

Utility-scale solar plants can be located wherever the sun's radiation is optimal, on cheaper land away from residential centers, and then delivered to users the same way electricity is delivered today—via the transmission grid.

The main advantage of large, utility-scale solar plants is cost reduction brought about by economies of scale. "Utility-scale solar is probably the only way to achieve real scale and reduce our carbon emissions,"[85] says Vinod Khosla, one of the leading investors in the clean technology space.

Utilities are comfortable with turbine-generated electricity—a century-old technology that relies on the electromagnetic effect explored by Faraday and Maxwell in the early to mid-nineteenth century. Most electricity in America and the world is still generated using a steam-driven or water-driven turbine.

Typically in a conventional power plant, coal is burned to heat water into steam. Inside the turbine, the steam turns blades on a shaft that spins a tight winding of heavy copper wire inside a big cylindrical array of magnets, using the electromagnetic effect to generate electricity. Gas turbines work the same way, using hot gases from the combustion of other fuels such as natural gas or diesel oil. Hydroelectric generation relies on falling water (channeled into high-pressure pipes) to run the turbines. Nuclear power is also generated by heating water into steam for the same purpose. These sources accounted for about 85% of electricity generation in America in 2006. Coal (49%), nuclear (19%), natural gas (7%), and hydro (7%) were the top four.

Between residential-scale and utility-scale production are commercial and industrial scales. Commercial scale includes office buildings, malls, and hotels. Industrial scale includes manufacturing plants, aluminum smelters, cement factories, and large computer data centers. While there may not be a clear definition or demarcation between these four scales in terms of actual plant size, it is clear that each one of them provides large-scale market opportunities.

In this book I also introduce the concept of "island-scale" or "village-scale" solar. Most populated islands are too small to merit a standard 1-GW (1,000-MW) coal plant— or even a 500-MW plant. These islands end up depending on diesel or other fossil fuels to produce electricity. Hundreds of thousands of villages around the world are not on the grid, so they are effectively isolated like islands and generate their power just like islands.

Solar energy is unique in that it can come in all sizes. You can buy a solar lamp or a solar calculator that runs a small LED light or display off a PV panel and battery. You can power a house, a hotel, a chip factory, or a whole city with solar energy.

"Solar can scale as no other energy source can."

In other words—as I will end up emphasizing throughout this

book, because it is such a vital point—solar can scale as no other energy source can.

Solar Power-Tower Trillions

Parabolic trough dominates solar thermal (CSP) electricity production today. During the time I was researching this topic (early 2009) there were hundreds of megawatts of trough CSP capacity deployed around the globe, while PS10 at 11 MW was the world's only operating commercial power tower.

I was still jet-lagged from my first visit to PS10 when Brightsource, a Silicon Valley company, trumpeted a deal with Southern California Edison to develop 1.2 GW of solar power. Brightsource had announced a grand total of 4.2 GW of new capacity to be built in the Mojave Desert. Not to be outdone, Pasadena-based power-tower competitor eSolar made public a 500-MW deal with NRG Energy. This was not long after eSolar was featured on the American cable news network CNN announcing a 245-MW solar plant agreement, also with Southern California Edison.

Announcements from India have come pouring in since then, including the largest solar plant in the world at 3.26 GW. (This is about 10 times larger than all the SEGS plants put together.) The Clinton Foundation has proposed 5-GW solar power plant in India. The state of Gujarat wants to be the solar hub of India and is attracting companies from South Korea, Japan, and Spain. It has also set aside 1,500 acres for solar development and invited companies like Abengoa and Moser Baer to participate.[86] In light (so to speak) of all these announcements, the Indian government goal of 20 GW by 2020 and 200 GW by 2050 does not seem farfetched. If anything, it seems rather tame.

As I've explained, solar generation on the utility scale is likely to be dominated by concentrating solar thermal power (CSP). So far the parabolic-trough design has dominated the market. However, both Brightsource and eSolar use what they believe is the most promising mechanism for large, utility-scale production of solar energy: solar power tower, essentially similar to Abengoa's PS10 and PS20.[87] According to Brightsource, solar power tower is expected to produce electricity at a cost 30% to 40% lower than that produced by parabolic trough, the CSP market leader[88].

Since one of the largest slices of the terawatts generated by solar energy in the foreseeable future is likely to be on the utility scale, the companies that dominate the CSP value chain will have a chance at the trillions of dollars that the market will likely invest in building and operating plants and supplying products and services to this nascent industry as well as selling CSP-generated energy. Furthermore, these dominant companies will have a good chance of profiting from innovations being developed as other companies invest in improving the technology and finding new applications for it.

Market size estimates for utility-scale solar power range into the trillions of dollars. Building a CSP plant (solar power tower or parabolic trough) currently requires an investment around $4 to $6 per watt. This figure varies depending on the size of the power plant (larger plants require smaller capital investment per watt) and will certainly decrease as product innovation pushes the performance/price curve down and as building techniques improve.

As we saw in the previous chapter, multiple generation technologies, including wind, hydro, geothermal, and ocean/tidal, will be required to form parts of the minimum 16-TW clean-energy infrastructure that the world will need by 2050. However, even with wildly optimistic assumptions, none of them can possibly generate more than a 1-TW-or-so slice of that pie. Unless something dramatic changes the nature of energy production (energy from supersymmetric particles?), solar energy will be the only clean source that can possibly scale to multiple terawatts beyond 10 TW and even deliver the bulk of the 30 TW we will need. A large proportion of those terawatts will likely be generated at the utility scale.

For high-solar-intensity desert areas, CSP today has technical advantages over photovoltaic at the utility scale. The central advantage is the availability of cheap and proven thermal-energy storage using molten salts (more on this later.) Thermal storage is what allows solar CSP to provide power seven hours after the sun goes down. Energy storage for solar PV and wind, by contrast, is still an order of magnitude more expensive on a per-kWh basis. CSP fans also talk about its higher conversion efficiency (25% to 33% of solar energy converted to electricity versus about 14% for PV), though that may change in due course with improvements in PV technology. And there are other applications for which solar CSP is better suited than any other technology, such as desalination (See Chapter 7) or industrial process heat (think factory-scale melting, boiling, and baking).

Desert CSP also has efficiency advantages in energy storage. According to Carnot's Theorem, the maximum efficiency of a heat engine equals the difference in temperature between the hot and cold reservoir divided by the temperature of the hot reservoir[89]. That's a mouthful, but basically it says that you can achieve higher thermal energy-storage efficiencies with higher temperatures for the hotter tank. Because solar power-tower technology can achieve higher temperatures for the molten salt (or other thermal fluid medium) it can achieve higher generation and storage efficiencies. This makes power tower a modality with a bright future in the energy universe.

That said, many challenges remain to take this technology to the next level. The companies that meet these challenges may create franchises that will dwarf today's Google, Intel, or General Electric. Just look at the numbers.

Mind-Boggling Market Size: Europe and India See the Light

Necessity is the mother of investment. Find a need or a problem and invest in creating products and services to solve it.

With its coal mined out, its "easy" hydro tapped out, no oil of its own, and North Sea natural gas well past peak, the European Union is facing tough energy choices. Nuclear is brutally expensive, dangerous, and insufficient anyway, and the other remaining traditional source, Russian natural gas, carries huge political and economic risks, as recent experience has shown. Wind is helping but (as we've seen) cannot scale nearly big enough to address the growing energy gap. Wind also has an energy storage issue that we will come back to in Chapter 8.

However, one resource Europe does have in large amounts is capital. In July 2009 a European consortium that included global powerhouses like ABB, Abengoa, Siemens, and Deutsche Bank announced that they had signed an MOU to raise $555 billion to build utility-scale concentrating solar power (CSP) plants throughout the Sahara desert and transmission lines across the Mediterranean to power both Europe and Africa[90]. Half a trillion dollars is a large number. Anyone who still thinks solar is something that might happen sometime in the future should be taking notice.

Wait a minute. The Sahara? But that's thousands of miles from most of Europe. Won't much of the CSP power be dissipated on the way to Paris, let alone Stockholm or Riga? Simple answer: no. With new high-voltage direct current (HVDC) transmission technology, electricity can be transported with minimal loss for thousands of kilometers. HVDC loses just 3% every 1,000 Km (620 miles), which means that plants can be built where the solar (or wind) resources are and transmitted to where the demand is.

You don't live close to a desert? Think again. It turns out that 90% of the world's population lives within 3,000 km (1,860 miles) of a desert[91]. Do you live in Tokyo, Berlin, or Chicago? Look it up on Google Earth. You live that close to a lot of sand and open sky. In fact, 90% of the major consumers of energy like China, Europe, India, and America are within 3,000 km (1,860 miles) of a desert—like the Gobi desert, the Sahara, the Thar, or the Mojave and other deserts in the US Southwest. All these consumer nations can be supplied with utility-scale solar electricity generated in the deserts.

The Indian government has also literally seen this light. A report called "National Solar Mission" outlines the goal to build a total of 200 GW of solar energy generation infrastructure by 2050[92]. Much of this infrastructure is expected to be on a "grid-connected" utility-scale level. India, of course, is endowed with some of the best solar resources in the world. The "Solar Mission" report states that India receives 5,000 trillion kWh of solar energy every year. (That's more than a thousand times America's 2007 consumption of nearly 4 trillion kWh of electricity.) Some areas in India receive up to 7 kWh per square mile per day. This is on a par with Arizona and Egypt and much higher than Spain or Germany. (The average American household consumes 31 kWh/day.)

Doing the Numbers

It's time to break this down step by step and really grasp the full scope of the utility-scale solar opportunity from the standpoint of capital investments.

1. In mid-2009 it took $4–6 in capital costs to build 1 watt capacity of utility-scale solar thermal power plant, such as power tower or parabolic trough. (The range of course depends on technologies used, size, location, and other features.)

2. Given this figure, a simple calculation shows that the capital investment needed to buy the goods and services to build 1 TW of concentrating solar power at $4–6 per watt is $4–6 trillion.

3. As I've explained in Chapter 2, absent another *entirely new* clean, financially viable, and scalable energy technol-

ogy to complement solar power, we'll need to build a solar infrastructure of about 10 TW by 2050.

4. This would generate a need for ten times the above number: $40–$60 trillion in capital investments over the next 40 years.

These numbers are truly staggering. But lest you still think that "solar is expensive" and that it would be cheaper to go with other options, read on.

Take nuclear (please). Nuclear power finances are, as I've said, treated like a state secret, but capital costs are believed to be around $8-$12 per watt[93]. A *Wall Street Journal* article on nuclear power plants quoted Florida Power and Light (FPL) officials saying that the cost of a GE-powered 1-GW nuclear plant would be $12 billion—or about $12 per watt. *This is 2 to 3 times the cost of solar thermal plants today.* Furthermore, as I noted in the previous chapter, the cost curve for nuclear power has gone steadily up since its inception in the 1950s, while according to the US Department of Energy's National Renewable Energy Labs (NREL) the cost curve for solar has gone down 20% per year and will continue to do so for the foreseeable future.

Building coal plants will not be less expensive either. When NV Energy postponed its 1,500-MW coal-fired plant in eastern Nevada, it quoted capital costs of $5 billion[94]. That is a little more than $3 per watt. This, mind you, is *not* the price structure for a (still entirely imaginary) "clean coal" plant. This is for "new coal," which is the same old dirty coal with a happy face—typically, some steam pumped into the emissions from the stacks to make them white and pretty.

If current trends persist—and by now, given the evidence I've presented, I hope you share my conviction that they will—solar thermal CSP plant investment costs will be about this much in a few years. Certainly in less than a decade. And certainly without the pollution. "Clean coal" plants, should they ever happen, are expected to cost twice what dirty coal plants cost. That means that in a decade (when proponents claim clean coal plants will be ready for prime time) they would cost $6/watt. At that point solar will likely cost less than $3/watt. So the dirty option will cost twice as much as the clean option. That's just for building the plant. Burning billions of dollars in fuel is yet another expense that coal will have—forever.

Bottom line: Investments in new energy generation over the next few decades will be in the tens of trillions, no matter what sources of energy are used.

Energy and Real Estate

Building power plants is conceptually similar to building a residential or commercial building. Despite a century of massive investments, industrialization, and commoditization of the raw materials, labor, and components for building a residence, the cost of building and maintaining *real estate* has not gone down.

Land is currently a small component of overall solar-plant construction price. The reason is that these plants are sited on the most inhospitable desert land: the higher its solar irradiation (insolation), the better a site is for a solar plant. All that insolation keeps these lands extremely hot and arid, and they lack topsoil for agriculture, making them less desirable for human habitation. Most flora and fauna also shun these desert lands as unfriendly.

This is in marked contrast to land use for many other sources of "alternative energy." The rise of biofuels has reportedly accelerated deforestation in places like Brazil, Malaysia, and Indonesia. The Brazilian Amazon and savanna, with their thousands of unique species, are disappearing at an increasing rate under the bulldozers of sugarcane and soybean ranchers in order to produce biofuels to power automobiles.[95]

In the United States, the Federal government owns and leases much of that hot, dry, inhospitable land that's perfect for

CSP plants through the Bureau of Land Management (BLM). On June 27, 2008, the BLM announced that they had received so many applications for siting solar plants in Federal lands that they were freezing the application process for 18 months.[96] According to the BLM, they were reviewing 125 applications covering more than one million acres for solar projects that had the potential to power more than 20 million homes. BLM officials said they were simply not equipped to handle so many applications. Now that's an interesting claim in light of the following fact: since 2004, the BLM "has issued 28,776 permits to drill (oil and gas) on public land," according to a 2008 U.S. House of Representatives energy report[97]. How can you issue nearly 29,000 permits to drill oil but be unable to handle 125 solar applications?

Confronted with a public outcry against this blatant unfairness, the Bureau quickly reversed its announcement and said that that its staff would continue reviewing such applications "in the interest of solar energy development."[98]

Follow the Sun, Follow the Money

Let's assume that utility-scale solar capacity will be just a tenth of the 10-TW "clean energy gap," that solar plant costs will drop to $2 $3 per watt (about a half of the current $4 6 per watt). This would still mean an opportunity for utility-scale solar infrastructure of anywhere from $2 trillion to $3 trillion in capital investment by 2050. If 30% of the 10-TW gap is filled with desert power, then the market opportunity is *six to nine trillion dollars.*

> *"Desert power could be a $6-$9 trillion market opportunity."*

Want a comparison? Google's 2008 revenues were roughly $20 billion or about 1% of the low end of the above capital investment estimate. General Electric, which is regarded as one of the best-run companies in the world, had 2008 revenues of about $180 billion or one-sixth of 1% (0.006%) of the high end of the $30 trillion estimate. It took GE a century to achieve these revenues, but it took Google just a decade to grow to that size. No wonder both these companies want to play a major role in the clean energy business.

Who Wants to Be a Trillionaire?

With a market that large, the rush to invest in and capitalize on that growth has already started. Abengoa Solar is off to a great start, but it is far from alone in this race.

In 2001, U.S. venture capital funds invested a grand total of just $5 million in solar technology companies. By 2008, solar companies were amongst the largest venture investment recipients. Companies like BrightSource, eSolar, and Solar Reserve received nearly $200 million each to build solar power tower plants in the US Southwest.

Spanish companies such as Iberdrola, Acciona, and Sener have moved quickly into the utility-scale solar plant development (and operations) opportunity by taking advantage of their presence in traditional power plant construction and operations. These companies are looking to be the AT&T or Edison Electric of the twenty-first century. They are well financed. They have hundreds of millions and even billions in the bank. They can buy the land, the technology, and the talent they need to succeed.

How important is it for a given country to be the headquarters of the AT&T of the twenty-first century? AT&T was one of the great companies of the twentieth. Its Bell Labs produced seven Nobel-prize winners and many of the great inventions that would define twentieth-century American ingenuity and lifestyle: radar, teletype, sonar, radio broadcasting, stereo audio, hearing aids, and talking movies—just to name a few. In 1946, AT&T began offering mobile telephone service; in 1947, it developed the transistor; in 1958, it launched the first modem; in 1962, it introduced the first communications satellite; in 1971, it created the Unix operating system and the C programming language; and in 1976, it built the first computerized switch network[99].

So AT&T's last round of great technologies became the basis on which Silicon Valley was built. I'm writing this book on a Macintosh computer that runs OS X (a Unix derivative) on an Intel Pentium (a descendant of the original transistor), connected to a Netgear router (a modern wireless modem), which of course links my machine to the Internet (a computerized network that runs mostly on Unix-derivative operating systems). Any way you look at it, AT&T generated trillions in wealth for its shareholders, its employees, its business partners, and the country in which it was headquartered.

"Abengoa Solar is in a position to win big in this market," said CEO Santiago Seage when I talked to him in his office in Madrid's Castellana district. "Many of the companies entering the market are technology companies with no experience building or operating solar power plants." At the other end of the spectrum, Sr. Seage explained, are companies (such as Iberdrola and Acciona) with experience building power plants but a small research and development budget. Then there's Albiasa, which comes from a construction background. All this makes Mr. Seage sure that Abengoa is "uniquely positioned in combining the best of a Silicon Valley technology startup company with high R&D budgets and the experience of developing and running large commercial power plants." Abengoa even has a small "venture fund" to invest in technology companies that show promise and can help Abengoa gain a competitive edge. (Silicon Valley networking giant Cisco Systems pioneered and perfected this venture-and-acquisition concept, which helped make it the market leader it has become.)

The CSP Race Today: Spain in Front

While most of its competitors were rushing to get into the market, Abengoa Solar had been there for almost a decade already and had made $100 million in revenues in the 2008 fiscal year. They also had planned on doubling this amount for the foreseeable future. In 2008 Abengoa Solar had a research and development budget of about $30 million –about 30% of revenues. To keep innovating and differentiating the company, it expected to keep that ratio in the near term.

The 280-MW Solana plant in Arizona is expected to make Abengoa $4 billion over the life of its 30-year contract with the Arizona Public Services utility. That's about $130 million per year, on a capital and operating cost of about $1.4 billion. A nice return on investment—especially considering that a large percentage of the capital cost is paid with borrowed funds. It's just like a mortgage.

It can get better than that. Assuming that Solana's "mortgage" runs the 30-year length of the contract with APS, Abengoa would be in a position to produce electricity at about 1 cent per kWh by the end of the contract. The deal calls for a set price just under 15 cents per kWh. That price may not persist through 30 years. However, "peaking power"—power produced and used during peak consumption times each day—is the most expensive power on the market. Peaking power may run two to four times the average price for electricity. Since that price is expected to keep rising, and since Solana produces peaking power, they may actually get better prices in the open market after their 30-year contract runs out. And their cost will drop to around *1 cent per kWh or less*. Solana will essentially give Abengoa Solar a free cash-flow machine powered by the sun.

Other early contenders for the trillion dollar prize are Acciona, Iberdrola, Sener, BrightSource, eSolar, and Solar Millennium (or Milenio Solar). BrightSource alone has announced contracts to build more than 4 GW of utility-scale solar plants— enough power for 1.4 million homes. This includes the two largest solar contracts in history, according to the company: 1.3 GW with Pacific Gas and Electric, and another 1.3 GW with Southern California Edison.[100] The first project is a 400-MW solar complex in Ivanpah, California, near Death Valley and Interstate

15 between Los Angeles and Las Vegas. The company plans to break ground in 2009 with the first 100-MW plant, followed by another 100-MW plant and a 200-MW plant.

The capital investment to develop 4 GW of solar power tower capacity is anywhere from $16 to $24 billion. Bright-Source has chosen the solar power tower method to create all this electricity. Pasadena-based eSolar and Los Angeles-based So-larReserve have also chosen solar power tower as their core technology for utility-scale solar power generation. Together, they will give this method the largest market share for solar power generation in America—if not the world. The Mojave desert is about to get very busy with concentrating solar power! But CSP desert power is only the largest-scale opportunity space in solar energy. Let's look at the next scale down.

"The significant problems we face today cannot be solved with the same level of thinking that created them."

—Albert Einstein

"Hey, we don't need you. You haven't got through college yet."

—HP managers to Apple co-founder Steve Jobs

"By harnessing the power of the sun, electrical power
will become more available around the world.
That will help humans turn seawater into fresh
water and eliminate environmental problems. If you have
enough energy you can solve a lot of other problems."

—Charles Munger, Berkshire Hathaway

CHAPTER 4

OPPORTUNITY II— POWERING INDUSTRY: INDUSTRIAL SCALE SOLAR

On Monday June 12 2006, the United States soccer team disappointed again by losing 3-0 to the Czech Republic at the FIFA World Cup in Germany. Five million individual soccer fans worldwide viewed 226 million pages and 425,000 video streams on the FIFA website hosted by Yahoo, Inc[101]. To serve all those millions of pages the company has built data centers around the world comprising about half a million computers that search, store, manipulate, and distribute documents, photos, videos, and other data. The energy to power those computers and the air-con-

ditioning to cool them costs Yahoo about $100 million per year.
Energy is Yahoo's second largest expense, after employee payroll.

Google, the largest web company on Earth, does not di-
vulge its energy spending. Using publicly available information,
though, I can deduce that during fiscal year 2008 Google spent
about half a billion dollars to power their massive data centers.
Here's how I arrived at that staggering figure:

1. In its publicly available Securities and Exchange Com-
    mission (SEC) filings, Google states that it spent a total
    of about $1.65 billion running its data centers in 2008.[102]

2. Yahoo spends about $100 million per year in energy to
    run its half million computers (about $200 per computer
    per year).

3. Google is about seven times larger than Yahoo, which
    means they may have spent $700 million to power their
    data centers.

4. Assuming Google is 30% more efficient than Yahoo
    managing its data centers puts the energy figure at $500
    million or so.

Google is very well known as a web company. What is
less well known is that Google is also an energy company. Half a
billion dollars in energy puts it squarely in the energy business—
only not in the traditional energy-consumer market. Google has
no desire to compete with Pacific Gas and Electric or Southern
California Edison. Google has enough on its plate competing
with Microsoft, Yahoo, Facebook, and other web and information
technology providers. But Google is a massive energy-guzzler. In
its own mind, the search-engine king may be a hybrid, solar-
powered, low-carbon-emitting Prius—but in reality Google is
the Hummer of Silicon Valley companies.

It's not that Google hasn't tried to stop itself from sucking up massive quantities of energy. Google works hard to make its business energy-efficient. It provides accessible, comfortable, and free buses to transport its employees from San Francisco to and from its headquarters 40 miles south of the City. It provides bicycles for commuting on the Google campus in Mountain View. The company has a water treatment facility at its data center in Belgium.

But the web colossus has taken further steps into the cleantech market. Google's not-for-profit arm, Google.org (now Google Ventures) has invested in companies whose goal it is to make solar energy cheaper than fossil fuel energy. Its slogan "RE<C" (Renewable Energy cheaper than Coal) has shown the world how companies can influence the energy conversation in a positive way. Google Ventures has invested millions in companies like eSolar and BrightSource that aim to build gigawatts of solar power plants. This is a good thing for the planet—and ultimately a great thing for Google's bottom line.

Data centers are the aluminum smelters of the information age. They consume massive amounts of energy and need to be located near plants that produce "cheap" and abundant power. The average data center in 2008 was 50,000 square feet and needed 5 MW of energy capacity.

> *"Data centers are the aluminum smelters of the information age."*

Just like Walmarts, Home Depots, and supermarkets, however, data centers are being supersized. The "average" data center in 2020 is expected to be ten times larger than its 2008 "small" siblings: 500,000 square feet. It's also expected to need a capacity of 50 MW.[103] The cost of the power to run data centers in 2005 was $18.5 billion. The following year, 2006, data centers consumed 61 billion kWh, or about 1.5% of all U.S. electricity demand[104].

By 2020, the energy cost for data centers in the United States is expected to rise to a staggering $250 billion. This is about twice New Zealand's Gross National Product in 2007 ($128 billion[125]). According to IBM, information technology energy consumption "is expected to double in the next five years."[106] Given all this, Google's energy expenditure could run north of $1 billion in that period. If Google keeps following the same cost curve, its energy bill in 2020 will be ten times what it pays now, or about $5 billion. Where is all that energy going to come from?

Heating and Chilling

While it takes lots of electricity to power millions of computers, most of Google's energy bill goes to the cost of cooling the computers in the data centers, not to powering them. Computers heat up when operating. Pack tens of thousands of them tightly in floor-to-ceiling racks row after row, and the heat is so intense it can melt the machines. Only about one third of energy consumption in a data center actually goes to running the computer equipment.[107] As a result, Google, Yahoo, Microsoft, Facebook, and other data-center-intensive companies spend hundreds of millions of dollars every year in air conditioning. Right now, that air conditioning is being provided the expensive way—by systems powered with electricity generated elsewhere. As we'll see, there is a much cheaper, more efficient, and less polluting way to provide cooling—with "waste" heat from solar thermal generators.

Silicon Valley web companies are not alone. Heating, Ventilation, and Air Conditioning (HVAC) accounts for most of the energy we use in our homes and businesses.

- According to the U.S. Department of Energy (DOE) "residential and commercial buildings account for 36% of the total primary energy use in the United States, and 30% of the total U.S. greenhouse gas emissions."[108]

- About 65% of the energy consumed in the residential and commercial sectors is for heating (46%), cooling (9%), and refrigeration (10%)"[109]

- Process heat accounts for 36% of energy used in industrial manufacturing in the U.S. This is an across-the-board average of all industries. Some industries, obviously, require much more heat than others. In the glass industry, for instance, process heating accounts for about 80% of energy consumption[110].

Solar Chips

Frito-Lay is one of America's largest snack and "potato" chip manufacturers. Brands like Doritos, Tostitos, and SunChips have been satisfying (and growing) America's taste for crunchy eats for decades. Frito-Lay, a subsidiary of PepsiCo, makes these chips in seven plants around the United States, including Arizona; Plano, Texas; and Modesto, California.

It is ironic that Frito- Lay's SunChips, which are manufactured in Modesto, one of the sunniest places in America, lacked one key ingredient: the sun[111]. Granted, FossilChips would not sound right. Nor would GasChips, even though the chip manufacturing process in these plants has traditionally relied on natural gas to heat the oil that fries the chips. Not any more.

In 2008 Frito-Lay unveiled a 2.4-MW solar thermal plant (built by Abengoa Solar) to generate steam directly and power its industrial process heat. This plant consisted of 5,065 m² (54,500 square feet) of aluminum parabolic-trough collector mirrors that heat pressurized water to temperatures of up to 249°C (480°F). SunChips are now truer to their brand name because they're made using the sun. The solar-heated water is pumped into the manufacturing plant's boiler system, which routes it to the cereal (wheat or corn) heater and the cooking oil heater. As usual in this solar technology, the water is then recirculated in a closed loop to be heated again.

Figure 4.1. Parabolic troughs following the sun (Source: NREL)

It's time to talk in more detail about parabolic troughs, the oldest commercial CSP technology. (From 1912, remember?) A parabolic trough is a solar-power collector in the form of a long parabolic mirror, like a mirrored half-pipe, that concentrates the sunlight on a *receiver tube* running above (at the focal point of) its entire length. The tube has a fluid flowing through it that absorbs the heat. This *heat transfer fluid* is either water or (more often today) a synthetic oil that can heat to higher temperatures than water. Typically, the transfer fluid is then used to vaporize water into steam that runs a generator turbine. At any parabolic-trough CSP plant there are several rows of troughs aligned north-south. They track the sun east to west along their main axis to maximize the irradiance they absorb and therefore the power they generate. This is the technology that has been used at SEGS for more than two decades.

One of the advantages of parabolic trough technology over newer designs, though, is that it can generate hot water or steam *directly*. This is important, because traditionally a lot of energy is wasted in the process of generating hot water for industrial processes.

Generating electricity to heat water (or anything else for that matter) is an inherently wasteful process. In a coal-fired power plant, only about a third of the fuel is turned into actual electricity—the other 65-70% is wasted. Then there are transmission losses, and when that electricity arrives at its destination and is used to boil water, still more energy is lost. In the end *up to 85%* of the primary energy is dissipated. But solar parabolic trough technology can heat water or steam directly with the sun, without wasteful intermediate steps. To do this, a power plant simply uses water rather than oil as the heat transfer fluid in the receiver tubes. This is what Frito-Lay did in its Modesto SunChips plant.

By boiling water directly, companies save on the inefficiency of having to generate electricity to do it. Heat doesn't travel well, so the solar thermal (parabolic trough) plant needs to be close to the user of that heat or actually onsite. Frito-Lay manufactures more than 145,000 bags of SunChips per day using its own onsite 384-collector system, and in the process the company avoids causing the emission of 1.7 million pounds of CO_2, the carbon cost of generating the needed energy in a coal-fired plant.[112]

Industry Is the Biggest Consumer of Energy

Industry consumes about one third of all energy produced in the United States. The top 10 industries account for 75% of all industrial energy usage.

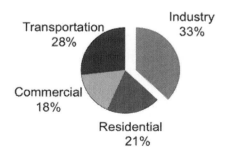

Figure 4.2. Energy usage across sectors in the United States, 2004. (Source: USDOE[113])

Eight energy-intensive industries collectively produce 90% of the materials we use, according to the U.S. Department of Energy. They have revenues of $1 trillion, they employ over 3 million people directly, and they indirectly generate 12 million more jobs[114]. These industries are: aluminum, chemicals, forest products, glass, metal casting, mining, petroleum refining, and steel. All are twentieth-century industries that exploded using cheap and abundant energy.

A lot of energy. The U.S. chemicals industry alone used 2.3 trillion kWh (7.8 quadrillion BTU) in 2004. To put that number in perspective, the whole country of Japan, the second-largest economy in the world, used a total of 6.6 trillion kWh[115] (22.4 quadrillion BTU.) This means that including every residence, farm, car, office building, aluminum smelter, semiconductor factory, and yes, chemical factory put together, Japan consumed just three times more energy than that one single American industry. Yet except for petroleum refining, the "big eight" list I just enumerated is also a list of American industries that have gone through tremendous shrinkage over the last decade or two—as energy costs have gone up.

Process heat—thermal energy used in industrial production process—is one of America's and the industrial world's largest users of energy. In Europe, process heat accounts for two thirds of industrial energy use.[116] Electricity is just one third. Another way to look at this number: industrial process heat represents 18.6% of all the forms of energy used in European Union (EU-15) countries.

The market potential for industrial process heat is enormous. About 50% of industrial process heat needs temperatures below 250°C (482°F). This represents an energy demand of 300 TWh in the European Union alone[117]. In 2007, industrial electricity prices in Europe were between 10.2 and 15.4 Eurocents per kWh[118] or an average of about 12.8 Eurocent/kWh (17.8 ¢/kWh). These figures result in a market potential for low-temperature industrial process heat in Europe of €38.4 ($53.8) billion per year.

The following table shows some examples of industrial processes that use relatively low-temperature heat (below 250°C or 482°F).

Industrial sector	Process	Temperature level [°C]
Food and beverages	Drying	30—90
	Washing	40—80
	Pasteurizing	80—110
	Boiling	95—105
	Sterilizing	140—150
	Heat treatment	40—60
Textile industry	Washing	40 –80
	Bleaching	60—100
	Dyeing	100—160
Chemical industry	Boiling	95—105
	Distilling	110—300
	Various chemical processes	120—180
All Sectors	Pre-heating of boiler feed water	30—100
	Heating of production halls	30—80

Figure 4.3. Industrial sectors and processes with the greatest potential for solar thermal uses.[119]

Parabolic-trough solar technologies like the one that the Frito-Lay plant uses today in California can easily generate heat up to about 250°C. It is not coincidental that Frito-Lay, as an early adopter of solar process heat, is in the food and beverages industry. Look at the range of processes for which food manufacture needs heat.

Generating solar hot water or steam directly for process heat can be far more efficient than using fossil fuel. On average, half the energy input to industrial-process heating equipment is lost—the range is 15% to 85% depending on the process and equipment[120]. The energy can be dissipated via flue gases, wall loss, operating loss, or in many other ways.

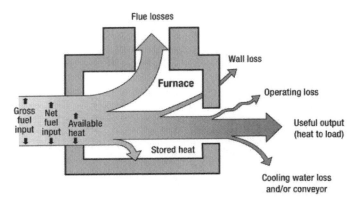

Figure 4.4. Energy loss diagram in a fuel-based process heating system[121].

The world demand for process heat is several times larger than Europe's alone. Assuming that America's market is similar to Europe's and that Japan, China, India, and the rest of the world use another 300 TWh, this back-of-the-envelope calculation yields a 900-TWh low-temperature process heat demand globally.

Multiplying this number by the power cost per kWh yields a round figure for the size of the opportunity. At 10 ¢/kWh you get a $90 billion/year market. *Over the 40-year period to 2050, you are looking at a $3.6 trillion opportunity.* (For those still skeptical: the SEGS parabolic trough plants

"In solar-generated process heat, you're looking at a $3.6-trillion-dollar market opportunity."

in California have been operating for about 25 years and have returned more than $2 billion to their investors.) And this is just for *low-temperature* process heat—which represents 50% of the industrial process heat market.

Egyptian Cotton

Remember Frank Shuman from Chapter 1? Shuman was a celebrated inventor in an era when inventors were like today's rock stars: Edison, Bell, Marconi, Tesla. Born in 1862 in Brooklyn, NY, Shuman had hundreds of patents in his name by the time he died and was featured in *Scientific American* twice in a single year.[122] His invention of shatterproof glass was an immediate commercial success that made him famous and wealthy before he was 30 years old.

Shuman's real passion in life was solar energy. At a time when Egypt was the largest producer of cotton in the world, Shuman engineered, raised financing for, and built that solar power in Maadi. The plant generated 65 horsepower to pump 6,000 gallons of Nile river water per minute and irrigate the cotton fields. To make his design work, Shuman invented many components used in solar plants with only slight changes today. For instance, he created a low-pressure steam turbine that processed four times more energy than anything then available in the market.

Figure 4.5. A closer view of Shuman's Parabolic Trough
Solar collectors at Maadi,, ca. 1912[123].

Some of the largest concentrating solar thermal power (CSP) plants today, like the SEGS in the Mojave, which generated up to 90% of the world's solar power in the early 1990s, still use Shuman's parabolic trough design.

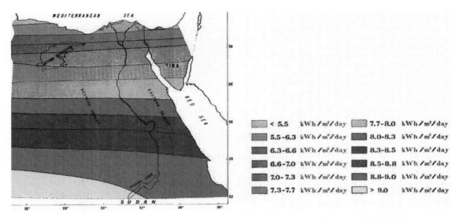

Figure 4.6. Egypt's direct normal insolation. (Source: IEA[124])

Egypt provided Shuman with some of the best direct solar radiation in the world, a ready market for the product, and the British colonial investors who saw the value that this technology could return. A map of Egypt's direct normal insolation (DNI) in Figure 4.6 shows how strong the sun's energy is there. Cairo receives more than 5 kWh per square meter per day, while some of the desert areas south of the capital receive more than 6.5 kWh over the same area and time. (Germany, the number one solar market in the world, receives on average less than 40% of that amount[125].) Some areas in the south of the country receive more than 9.0 kWh/m^2 per day! Think about it this way: the average American household consumes about 31 kWh/day. An area slightly larger than 3.2 m^2 (34.4 square feet) receives solar energy equivalent to that consumption.

Today's solar technology doesn't convert all that energy—but it can get close. Solar photovoltaic panels convert 14-15% and solar thermal CSP technologies convert about 33% of the energy from the sun into electricity. However, by combining heat and power generation, a plant can convert up to 80% of solar energy. Since much of the electricity we use in summer heat goes to air conditioning, we can use the sun to heat water to power air conditioning directly.

Huh? That seems counterintuitive. How and why is hot water used to cool air? The why is obvious: energy is energy, and that still very hot water coming off the generator turbine blades has lots of it that would otherwise be wasted. So the remaining question is how to use that energy for refrigeration with high efficiency. There are actually several technologies that do this, but the essential feature is that the still very hot water flowing from the turbine is compressed, then used to drive a compression-evaporation cycle much as in your fridge at home. As in your fridge—or on your skin when you perspire—the evaporation process chills the coolant (in this case water) and this in turn chills air pumped through pipes around the evaporator. Its energy extracted, the water is recycled back into the solar thermal system.

The hot water from CSP plants can also be used for industrial process heat, residential heating and cooling, or seawater desalination. (More on these topics later in the book.)

Egyptian Hot Medicine

As I've just explained, Egypt has some of the world's best solar resources. Almost a century after Shuman's parabolic trough plant was shut down, a new one was opened in Egypt. Located a few miles west of Cairo, this solar plant provides low-temperature process heat to the El Nasr Pharmaceutical company. Like the Frito-Lay plant in Modesto, the El Nasr plant produces hot water—not electricity. On-premises solar water heating is both more efficient and cheaper than today's methods of boiling water.

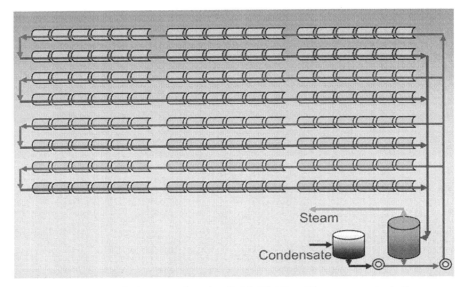

Figure 4.7. Parabolic trough solar field. El Nasr Pharmaceutical, Egypt
(Source: Lotus Solar[126])

The layout at El Nasr is typical of parabolic trough solar plants. It has 144 trough-shaped collectors, each measuring 6 meters (18 ft) long and 2.3 m (6.9 ft) of aperture, to a total of 1,900 meters (6,234 feet) of reflective surface. The collectors are arrayed in eight "horizontal" rows of 18 each. The eight rows form four closed loops: unheated water is fed to the four "odd" rows, circulates left through that row and then right through the "even" row below it—in this way circulating through a total of 24 collectors. The water is heated to the intended temperature (175°C) and fed into the company's steam network.

With most of its heat extracted, the water flows into a condenser and is fed back into the parabolic trough loops to be heated again in yet another heating cycle. This plant delivers 1.9 tons of saturated steam per hour at a pressure of 7.5 bar (108.8 psi)—the equivalent of 1.33 MW of thermal power.

The plant cost about $2.2 million to build—less than $1.60 per installed watt of power. This investment price is equivalent to half the capital cost of a new coal plant. The other main difference, obviously, is that the El Nasr plant can run with zero fuel costs and zero carbon and mercury emissions. Also, you cannot profitably operate an industrial coal plant at less than 500-MW capacity or a nuclear plant at less than about 1, 000 MW. A solar thermal plant like the one at El Nasr can be profitably built at smaller scales, like 1 MW.

Furthermore, according to the European Solar Thermal Industry Federation, the capital costs of building a solar thermal plant will fall to $0.40 or just about a fourth of El Nasr by 2030[127]. At that time the levelized cost of energy produced by these plants will be as low as 2 c/kWh in Southern Europe.

If Egypt were to realize even a small percent of its solar energy potential, it could be a net exporter of solar electricity to Europe. How large is Egypt's potential? A CSP plant the size of Lake Nasser (which powers the Aswan hydro plant) could "harvest an amount of energy equivalent to the present Middle East oil production."[128] That's the equivalent of about 9 billion barrels of oil per year!

> *"A concentrating solar power plant the size of Lake Nasser could harvest an amount of energy equivalent to the Middle East oil production."*

How would Egypt distribute all that energy to gigawatt-hungry nations? Right now, Egypt's transmission grid is connected to Jordan, Syria, and Turkey to the northeast. To the west it is building an interconnection with Libya, which is also working on a link with Tunisia that will be connected to Morocco and Spain. Spain is connected to Portugal and has a small connection with France.

Of course, selling to Europe through that old grid would not be efficient. However, there is a plan (called Desertec) to build HVDC lines to link solar plants in the Sahara to the consumption centers in Europe—that's the one that Deutsche Bank and its consortium partners are raising the half-trillion dollars for right now. New Zealand already powers the North Island with power generated in the South Island—with HVDC transmission lines underwater between the islands.

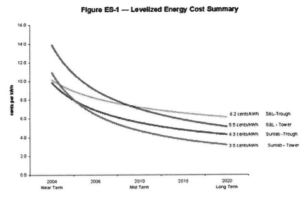

Figure 4.8. Cost of electricity produced by parabolic trough and power tower to 2020. (Source: Sargent and Lundy[129])

Furthermore, the cost of producing solar electricity is rapidly falling. It is expected to fall to the equivalent of oil at $20 per barrel by 2020 and to $15 per barrel beyond that point. That's 3.5 ¢/kWh. *By 2020, unsubsidized solar will be cheaper than subsidized coal.*

As Google, Yahoo, and Microsoft look for areas with cheap electricity to power their massive data centers, they could do much worse than 3.5 ¢/kWh in 2020 and 2 ¢/kWh by 2030.

Yet despite Egypt's superior solar resources and export possibilities,

> *"The cost of solar is expected to go down to 3.5 ¢/kWh by 2020. Unsubsidized solar will be cheaper than subsidized coal."*

83% of that nation's electricity today comes from burning oil or natural gas—which released 34 million tons of carbon into the atmosphere, (about half a million tons per Egyptian.)

Egypt has built massive civil engineering projects like the Aswan Dam and the Suez Canal. Can this country rise to the challenge of making itself an energy world power? Two centuries after Napoleon's military power invaded Egypt, Cairo can turn the tables by exporting solar power back to Europe. This time, though, it would be a peaceful mutually beneficial endeavor—using HVDC lines.

Solar Millennium

Solar Millennium's office is in an unimposing building in an unimposing part of Berkeley, California. My first conversation with Rainer Aringhoff, the President of Solar Millennium (USA), lasted about two and a half hours—but it occurred to me that if I had brought good beer or wine instead of coffee, we could have talked into the wee hours of the morning.

Or rather, I could have listened to him all that time. Mr. Aringhoff is one of the few executives who have been in the solar industry since the early 1980s. He is still very much of this industry, and he's certain that this time, the conditions are ripe for solar to make a significant leap. Back when President Jimmy Carter funded the fledgling solar industry to achieve American "energy independence" from Middle East oil in the late 1970s, Aringhoff was working to make that vision come true.

After Carter left the White House, the solar industry faced rapidly diminishing research and development budgets until it almost disappeared from the map. (One of the first things that newly inaugurated President Ronald Reagan did in 1980 was to have the symbolic solar panels installed by his predecessor ripped from the White House roof.) Partly as a result, today America is even more dependent on Middle East oil than it was three decades ago.

In 1972 the United States imported 811 million barrels of oil, or 19% of our total consumption. In 2008 we imported 3.3 billion barrels or 62%[130]. We now consume more oil and are more dependent on importing it. And it costs more, too. In 1972, oil cost $1.92 per barrel, while in 2008 it averaged $94.34, according to British Petroleum's statistical Review of World Energy. According to these figures, we went from paying $1.6 billion in oil imports in 1972 to more than $350 billion in 2008. So much for energy independence!

Not only have the prices of oil and other fossil fuel inexorably trended up, but just to confuse matters, this upward trend has been anything but smooth and continual. There's tremendous volatility in the price of oil (as of other commodities). It's easy to see in hindsight why short-term-oriented U.S. policymakers and investors have ignored solar for so long. As oil slid to $10 per barrel during the 1990s, General Motors happily paid $500 million to acquire Hummer. Oil was supposed to be cheap and plentiful forever. Ha. (You have to ask yourself: if the then largest and most petroleum-dependent company on earth could not forecast oil prices, how can the rest of us?)

So like a kid genius in a schoolyard full of bullies, the solar industry was pretty much scorned and pushed into a corner. Through the middle and late 1980s, Aringhoff worked with the team building SEGS in Southern California—a project which offered a glimmer of hope that solar would someday come back. When there were no more solar plants being built anywhere in the world, he went to Brazil to consult on power plants. Then, when Germany singlehandedly revived the solar photovoltaic industry in the 1990s, Aringhoff took the first airplane to Frankfurt to join in. After that, he went to Spain to start what would later become the largest solar thermal market in the world.

Today, Rainer Aringhoff's goal is to help turn the U.S. Southwest into the planet's biggest generator of concentrating solar power. Over the last few years, Aringhoff has been crisscrossing the country (and the world) giving presentations about solar thermal power, the transmission grid, and America's potential to lead the field of clean energy.

Energy From Sunshine, 24/7: It's Here!

Aringhoff's journey reminded me of Al Gore's. Back in 2004, I saw Al Gore give a presentation about global warming in a converted warehouse at Fort Mason in San Francisco to a small group of people attending a Green conference. For years, Gore would talk about the topic to anyone who would listen. With the conviction of science and historical data on his side, the former Vice President traveled the globe with his presentation until everyone heard the message. Who knew then that it would be only a couple of years before the idea would enter the mainstream and Gore would win the Nobel prize, an Academy Award, and a Grammy? The first time I visited the PS10 solar power tower in Seville, they proudly told me Gore had recently visited the plant. Small world.

When I met with him in Berkeley, Aringhoff and I talked about Andasol-1, which was just then starting operations. Solar Millennium's Andasol-1 plant near Granada, Spain, which officially went online in July 2009, is a 50-MW plant with 7.5 hours of thermal energy storage. This plant uses 510,000 m² of parabolic trough collector surface (5.5 million square feet) and two tanks of molten salt thermal storage to generate a total of 280,000 GWh per year—about enough power for 170,000 people. Andasol-1's energy storage is the largest in the world and can generate on-demand electricity in the evening, during rain or cloud cover.

Andasol-2 and Andasol-3 are two identical solar plants that are being developed as I write this. Each plant has 50 MW of capacity, 7.5 hours of energy storage, and a total production of 280,000 GWh per year. More than half million people will get their electricity from these three plants—plus, their clean operation will spare the Earth's atmosphere from 450,000 tons of carbon dioxide per year.

I mentioned earlier in this chapter that the expected size of a data center in 2020 will be 500,000 square feet. Such a center is also expected to need a capacity of 50 MW.[131] Andasol-1 produces that 50 MW, but only 7.5 hours of storage. Meanwhile

> "Gemasolar is a CSP plant with 15 hours of energy storage. 24/7 solar power is here."

Google, Yahoo, or Microsoft cannot afford to be down even for a minute. They need a steady flow of power 24/7/365.

Before you say "lump of coal," let me tell you about Gemasolar. Gemasolar (formerly called "Solar Tres") is a solar power tower plant with a 17 MW capacity and 15 hours of energy storage. Yes, a solar power plant that will deliver electricity at 10 pm., at 1 am., and at 4 am.

There you have it: *a 24/7 solar plant*. Combine the 50 MW capacity of Andasol with Gemasolar's salt storage and you can power the typical data center in 2020 round the clock. Still, Google can't possibly risk any downtime. What if there are three full days of rain in a row?

I took a look at the weather pattern in Yuma, Arizona. According to the US military, the Yuma Proving Ground (an Army test base) has "sparkling clean air, low humidity, skimpy rainfall— only about three inches per year—and an annual average of 350 sunny days."[132] The other 15 days, the data center can buy power from the grid. So the data centers would not be totally off grid— but the sun can meet 96% of their energy needs. What's more, the rest of the energy doesn't have to come from polluting plants. Wind, geothermal, and other clean energy sources can power that other 4% of the time. Bottom line: solar today *does* have the ability to bring us "baseload" electricity. Clean energy opponents will have to invent a new excuse for our society not to go with solar.

Data center operators, as I've explained, spend billions of dollars per year in energy—a figure quickly rising to tens or hundreds of billions per year. How large is this market? As I said before, the cost of the power to run data centers in 2005 was $18.5 billion[133].

This cost is expected to rise to $250 billion by 2020—a compounded growth rate of 26.5% per year. Assume that the industry makes massive energy efficiency gains so that energy costs go up only 6.5% per year—to just $38 billion in 2020 and $250 billion in 2050. You're still looking at $3.7 trillion in energy expenditures just to run data centers over the next 40 years (the life of a power plant).

This will be a market opportunity in the trillions of dollars for producers who are able to gener-

> "You're looking at $3.7 trillion in energy costs to power data centers. That's a huge market opportunity for solar energy providers."

ate electricity (to power the computer equipment) and air conditioning (to cool it.) CSP technology is uniquely positioned to produce both the electricity and the steam (to feed the chillers for air conditioning) with a high degree of efficiency. Add thermal storage and connect it to the grid, and data centers can run 24/7 with mostly solar energy.

Six months after my first meeting with Rainer Aringhoff, Solar Millennium announced that it had signed a Power Purchase Agreement (PPA) with Southern California Edison for the development of 726 MW of solar electricity capacity to supply the California grid. That capacity would by itself triple the solar-thermal capacity in the state, with the greatest solar-generation capacity in the United States. The contract is divided into two 242-MW plants with an option for a third one of the same size. Each plant would cost around $1 billion to build (about $4 per watt.)

The sites chosen for these plants are the towns of Ridgecrest, Desert Center, and Blythe. Together, these sites get some of the highest Direct Normal Incidence (DNI) solar radiation in the world—about 2,800 kilowatt-hours per square meter per year ($kWh/m^2/yr$). I'll remind you that the average US household consumes 936 kWh per month.[134]

Think about it. Harvesting about 4 square meters (43 square feet) of Southern California desert can already, with proven technologies, yield solar energy equivalent to what each American household consumes in electricity. Solar can power your mobile phone or PC when you do a Google search, and it

"Harvesting about 4 m^2 (43 ft^2) of Southern California desert gets solar energy equivalent to what each American household consumes in electricity."

can power Google's industrial-scale data centers when they crunch the bits and push the results back to you.

Aringhoff was right. This is the time solar is happening on a major industrial scale. The Solar Millennium is not just a company name any more. It's here.

"This 'telephone' has too many shortcomings to be seriously considered as a means of communication. The device is inherently of no value to us."
—Western Union internal memo, 1876

"Airplanes are interesting toys but of no military value."
—Marshall Ferdinand Foch, Ecole Superieure de Guerre.

"Any intelligent fool can make things bigger, more complex, and more violent. It takes a touch of genius—and a lot of courage—to move in the opposite direction."
—E.F. Shumacher

CHAPTER 5

OPPORTUNITY III— BIKINI POWER: ISLAND AND VILLAGE SCALE SOLAR

The Marshall Islands consists of 70 square miles of land spread over half a million square miles of South Pacific ocean water. Its white sand, coconut trees, and warm idyllic climate would make a perfect backdrop for a tropical beer commercial or for a drink with a twist of lemon and a little umbrella. Formerly part of the United States, the Republic of the Marshall Islands (RMI) became self-governing (in "free association" with the United States) in 1986. Of its many atolls, islets, and reefs, one is indelibly embedded in world consciousness: the Bikini atoll, where the U.S. exploded the first hydrogen bomb in 1952[135].

Fifty years later, things were not better in this country of 54,000 inhabitants. On July 3rd 2008, the Marshall Islands declared a state of economic emergency as the price of oil hit $147—an all-time high. President Litokwa Tomeing announced that the national power utilities faced a deficit of $17.5 to $21 million. This was equivalent to 20% of the total national budget[136]. The country ran the risk of going without electricity if the government did not come up with that money quickly. This would have been a "disaster of unimaginable magnitude," according to President Tomeing.

The RMI got in trouble because it derives essentially all its primary energy from fossil fuels. Its industry, businesses, and homes run on electricity produced by diesel generators, and its cars run on gasoline. Prices that go up an order of magnitude in less than a decade are bad enough. That's not the worst part of buying fossil fuels like coal, oil, and gas. An even bigger problem with fossil fuels is the volatility in pricing.

Imagine buying a home where the interest rate is reset every day and could in fact increase by 700 percent over a decade. You would not know from one month to the next what your mortgage payment would be—or if you could afford to pay at all. That $2,000/month mortgage payment could turn into $8,000 next month and $16,000 a couple of months after that. You would have no ability to plan your future and that of your family.

Welcome to the world of commodity fuels.

The price of a barrel of oil went from $16 in 1999 to a peak of $147 in 2008—just a week after the Marshall Island crisis (fig 5.1). Oil then went back down below $40 before it rebounded back above $70. Commodities derived from oil such as diesel, kerosene, and gasoline follow a similar pattern. Natural gas and coal are more regional commodities but also go up and down with world economic and financial markets.

The things that affect the price of oil can be mind-boggling. Imagine your mortgage payment going up 10% or 20% in a single day because the leader of a Middle Eastern nation said something that the hedge fund managers in New York liked (or didn't like).

"Natural gas is one of the most volatile commodities in the marketplace today," according to Arizona Public Services. "APS's current hedging program is based on a systematic approach looking three years forward on a rolling basis and using financial model simulations containing built-in assumptions, such as load growth

> "Natural gas is one of the most volatile commodities in the marketplace today."

and outages at power plants."[137] The hedging works like this: APS pays a premium to hedge (guarantee the price of) 85% of the anticipated volumes for year 1, as well as 50-65% of year-2 and 30-40% of year-3 anticipated volumes. Given the gas-market volatility, APS in 2008 was looking at extending its hedging for five years instead of three years. That is, they would pay even more money to guarantee prices for an additional two years.

Whole industries outside energy can be affected by this volatility. Take the airline industry. Airlines have been ravaged by their inability to plan one of their highest-cost items: gasoline. They sell a ticket for a trip a month or eight months into the future but have no way of knowing what that ticket will cost them in fuel. Sure, they can engage in financial hedging and "buy" oil futures. Because of volatility, this exercise is no more than guesswork at best and gambling at worst. Guess what the price of oil will be a year from now, let alone two or three? *This is not about demand and supply.* What will the cover of the *Wall Street Journal* say about which Middle Eastern leader on a Tuesday in September five years from now and how will that affect the price of oil—and your company?

Southwest Airlines bet right and was able to contain fuel costs. They "hedged" and assured that most of their oil would be priced at $73. When oil shot up to $147 they looked really smart. Most other airlines didn't and lost billions. Was Southwest smarter? Not really. After they bet right, they bet wrong. When

oil prices fell back to $61, Southwest had to take a $247 million
charge for their first quarterly loss ever[138].

Gambling on energy prices should have nothing to do with
operating a healthy company. Yet energy price volatility exacts
an immense cost on companies in many industries—or entire
small or poor nations—that depend on oil and other fossil-fuel
commodity prices. The Marshall Islands went dark when it got
caught up in a world of rising fuel prices and a level of volatility
that it was unable to handle.

With solar energy you know what the cost is going to be—
forever. Whether you are an individual who needs to heat the
house in the winter, a data-center company that needs to budget
for increasing power needs, or a city (or country) that needs to
take care of its citizens' energy needs without going bankrupt,
solar energy can give you that cost stability that no fossil fuel can
or ever will.

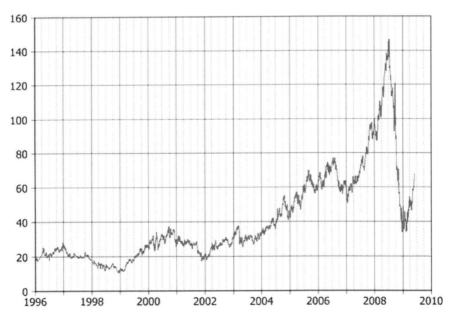

Figure 5.1. Oil prices 1996-2009. Dollars per barrel for NYMEX
sweet light crude WTI (Source: Wikipedia[139])

What is Village-Scale Solar?

I invented the terms "village-scale solar" and "island-scale solar" to describe the market need for energy on the part of "islands," "villages," or other users that are either off the larger grid or too small to warrant a "standard-size" coal plant (I GW or 0.5 GW.) Much of the developing world still consists of relatively small and isolated villages. In India alone, for example, there are more than half million villages of all sizes—most of which are not on the grid. These communities mostly depend on diesel-run generators to produce their electricity. The diesel fuel is brought in from somewhere else by ships or trucks, which makes it prohibitively expensive.

In 1994 the operating cost of village-size diesel-produced electricity was between $1 and $2 per kWh[140]. That's before diesel prices more than tripled as oil prices rose in the following decade. Should I remind the reader that solar photovoltaic electricity is around 20 ¢/kWh today? Or that there is no fuel cost?

Gary Zieff, President of Dissigno, a San-Francisco-based company, wants to get five billion people to switch from fossil fuels to solar PV.

> "The cost of diesel electricity was between $1 and $2 per kWh. Solar PV is 20 to 30 cents per kWh."

"Kerosene and fossil fuel-based energy are keeping a vast population in poverty," says Mr. Zieff. "Kerosene costs $1,000 per lumen, which is two orders of magnitude more than we pay in the U.S. The light is so bad that children reading have to get closer and closer to the tin can, which means that they'll breathe the noxious fumes or be at risk of fire."

If these families can't afford the kerosene, they have to set out to find firewood. "The mothers may need children's help with all the errands to just get basic energy to cook or read. We just flip a switch," says Mr. Zieff. "Improved solar lighting is the first step on the road to a better life. Children can read at night and mom can sew apparel for income generation. Light is the way for them to understand the power of power. It's so simple!"

Dissigno has a different business model. They rent a battery-powered LED lights on a monthly basis. A person or organization in a poor off-grid community acts as a "community bank." He or she educates the users, rents the LED lights, and collects the monthly fee. The "bank" also has an inventory of batteries that are charged using solar PV panels. Once a month the users come to pay the fee and swap the low battery for a full one. The price? About $2.25 per month. This is about what users pay for kerosene today (although fossil prices vary depending on local conditions and number of intermediaries.)

"We had a project in Tanzania where he turned a profit after just 6 months. Then he hired someone else to help him grow the business. There are new jobs created, children can read and study, moms can sew, their indoor environment is clean. Something as simple as clean energy is the solution to so many of the world's problems," says Mr. Zieff

Patrick Walsh is an American entrepreneur who won the prestigious Lemelson-Illinois award in 2008 for the invention of a solar-powered LED light powered by a small solar panel[141]. "There are about 600,000 villages in India, and half of the villagers used kerosene lamps,[142]" said Walsh. "They spend $38 billion a year, or about 5-10% of their meager income, buying kerosene."

Walsh founded a company called Greenlight Planet to produce and market the "SunKing," a solar-powered LED light with built-in battery that can provide up to 16 hours of light per day powered purely by the sun. This light is twice as bright as kerosene light and doesn't cause any dangerous indoor pollution.

But these people are so poor—it can't be much of a market, right? *Wrong*. At $60 per solar lamp and a market of 1.6 billion kerosene users, the market opportunity is *$96 billion*. Assuming a replacement rate every four years that's about $960 billion over the next four decades.

As the Indian government builds the national grid, many villages will eventually be connected to it. However, building the grid will be a long process, and many more villages will never join it—they're too small, or too remote, or the terrain is too difficult to bring lines across, or all three.

The good news is that they don't *have* to be on the grid. Many of them can do fine with solar power plants that deliver power locally without a major interconnect. Should the grid ever connect with them, they will be able to balance the load, but they won't have to be dependent on it for local energy needs.

And, as I've already mentioned, if you think this is a "developing" region problem, think again. Hawaii fully qualifies as a state in need of island-scale solar energy. Hawaiians pay some of the highest average rates for energy in the United States. In 2007 their electric rates were about triple the national average, with users on Molokai paying up to 41.64 ¢/kWh[143]. That's before oil prices tripled again the following year.

> "Hawaii residents paid up to 41.64 ¢/kWh in 2007. That's before oil tripled."

Another form of solar technology that can generate electricity efficiently for off-grid businesses or villages is the solar-dish Stirling engine system. This system, as I discussed in Chapter 3, looks like an inverted umbrella, usually mounted on a tracking system. (See Figure 5.2.) The mirrored "umbrella" dish focuses the sunlight on a receiver that juts out of it, much in the way a satellite dish focuses the signal. This receiver has a piston-based engine that turns the heat into power. Companies like Infinia and Stirling Energy Systems (SES) are developing products that vary in capacity from 3 kW to 25 kW.

A 25-kW dish Stirling engine could generate power equivalent to the demand of about 20 American households—or several hundred households in an Indian or African off-grid village.

Figure 5.2. EuroDish Stirling engine solar power system
(Graphic: Wikipedia[144])

A company called Terrafore, headquartered in Riverside outside Los Angeles, is developing a larger system aimed at villages and businesses. Using a type of CSP called Linear Fresnel, Terrafore is developing a 200-kW system that could generate both electricity and hot water. According to Terrafore CEO Rajan Kasetty, this system is so lightweight that it can easily be placed on a rooftop without the kinds of support structures that many industrial systems might require.

This company is also working on a more efficient and compact form of salt energy storage. (See Chapter 7 for more on energy storage.) Terrafore cofounder Anoop Mathur was part of the Honeywell team that worked on the original Solar One power tower in the Mojave desert. "We want to take this technology out of the desert and into the communities where they are also needed," says Mr. Kasetty.

A 200-kW solar CSP system could generate electricity for a village of hundreds of households. A compact inexpensive solar salt system could help a town store energy for nights or during cloud covers. A smart microgrid system could help manage this type of village-scale solar infrastructure.

But I'm getting ahead of myself. Before I discuss storage and grids, let's talk about some other kinds of "islands" that could use this intermediate scale of solar power.

Military Bases

In 2007 the United States military consumed more energy than the entire country of Nigeria (population 140 million) and more oil than all but 35 countries in the world, according to the *Energy Bulletin*[145]. The price tag: $20 billion.

Military bases can be like islands: they are independent, sometimes isolated, and self-contained communities. Many military installations have their own electric generation facilities and may also connect to the grid to complement this power. They need reliable energy services and cannot afford to lose power under any circumstances. (The military's energy consumption is probably not accurately disclosed. Energy is a key indicator of activity. A third party looking at a graph showing a spike in energy consumption or a "hockey stick" curve could accurately predict that the military was preparing for action outside the ordinary.)

The military is also an early adopter and investor in technology. A notable example of military investment is the Internet, which came out of a research and development project started four decades ago (August 1969) as ARPANET. The Defense Advanced Research Projects Agency (DARPA), then called simply ARPA, conceived and funded this far-fetched technology infrastructure for years before the rest of the world fully came onboard[146].

Furthermore, decades after politicians started talking about "energy independence," the military finally sees energy as a national security issue. According to Robert Redlinger of Chevron, most of the world's oil and natural gas reserves are owned or operated by national oil companies in countries like Saudi Arabia, Iran, and Russia[147]. Furthermore, the 13 largest oil companies by "proven reserves" are national companies—Chevron being the largest 'international' company at number 14.

A recent Department of the Navy report titled "Powering America's Defense: Energy and the Risks to National Security" concludes that *"U.S. dependence on oil weakens international leverage, undermines foreign policy objectives, and entangles America with unstable or hostile regimes. Inefficient use of and overreliance on oil burdens the military, undermines combat effectiveness, and exacts a huge price tag—in dollars and lives."*[148] For these reasons it makes sense for the military to invest in and operate its installations with solar power.

At least some in the military apparently concur with this logic. The largest solar photovoltaic array in North America consists of 72,000 solar panels with a capacity of 14 MW. It went online December 2007 at the Nellis Air Force base in Nevada, and it was designed to generate a total of 30,000 kWh per year. "That's the equivalent of powering about 13,200 homes during the day," said President Obama on a visit to the base. "It will also save the U.S. Air Force $1 million per day[149]."

The US Army also announced that it was planning to build a 500-MW solar thermal plant at Fort Irwin in the Mojave desert in California. This plant would "provide the sprawling Army post with added energy security against disruption of power supply."[150] Spanish giant Acciona, which built and operates the Nevada Solar One 70-MW solar thermal CSP plant outside Las Vegas, has been announced as a developer of this project, together with Clark Energy Group.

Lockheed Martin, one of the largest defense contractors in the world, is also getting into the solar plant development business. On May 22, 2009, Lockheed Martin announced that it would build a 290-MW solar power plant in Harquahala Valley, Arizona, 75 miles west of Phoenix[151]. According to the news report, this plant would provide "dispatchable" electricity, which means that it will have several hours of molten salt thermal energy storage. This is in line with Abengoa Solar's 280-MW Solana solar plant which is expected to have 7 hours of storage.

In 2008, Lockheed-Martin had revenues of $42.7 billion and assets of $33.7 billion, with only $3.8 billion in debt.[152] Is this company expanding into the civilian market? Not likely. Eighty-four per cent of Lockheed Martin's 2008 revenues came from the U.S. Government with the company either as a prime contractor or subcontractor. 13% of revenues came from foreign governments "including foreign military sales funded in part or in part whole by the U.S. Government," while only 3% of sales were to "commercial and other customers." I'm just guessing this Arizona plant is part of Lockheed-Martin's learning curve and that other announcements of military solar thermal plants will be forthcoming.

How large is the market for military solar? Take just the two bases mentioned above. The Nellis solar array cost about $100 million, while the Fort Irwin plant, if built, will likely cost around $2-3 billion (500 MW times $4 to $6 per watt). The military has probably 1,500 bases in the United States[153] and more than 700 around the world.[154] Do the numbers.

At the most recent (July 2009) Concentrating Solar Power Summit USA in San Francisco, several prominent multibillion-dollar infrastructure construction firms like Bechtel and CH2M Hill (and Lockheed-Martin) sent multiple representatives each —they may have sent none the year before.) Construction and defense giant Fluor recently announced a deal to build a 49-MW power plant using eSolar's technology[155].

Extrapolating from the U.S. military's self-reporting, its energy spending over the next four decades will be north of $800 billion dollars. The rest of the world's military spending put together is about the same as America's[156]. Assuming the same ratio applies to energy spending, then the rest of the world's military will also

> "The U.S. military will consume $800 billion in energy by 2050."

consume about $800 billion. That's a total $1.6 trillion in world military energy spending to 2050.

Energy will increasingly become a "homeland security" issue. Given the distributed (decentralized) basis of solar and clean energy, it only makes sense that the military will adopt solar electricity, heating, and cooling. The business opportunities for the entrepreneurs who invent new clean energy solutions and those who build and supply that energy are enormous.

The race for military solar power generation contracts is on.

Masdar: A City 105% Powered by the Sun

The desert in Abu Dhabi defines hot. When I visited in late fall (November) the temperature was above 38°C (90°F), but during the summer it habitually reaches 50°C (122°F), which makes it unbearable not just to visitors like myself but also to the local people. Air conditioners are standard in every new home. Whoever can afford it—and isn't there to make a lot of money as quickly as possible—leaves for Europe, America, Lebanon or other cooler locales.

The United Arab Emirates, of which Abu Dhabi is part, is the worst carbon-dioxide emitter per capita in the world. But they are planning on changing this. A few miles outside the capital city of Abu Dhabi lies a massive construction site. One of the largest airports in the world is rising where there is mostly desert sand today. Next to the airport is the site where the government has broken ground on the development of what it intends to be the world's greenest city: Masdar.

Today Masdar consists mostly of cranes, parking lots, and lots of sand and sun. When finished, this $20 billion city will house 50,000 people, commerce, and a science and technology university.

The plan is for Masdar to produce all its power from solar energy—and have a small electric surplus to pump to the Abu Dhabi grid. When I spoke with Masdar's builders, they proudly said that it will be powered 105% by the sun. The drinking water will be desalinated or recycled, the air conditioning will be powered by chillers fed with solar hot water and solar electricity, and local transportation (no cars will be allowed) will be centrally powered.

Figure 5.3. Future site of Masdar city, Abu Dhabi, U.A.E. (Photo: Tony Seba)

District Heating

District heating makes use of a centralized power plant that generates both power and heat and distributes them to users within a "district" or relatively small geographic area. In general, as I've already pointed out, power plants convert only up to a third of the available energy into electricity. The rest is released into the environment as so-called "waste heat." This waste heat take the form of hotter water released back into the river or lake, or hot air released from those ubiquitous cooling towers (Fig. 5.4), or both.

Figure 5.4. Cooling tower and cooling water discharge of a nuclear power plant (Graphic: Michael Kaufman, Wikipedia[157])

A Combined Heat and Power (CHP) plant, by contrast, converts much of this waste heat into usable heat in one form or another. A very common form is District Heating (DH).

District heating is not a new concept. The Romans used to distribute heat from centralized steam plants. There is a working district heating system in France that has been operating since the Middle Ages[158]. According the U.S. Department of Energy there are more than 30,000 district heating systems in the United States[159].

A DH system can scale from a single residential or commercial building to a whole village or a large urban neighborhood. Apartments get heat and hot water from a centralized location instead of having their own (inefficient) heaters, laundromats get steam and hot water to wash clothes, and stores just have to turn a thermostat to calibrate the temperature inside.

The oldest and largest DH system in the United States is in Manhattan. Consolidated Edison Steam Operations provides

14 million tons (30 billion pounds) of steam to more than 100,000 commercial and residential establishments in New York City[160]. The New York Steam Company started this system in 1882 in lower Manhattan, and it has grown throughout the years to encompass an area from the Battery in lower Manhattan to 96th Street.

District heating has had an uneven adoption curve throughout the world. In Iceland, up to 95% of all residences enjoy centralized district heating, while in the U.S. the penetration is less than 1%. However, the rise in energy costs and the volatility of world energy prices has made many governments take notice of district heating and cooling. From Abu Dhabi to Barcelona, there are now many efforts around the world to use this method as a way to increase energy efficiency.

Figure 5.5.
Manhattan: underground steam rising at Lexington Avenue
(Graphic: Wikipedia[161])

While district heating goes back to the Romans, district *cooling* is relatively new. Luckily, district cooling can rely on the same infrastructure as district heating. Masdar is planning to provide district heating and district cooling—both from solar energy.

District Cooling

Masdar's 105% clean-energy infrastructure is being planned to air-condition the whole town using solar powered air conditioning. No individual air conditioners will be allowed. The whole city will be centrally chilled. This is district cooling.

Just like district heating, district cooling takes advantage of technology and energy efficiencies that a village-scale geography can bring. Unlike electricity, which can and does flow efficiently over long distances, heat does not. What sorts of savings and efficiencies can be achieved by district cooling over individual air conditioning in every apartment or office? According to a report presented to the 2008 Euroheat & Power Conference:

- 30% in electricity savings;

- 80% in fuel savings;

- Removal of CFCs (chlorofluorocarbons that destroy the ozone layer);

- 65% CO_2 reductions.[162]

Note that these figures are for non-solar (fossil-fuel) sources. Solar would of course totally eliminate the CO_2 emissions.

Most of the energy generated at Masdar will come from concentrating solar power (CSP), with a considerable percentage also coming from solar PV. As I explained in earlier chapters, CSP can generate both electricity and hot water, while PV only generates electricity. Masdar will generate air conditioning through three different technologies: electrical chiller, absorption chiller, and dessicant/dehumidifier. Each method serves a different purpose. A dehumidifier captures the water vapor in the air—all water is a precious commodity on the Arabian Peninsula—and collects it for recycling, An electrical chiller just compresses and evaporates a refrigerant, like most home air conditioners, in this case running directly off solar electricity. An absorption chiller is a large (industrial-scale) air conditioner whose main input source is *hot water*. Yes, you need heat to get cold air[163]. An ordinary refrigerator uses heat too—see Chapter 4. The absorption chillers in Masdar will use the superheated water from the CSP turbines.

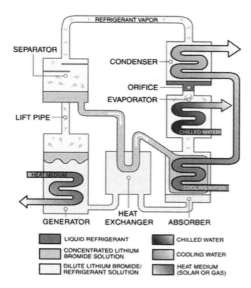

Figure 5.6. Single-Effect Absorption Chiller (Source: USDOE[164])

There are five million commercial buildings in America alone. A lot of their roof space is taken up by industrial equipment (chillers and heaters) to operate and maintain the building's environment. Cooling and heating uses 39% of all the energy consumed in U.S. buildings. Given this figure, it will be no surprise that many of the heaters and chillers they employ are inefficient. With its own efficient equipment that uses thermally activated technology, a building or district can avoid the inherent losses in electrical generation and transmission—which are at least 70%.[165] District cooling systems reach efficiencies that are 5-10 times higher than those of traditional electricity-driven equipment.[166]" Furthermore, because it avoids electricity use during peak loads (the hottest times during the hottest days) district cooling can help reduce electricity demand by up to 80%.

"District cooling systems reach efficiencies that are between 5 and 10 times higher than with traditional electricity-driven equipment."

The opportunity here is to use the sun, probably through CSP, to heat the water and directly feed it to a chiller. The efficiencies gained by this approach in district cooling and commercial cooling could be quite large. The global chiller market was around $4.5 billion in 2006.[167] Asia-Pacific comprised $2 billion of that figure, with China growing at 13.1% while the U.S. grew 6.2%.

Masdar engineers and architects are designing from the ground up with the most energy-efficient district cooling configuration possible. This means CSP hot water feeding a large absorption chiller. The cold air is piped to the apartments, offices, and businesses as needed via district cooling.

To sum up: the distributed nature of solar energy allows off-grid houses, businesses, villages, and islands to generate electricity, heat, and air conditioning effectively and efficiently. Billions of people around the world live in millions of villages with no access to electricity. Most of these villages are just like islands—relatively isolated and with little chance of gaining access to an electrical grid any time soon.

From a single solar-powered LED-light to district heating and cooling, solar ends up being not just a cleaner but also a more energy-efficient solution. Traditional electricity generation, as I just mentioned, has energy conversion losses of 70%. On-site solar energy generation cuts down on those losses, while mechanisms like DHC can help bring scale efficiencies to relatively small communities.

The business opportunities for entrepreneurs who can create and implement these efficient solar-based ways to meet global lighting, cooling, and heating needs as we transition to a clean-energy society are huge. From the Marshall Islands to India to Abu Dhabi, solar energy is a big part of the solution to the besetting problems of energy insecurity, poverty, and ill health. In the US and Europe, as the twentieth-century "dumb" grid is replaced by smart one over the next decade, district solar heating and cooling can help reduce brownouts and blackouts as residential and commercial energy demand continues to rise. Let's talk about what else solar power can do for homes and businesses.

"I do not believe the introduction of motor-cars
will ever affect the riding of horses"
— *Mr. Scott-Montague, British MP, 1903*

"Every great and deep difficulty bears in itself its own solution.
It forces us to change our thinking in order to find it."
—*Niels Bohr, Physics Nobel Prize, 1922*

"One thing I feel sure of... is that the human race must finally
utilize direct sun power or revert to pre-civilization."
—*Frank Shuman, solar inventor, ca. 1911*

CHAPTER 6

OPPORTUNITY IV— POWER TO THE PEOPLE: RESIDENTIAL-SCALE SOLAR

Mark Twain once said that the coldest winter he ever spent was a summer in San Francisco. The best time to enjoy San Francisco "summer" weather is probably in the fall. That said, October 2008 was not particularly cold or hot in San Francisco. The news was dominated by the financial meltdown on Wall Street and the American presidential elections. That month, Pacific Gas and Electric (PG&E) charged me 11.55 cents per kWh (¢/kWh) for electricity usage in my San Francisco apartment. PG&E has to make a return for its investors, so I assume that their cost of producing and or procuring this electricity is below 11.55 ¢/kWh. If PG&E were to build solar plants or buy electricity from another supplier, its costs would have to be below 11.55 ¢/kWh.

Electric rates are wildly and widely variable. They vary from county to county and from state to state. According to the Nebraska Energy Office, average rates in July 2008 ranged from 5.66 ¢/kWh in West Virginia to 18.81 ¢/kWh in New York to 31.56 ¢/kWh in Hawaii. The United States national average was 10.52 ¢/kWh[168].

Even within the state of Hawaii there are different rates on different types of user on each island. According to the Hawaiian Electric Company, a Residential consumer on Maui was charged 28.06 ¢/kWh, while a "Type G Smaller Use Business" on Molokai was charged 41.64 ¢/kWh. (These are 2007 rates from before oil prices doubled again and peaked a year later.)[169] This variability has many contributing causes, including how the electricity is produced and the time of the day and the year.

Each island in the Hawaiian chain has its own generation plant and backup. More than three-fourths of all the electricity in Hawaii is generated by petroleum-fired power plants[170]. As I discussed briefly in the previous chapter, Hawaii imports all the fuel it uses to power these plants and is thus hostage to the vagaries of the global price fluctuations that are typical of the commodities markets. Hawaii drilling for oil or growing its own fuel from, say, sugarcane would not help at all, since domestic fuel is priced on a global parity level.

According to the Hawaii Electric Company, the state's terrain makes electrical transmission and distribution difficult.[171] Hawaii is composed of many small islands that would have to be linked via subterranean transmission lines to connect their separate grids. However, as I've mentioned, the technology to do this exists; it has been used to link New Zealand's South Island (where most of that country's energy is produced) and North Island (where most of its energy is consumed.)

Hawaii has the highest electricity rates in America while being blessed with wonderfully hot, sunny days most of the year. The reader who has read this far will probably share my opinion that this situation, given the potential of existing technology, verges on the absurd. But absurdity, like necessity, can be the mother of investment.

The Grid Parity Fallacy

One of the fallacies in the energy conversation today is that of "grid parity." As in, "when is solar going to achieve 'grid parity'?" Even many in the solar industry have latched unto this false question.

What is grid parity anyway? Grid parity is supposed to be *the point at which photovoltaic electricity is equal in price to or cheaper than grid power.* It's being reached first in areas with lots of sun and relatively high electricity costs. Grid parity has already been reached in Hawaii and other islands that otherwise use fossil fuel (diesel oil) to produce electricity, and most of the US is expected to quickly reach grid parity over the next decade.

But so what? When a region like Hawaii is paying 30-40 ¢/kWh for its electricity, the estimated cost of photovoltaic electricity, which is just above 20 ¢/kWh, makes total sense, and not just in Hawaii. Do we wait for "grid parity" in Atlanta or San Francisco before investing in solar? Meanwhile, much of the world pays electricity prices that are much higher than "grid parity" in America or Europe.

So while the media conversation about solar photovoltaic electricity has mostly been about its reaching grid parity in industrialized, grid-connected societies, one major number has been totally overlooked: *2.5 billion.* According to the United Nations Education Scientific and Cultural Organization (UNESCO) about 2.5 billion people in developing countries, mainly in rural areas, have little or no access to commercial energy services[172].

So for a third of humanity there is no such thing as home electricity—of any kind. No light-bulb, television set, or microwave oven. The transmission grid does not reach their homes. Many of these homes are in conditions that are closer to nine-

teenth-century life—or sixteenth-century life, for that matter—
than what we think of as the living conditions of the twenty-first
century.

A transmission grid to reach most of this population is
probably not going to be built anytime soon, if ever. Furthermore, most of the two billion human beings who are going to
join our planet over the next four decades will not do so in industrialized, grid-connected societies. In these markets, solar and
other forms of clean energy are competing with kerosene and
diesel fuel. They're also competing with "biomass," namely wood
that is used for heating and cooking.

When Deng Xiaobing announced China's "Four Moderni-
zations" policy in 1979, there were two million telephones in
China. By 1999 there were five times as many: about 10 million telephone users. Then the market truly exploded. As of May
2009, nearly 500 million people in China owned a telephone[173].
As an educator in entrepreneurship and the introduction of new
technologies and new markets, I find this growth unparalleled. In
just a decade, the phone market in China grew by 5,000%; more
people acquired a phone in ten years than the whole population
of the United States.

This kind of penetration would simply have been impossible under the old landline telephone model. It took AT&T almost
a century to give most American homes access to a telephone.
This company had a government-sanctioned market monopoly,
pricing and financial power, and the time to make mistakes and
invent the new technologies necessary to build the infrastructure.

In almost any country, let alone a huge and heavily populated developing nation like China, building a "telephone grid"
in 10 years to provide access to twice the number of users that
it took AT&T more than 90 years to reach would simply have
been impossible. Ripping out the city streets, setting up the poles
across the countryside, and laying the cables into hundreds of
millions of homes would have required financial, technological,
operational, and management resources that China lacked at the
time.

The way China provided telephones to half a billion people in a decade is same the way the world can provide power to 2.5 billion people who lack electricity: *off the grid*. China's half billion phones are mobile phones, so no landline infrastructure was required. They are essentially off-grid. The cost of adding each off-grid user is much lower than the per-user cost of laying a multi-trillion-dollar grid infrastructure in those regions.

> *"The way China provided telephones to half a billion people is the way the world can provide power to 2.5 billion people who lack electricity: off the grid."*

That's China, an emerging economic power, and phones, not solar panels. Can the world's poor countries and people afford solar energy?

Can The Poor Afford Solar?

Back in 1976, Dr. Muhammad Yunus, a Bangladeshi economist, started what most considered a crazy scheme: lend money to poor women and men in rural areas, without collateral, and at lower-interest rate cost than any alternatives available to this population. The goal was to help this population gain access to capital to buy working tools or livestock, become small business people, and lift themselves out of poverty.

In 1976 Dr. Yunus started with a first loan of $27 from his own pocket. That year he made a total of 10 loans. From that humble beginning, Bangladesh's Grameen Bank grew to about 690,704 loans in 2006. Incredibly, 97% of Grameen's customers were women, traditionally shunned by established financial institutions. Furthermore, these loans helped poor families build 641,000 houses[174]. By 2005, Grameen had loaned more than $5.1 billion to 5.3 million people[175]—with repayment rates better than those of American banks even before the 2008 financial crisis.

Dr. Yunus had created one of the most important financial innovations of the last few decades: the concept of *microcredit*.

As of December 2004 there were at least 3,200 microcredit institutions that lent cash to more than 92 million people around the globe. Incredibly, "almost 73% of them were living in dire poverty at the time of their first loan."[176] In 2006, Dr. Yunus was awarded the Nobel Peace Prize for developing microcredit into an "ever-more important instrument for the struggle against poverty."[177]

As a 69-year-old man who had the world's gratitude and a guaranteed place in history's pantheon, Dr Yunus could have easily and happily retired. Instead he has started several other ventures that bring jobs and resources to the poor.

Seventy percent of the Bangladeshi population has no access to electricity—a shameful number in a nation with such great solar radiation. Lack of energy makes it difficult if not impossible for people to better themselves socially and economically. Without energy you can't run an efficient poultry farm, a food catering business, or even a basic home sewing business. So Dr. Yunus started Grameen Shakti to bring solar power to the people. GS would employ the same principles as Grameen Bank: to give poor and rural people access to a resource with which mainstream institutions and "the market" had formerly neglected to provide them.

In 1997, Grameen Shakti provided the know-how and the credit for the installation of 228 solar panels. GS trains installers who go door-to-door in rural centers promoting the benefits of solar electricity. Since most homemakers are women, 50% of these installers or "engineers" are also women. Bangladesh is a socially conservative country. Having men performing these duties is problematic because it's not considered appropriate for women to be visited at home by a man who is not their husband or other close family member. But this very restriction on women at home creates an opportunity for other women to learn skills and earn money.

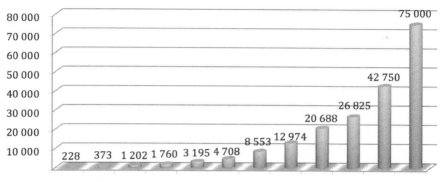

Solar Home Systems (SHS) Installations

Figure 6.1. Grameen Shakti: annual number of "Solar Home System" installations, 1997-2008. (Source: Grameen Shakti[178])

Over the decade after 1997 Grameen Shakti grew almost a thousandfold. By 2008 it had installed a cumulative 220,000 "Solar Home Systems" and was still growing at 100% per year. It had also provided "green jobs" to 8,000 people, of whom 4,000 were "engineers" or installers. Most of these 4,000 people were school dropouts (it's common in Bangladesh for girls to leave school very early in order to help at home) who might otherwise not have had a chance at decent jobs and economic advancement[179].

The cost of a Grameen Shakti solar home system (SHS) including the (Japanese) rooftop solar panels, the electronic components, and a battery is $350-$400. Buyers put down 10-15% of this cost and get a 3-year loan to amortize the system[180]. At this point they own a solar generating system that should provide electricity for 20 years.

The energy capacity installed by Grameen Shakti as of March 2009 is 11 MW, equivalent to the PS10 tower power plant in Seville. This capacity benefits up to 2 million people daily and produces 44 MWh per day.[181] The power lights up homes, powers television sets, and recharges cell phones at night.

These solar generators are mainly displacing kerosene, which is people's main source of light and cooking energy throughout Bangladesh—and throughout much of the poor world. Kerosene costs up to $2 per kWh, about 20 times what I pay for electricity in San Francisco. The poorest of the poor are paying much more than we are, both in absolute terms and as a percentage of their incomes! *What* "grid parity"?

What's more, kerosene also kills people, not just by fire but by producing noxious fumes. According to UNESCO, more than two million children died from acute respiratory disease in 2000; 60% of these deaths were associated with indoor air pollution and other environmental factors[182]. Kerosene is not just expensive. It's downright dangerous.

Meanwhile, solar energy is even more capable of distributed operation than cell phones are, since solar PV has no need even for transmission towers. The potential to reach everyone everywhere and give them access to modern energy is unique to solar. Can anyone say "democratization of energy"?

The sky is literally the limit for the growth of solar energy. Grameen Shakti plans to install one million solar home systems by 2012 and wants to create 100,000 green jobs by 2015[183]. Create jobs and advancement opportunities for the poor, save children's lives, and save the planet too? This sounds like another Nobel Peace Prize to me. In January 2009 Dipal Barua, who spun off Grameen Shakti from Grameen Bank in 1997 and has been its Managing Director since, won the $1.5 million Zayed Future Energy Prize[184].

> *"Grameen Shakti plans to install one million solar home systems by 2011 and wants to create 100,000 green jobs by 2015."*

Grameen Shakti proves that a profit-making, market-based enterprise with a social purpose can give millions of poor people access to electricity without a transmission grid, just as the Chinese government proved that similarly inexpensive processes can give phone access to hundreds of millions without a traditional telecommunications infrastructure.

Solar Water Heating

On December 1, 2008, General Electric announced that it was entering the solar water heater market[185]. The previous year a grand total of 12,000 such heaters were sold in the United States residential market. GE is one of the largest companies by revenues and market capitalization in the world. To move the needle at this company, a business has to sell in the billions and promise steady growth as far as the eye can see. Why would GE get into such a tiny market?

Let me take you back in time to mid-twentieth-century Israel. After the country experienced its first major energy crisis in the 1950s, it made solar water heaters compulsory. By 1983, 60% of Israeli homes had solar water heaters and now every new home in the nation has to heat water this way. In Israel today, 90% of homes have solar water heaters.[186] This is not some touchy-feely environmental movement: it's the law.

While the U.S. is playing catch-up, the solar water heater market offers tremendous growth opportunities. There are more than 90 million homes in this country, virtually all of which have a water heater. More than 1 million new houses are built each year and most of this growth is in the south and western parts of the country—the sunny areas.

Solar water heaters are three times more energy efficient than electric water heaters and twice as efficient as gas-fired heaters. Given that 15% of a typical residential energy bill goes to water heating, a homeowner could save up to 10% of that bill by switching to a solar water heater.

Each year 9 million (non-solar) water heaters are sold in the United States. A market penetration anywhere near Israel's, and GE's business would grow exponentially in this country. Water heater prices vary, but in 2006 consumers spent an average of $440 to replace their water heaters ($581 for gas units and $353 for electric units[187].) This would make water heaters a nearly $4 billion-a-year market—$160 billion over the next four decades. That's just in America!

Hawaii requires that all new homes built in 2010 and after come with a solar water heater. California's Solar Hot Water and Efficiency Act of 2007 has created a goal of installing 200,000 solar water heaters in the state by 2017. Other countries like Australia and Spain have also approved laws requiring solar water heaters for new construction.

While many companies are chasing the high-tech route to win in solar, there are multibillion-dollar opportunities like the solar water-heater market that are heating up right now. GE should know.

> *"This would make water heaters a $160 billion opportunity. That's just in America."*

Photovoltaic Solar Panels

As I explained earlier, solar energy consists of photons—packets of light. When photons strike atoms, they transfer their energy to those atoms, causing them to start vibrating faster (in a solid) or bouncing around faster (in a fluid). To turn the heat-energy into electricity, we use the heated fluid to drive a turbine that in turn runs a generator. Where you have motors, drives, pipes, and high heat, you have higher operating and maintenance costs. (Think about your car.) Solar thermal technologies seem to be well suited to commercial, industrial, and utility-scale applications where technicians can operate and maintain the plants.

Photovoltaic (PV) cells, by contrast, turn solar energy directly into electrons—and so into electricity. PV is easy to install and use. No water, turbines, or fossil fuels are needed. Photovoltaics are also as sturdy as any energy technology can be. The U.S. National Aeronautics and Space Agency (NASA) has used solar cells to power unmanned vehicles (satellites and probes) in space since the 1950s. In 1958 NASA launched the Vanguard 1, the first solar-powered satellite.

Figure 6.2. The Vanguard 1, the first solar powered satellite.
Launched 1958. (Source: NASA)

Forty five years later, in 2003, when NASA's Rovers were sent to Mars they had solar panels to power them. Conditions in space for any technology we can currently develop are as tough as they get. The Mars Exploration Rovers were designed to withstand those conditions. They were stuffed into a compartment on a space vehicle traveling 500 million kilometers (320 million miles) through extreme temperatures, hard radiation, and space dust. The landing, at 20-24 meters per second (53 miles per hour) alone would break almost anything on earth—even with the airbags they used to cushion the impact. (Imagine driving your car at that speed straight into a wall.)

Once the Rovers got to Mars, the 140-watt solar panels were their main power source. Motors, cameras, computers, antenna, and scientific instrumentation: the whole machine was powered by the PV panels using a lithium-ion battery for storage. Three years later, despite corrosive and toxic Martian surface chemistry, temperature extremes, and dust storms, the PV panels were producing about 300 to 900 Wh per Earth day.[188] No maintenance needed.

Figure 6.3. The solar-powered Mars Exploration Rover, 2003.
(Source: NASA/JPL)

Because photovoltaic cells convert the energy of the sun directly into electricity, they don't need to turn water into steam to drive a turbine or a piston. So they don't need the "power blocks"—the whole apparatus of boilers, condensers, compressors, turbines, and so forth—that solar thermal or fossil-fuel-based or nuclear-based power (90% of all electricity) generation require.

I'll say it again, because it's a point that bears repeating. *Alone among all power sources, PV works well on any scale.* Photovoltaic solar panels can be used to power anything from a single LED light-bulb, to a house, to an army base, to a utility-scale power plant. A home or a business can start with a small solar-panel installation and add more PV capacity as needs change.

The largest solar PV plant as of mid-2009 was the 60-MW Olmedilla Photovoltaic Park in Spain. The Nellis Army base in Nevada is powered by a 14-MW solar panel array. eBay's campus in San Jose, California is powered by a 650-kW solar installation on its roofs. A relatively large residential rooftop solar-panel system in Los Altos, near San Jose, produces somewhere between 5 kW and 10 kW. A solar street light could run on a little 80-W panel.

The smallest useful PV application I have seen is a tiny solar-powered LED light that can bring high quality, safe, and inexpensive reading to billions of people around the world. (I have a solar-powered flashlight / key-ring that a former girlfriend gave me. I'm sure it might be useful someday but I'm not sure how yet.) By contrast, the smallest "viable" nuclear plant is about 1 GW capacity and a coal plant about 0.5 GW.

The ability to work with sunlight of any quality is also where PV shines (metaphorically) brighter than CSP. Diffuse light is sunlight that is reflected off the clouds, the ground, buildings, dust, air pollution, and so on. Direct light, as the term suggests, comes straight from the sun on clear days and (at its best) from high angles—with minimal scattering by the atmosphere along the way.

Obviously, the quality and quantity of sunlight is affected by time of day, season, cloudiness, geography, pollution, nearby shadows and so on. But the difference between areas even at the same latitudes can be astonishing. Look at this map.

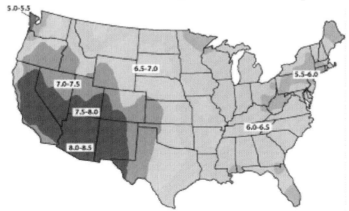

Figure 6.4. Quantity of solar radiation (in kWh/m2/day) striking the United States in June. (Source: USDOE[189])

The amount of solar energy that falls in Yuma, Arizona in June can be *nine times larger* than that falling in Caribou, Maine.[190] Based on this number alone, it might make sense for a Maine resident to contribute to building a solar power plant in Arizona and have it transmit the power to Maine! The 12% transmission loss is tiny compared with the 1,000% difference in solar energy production for the same power plant. (Of course, we would need a grid that can handle that kind of load, which is the subject of another chapter in this book.)

As we've seen, solar thermal technologies, like parabolic trough and power tower, work best where there is lots of high direct-incidence sunlight. But much of the world receives diffuse light—which makes PV attractive in many places that would not be appropriate for solar thermal. Photovoltaic cells can function at the South Pole or in Cairo—as well as on Mars or in interplanetary space.

Grid independence. Ruggedness. Scalability. Ability to work under nearly any light condition. These are some of the main reasons why photovoltaic is a preferred solution in most cities and towns around the world—for small, medium, and large applications. It works where no other power technologies can. In fact, for the billions of people who aren't on the grid at all, solar PV may well be the only real choice for electricity at this point.

This is the point in my speaking engagements where I get asked: Why don't we have more solar penetration? What can be done to make it happen? Money and politics? I went to ask one of my favorite couples in San Francisco.

Solar Finance

Alex and Helen Nigg live in San Francisco's Noe Valley district. It is a clear December day, and we can see downtown from their balcony. Alex is raising a venture fund with the goal of investing in cleantech software and services companies. Helen is a business development manager with a solar photovoltaic company and spends much of her time driving up to sell and oversee solar installations in Napa Valley wineries.

"Electricity is cash," says Alex Nigg. "If you look at electric flow as cash flow, then you can see how this whole clean energy build-out presents so many opportunities to financial industry players. Especially those who are interested in a predictable steady cash flow. As important as technology is, the big innovation in the solar industry is financial." Spoken like a true investor, I thought.

> *"As important as technology is, the big innovation in the solar industry is financial."*

One of the major spurs to the development of the mobile-phone industry was financial innovation. Back in the days when a (brick-sized) mobile phone cost $2,000, the mobile phone was the province of well-to-do early adopters or those who literally were doing business deals on the street or in the backs of their limos. The mainstream market was nowhere to be seen. Then the industry learned from some of its top customers: take our phone for free (or low down payment)—as long as you sign a one-year or two-year exclusive contract with us. The rest is history. Billions of cell phones later, this industry is a cash-flow machine. Would that model work in solar?

The most important financial innovation in clean energy came out of California in the 1980s: the Standard Offer Contract (SOC) between solar-installation builders and electric utilities. An SOC basically guarantees that a buyer (usually a utility) will purchase energy from a supplier for a set rate over the life of the contract. In 1982 the first SOC was signed, and within a year the first SEGS plant was built. This was followed by what became the biggest solar construction boom in history. It took at least a decade for the rest of the world to catch up to the power generation build-out that was spurred by this financial innovation.

The Standard Offer Contract later morphed into the Power Purchase Agreement (PPA) and later the feed-in-tariff (FIT) which has been used by European governments to accelerate the adoption of wind and later solar energy investments. Like an SOC, a PPA is a contract that guarantees that a buyer will purchase the energy output of a solar (or wind) producer at a certain price for a specified amount of time. For example, the PPA that Arizona Public Services signed with Abengoa Solar guarantees that over the next 30 years the utility will purchase its solar output of 900 GWh per year at a price of just under 15 ¢/kWh. So as the building and/or installation costs are amortized, the profit for the power supplier goes up.

The market opportunity in solar finance may in fact be larger than that in manufacturing or installing solar panels. The examples of twentieth-century manufacturing powerhouses like GE and GM are telling. GE's financial services arm produced 40% to 50% of the company's earnings while helping the company sell its high-priced items like medical devices, jet engines, and power turbines. Similarly GMAC, GM's financial services division, helped finance and sell GM cars to the point that it became more profitable than the "automotive division." (In the mid-2000s, GMAC would get disastrously into mortgage lending before it was spun off by GM.)

To learn what has worked in the solar residential and commercial markets, I went to the company that's making the fastest inroads in the largest solar market in America: California.

SolarCity and Solar Cities

"Our reputation in the industry is one of financial innovation," says David Arfin, SolarCity's Vice President of Strategy. "Yes, we are in fact financial innovators, but what we really brought was a customer-driven, turnkey-system approach. We put together all the parts from the panels to the wires, install them, connect them, and operate them."

When I was doing research for my last book (*Winners Take All—9 Fundamental Rules of High Tech Strategy*) I discovered that what had made the iPod successful was that Apple was the first company who put together the "whole product" in the mp3 player market[191]. Many competitors, including Rio and Creative, had come to market earlier with decent mp3 players, but they had left it up to users to put together the listening experience on their own: install PC Media Player from Microsoft, transfer the music from the CD by hand, download it from a possibly suspect site, or whatever. The moment Apple put the whole product together, its iPod took off and never looked back.

SolarCity is doing something similar in the residential and commercial photovoltaic business in America. Today, many consumers do the research for the "best" or most efficient photovoltaic panels, inverter technologies, software, smart devices, and connectivity to the grid. Then they look for an installer. And of course they look at bank financing: Can they take out (and handle) a second mortgage? What happens if they sell the house?

Clean energy is not different from high tech in that respect. Early adopters do a bit more in-depth work when they purchase technology, often from multiple suppliers—and then they need to put the pieces together and make them work as intended. Kind of like the way adventurous electronics buffs made home computers from kits and other off-the-shelf components circa 1980.

Financing is also a big part of the decision process. Mr. Arfin compared shopping for solar energy with shopping for mobile phones. "Imagine that someone told you to buy a $30,000 cell phone because you'd save much more than that on telecom costs over the next 30 years. Would you take it? Consumers don't think like that." I did the numbers: if you paid a typical $85 a month for the privilege of using AT&T's air rights for 30 years, you would end up giving the company $30,600. I wonder why no one is asking AT&T about "grid parity" with landline phone services.

SolarCity is putting together a business model that combines the mobile phone and the network provider (iPhone plus AT&T, or Blackberry plus Verizon if you prefer.) SolarCity owns the equipment, installs it, and provides the service. They lease it to the residential user in exchange for a long-term contract. The user gets the long-term benefits of the sun without the need to plunk down $30,000 for the equipment.

Part of what makes this business model work is driving the costs down—and the larger portion of the cost of solar is not the photovoltaic panels. While the mainstream and business media drone on about the cost of PV panels ("have you broken $1 per watt yet?"), the costs of installation, racking (or tracking), inverter, plus sales and marketing expenses come to twice the purchaser cost of the solar photovoltaic panel. So that's where the biggest cost reductions have to come from.

Leading PV cell makers are pushing down the cost curve very hard—about 20% lower prices per year over the last few decades. However, we need to push the price of the rest of the "whole product" down by an equivalent amount—or more. This isn't fair, in strict economic terms, because as I have already pointed out in Chapter 2, the playing field is anything but level. (More about this in the next section.) Solar industry leaders will say sotto voce: "Fossil fuels are subsidized, and realistically they will remain so for the foreseeable future. What we need to do is drive down costs over the next eight years so that unsubsidized solar can compete with subsidized coal or oil."

Meanwhile, cities in California, from San Francisco to Berkeley to Palm Desert, are not waiting for grid parity. They're creating incentives to make themselves clean. Palm Desert and Berkeley, for instance, are using financial innovation to spur the adoption of solar energy. These cities offer homeowners low-interest, long-term loans to finance the installation of solar panels. Home values rise, the municipality's tax base is higher which helps its coffers long-term, and the city cleans up its infrastructure.

"Our city's goal is to reduce [fossil fuel] energy use by 30% by 2011," says Patrick Conlon, director of Palm Desert's Office of Energy Management, which administers the loan program. "There's no way we can do that without lots of solar power and energy efficiency."[192]

Fossil Fuel Subsidies

On July 7, 2009, as I mentioned at the start of Chapter 2, Robert Bryce wrote an opinion piece for the *Wall Street Journal* complaining that the Obama administration was thinking about pulling the $1.92 billion in subsidies the U.S. government had been giving to the oil and natural gas industries[193]. That a government is subsidizing one of the largest and most profitable industries on earth is probably not surprising. That some see that subsidy as an inalienable right—even in the midst of the worst recession in two generations—boggles the mind.

According to the U.S. Energy Information Administration's "Federal Financial Interventions and Subsidies in Energy Markets 2007," the government subsidized the "Refined Coal" industry to the tune of $2.1 billion that year compared with $14 million for solar. The 200-year-old, (very) mature, profitable, dirty industry got hundreds of times more subsidy than the young, up-and-coming, clean industry. This amounted to a subsidy of 2.98 ¢/kWh for coal (vs. 2.4 ¢/kWh for solar). Is coal cheap? Sure. It's also heavily subsidized. And it's not America alone that does this. The governments of the world spend $250 billion per year in energy subsidies, according to the influential *Stern Review*.[194]

But it's not just the massive subsidies that the multi-trillion-dollar oil, natural gas, coal, and nuclear industries keep on receiving from governments around the world that tilt the energy-competition playing field. Discussion of energy economics should include an investigative reality check as to all the different ways in which the fossil-fuel and nuclear industries have biased the rules and regulations in their favor.

Paradoxically, then, government participation to help enable solar and wind is therefore a necessity—not because clean energy producers need subsidies *per se* but because the existing laws, rules, regulations, and yes, subsidies, are so stacked against them. In Chapter 2, for example, I examined the truly amazing regulatory structure that allows utilities to pass the construction costs of nuclear power plants on to consumers long before the plants generate a single watt of power. There are plenty of others. "The ITC (Investment Tax Credit) has less than eight years to run out. We have to drive costs hard over this time to the point that unsubsidized solar can compete with subsidized fossil fuels." So says SolarCity's David Arfin—who as a strategy vice president needs to be a little ahead of the market.

The Solar Photovoltaic Market

Installations of solar photovoltaic (PV) in 2008 amounted to 5.5 GW of capacity, according to *Solar&Energy*, a solar PV research company and publication[195]. That's 129% larger than the 2007 figure of 2.4 GW. The largest market by far has been Germany. This is a result of government policies requiring feed-in tariffs (FITs) for solar power generation.

Feed-in tariffs are government-set rates at which the utilities have to purchase power from the solar or wind producers for a specified number of years. FITs work slightly differently in different countries, but the basic concept is the same. At the end of 2007 Germany had 49.3% of the world's installed photovoltaic capacity, while Japan had 24.5%[196]. However, in 2008 Spain represented 41% of new PV installations while Germany was second at 28%.[197] This is a direct result of new generous FITs in Spain that spurred massive industry growth.

PV production has been doubling every two years since the 1990s and, as I mentioned, dropping in price by about 20% per year for several decades. Such technological improvement and production-for-price increase are reminiscent of Moore's Law, which has applied to semiconductors for several decades and has made computers accessible, untethered, and ubiquitous worldwide. (As a reminder: Moore's Law roughly states that the cost of a given unit of computing performance will drop by half every two years.)

Germany-based Q-Cells was the market leader in 2008, with production of 570 MW of solar cells. US-based First Solar came in close second at 504 MW with a wafer-thin lead over China-based Suntech at 498 MW and Japan-based Sharp at 473 MW, according to *Solar&Energy*. Those four companies are proxies for the world of photovoltaics. Germany dominated the PV-production market for many years—and still dominates the value chain including the PV whole product. Japan was close behind Germany, with the United States playing catch-up only recently.

Today, China has emerged as an industrial hub for solar photovoltaic production. Some of the largest and fastest-growing companies in the space hail from China or have major manufacturing facilities there. According to data from the China Association of Solar Energy, in 2007 the production of solar PV components was as follows[198]:

- China: 1,180 MW

- Europe: 1,062 MW

- Japan: 920 MW

- United States: 266 MW

However, as a consumer, China is lagging. Its installed base in 2007 was only 100 MW, less than 9% of its total PV production. This demand was expected to grow a thousandfold by 2050 to 100 GW, as China aims for 5% of total national power generation to come from solar PV[199]:

If China alone is expected to build 0.1 TW of solar PV capacity, how much is the rest of the world likely to build over the next four decades? According to Dr. Winfried Hoffmann, President of the European Photovoltaic Industry Association (EPIA.), the global photovoltaics market is headed up to nearly 1 TW of installed capacity by 2050[200]. Residential PV installations run about $6 to $8 per watt. This includes not only the solar cells but the "whole product": installation, tracker, electricity inverter, cables, and so on. That would make this a $6+-trillion market.

Solar cell manufacturers are assiduously working to cut costs below the $1/watt cost of producing PV. However, the other elements of the solar whole product also have to descend the cost curve further for the $6/watt figure to go significantly down. "Two thirds of the installed PV value chain is the balance-of-system," David Arfin of SolarCity reminds us. "PV manufacturers are doing a good job driving their costs down. We have to do the same with the rest of the value chain. This is process-driven innovation. We may have to cut 1% in 50 places to get a 50% reduction in price" so that the whole product can get to the $2-3 per-watt range.

What percentage of the 10 TW energy gap in 2050 will be filled by solar photovoltaics? A joint report from EPIA and Greenpeace sees 1.9 billion people powered by solar PV by 2030—to the tune of 1.8 TW. Of that total, 1.6 billion people would be off-grid.[201] Remember the China mobile phone model that provided half a billion people with phones in a decade? Logistically it can work. However, assume conservatively that it takes a little longer to achieve a little less than EPIA and Greenpeace believe: 1 terawatt of installed solar photovoltaic capacity in the residential market by 2050. Assume again that the whole product will go down to $2 or $3 per watt—and we're looking at a $2-$3 trillion market opportunity.

> "We're looking at a $2-$3 trillion market opportunity in residential solar photovoltaic."

Commercial-Scale Solar

One huge market that I haven't delved into so far in this chapter is "Commercial-Scale Solar." That's the eBays and the Adobes as well as the big-box stores and supermarkets and corporate HQs of the world that purchase solar systems for their rooftops or garages. Half SolarCity's revenues come from commercial installations.

There are more than five million commercial buildings in America[202]. These buildings receive solar energy greater than the energy that they consume inside, every day. Billions of square meters of walls and roofs are literally bouncing back the free energy that the sun is pouring down on them. America is building the equivalent of 5 GW of new roof space every year[203]. Since commerce takes place during the day, it's a no-brainer that solar is an appropriate energy source for commercial buildings. When they need to keep lights on after dark, of course, they just draw on the grid again. But the savings are spectacular nonetheless: countless kilowatt-hours for only the amortized installation and O&M costs.

> *"There are more than five million commercial buildings in America. These buildings receive solar energy greater than the energy they consume."*

While we think of photovoltaics in terms of flat roof solar panels, there is a whole new market opportunity in a concept called "Building Integrated Photovoltaics" or BIPV. As its name implies, PV is being designed to be part of the fabric of commercial buildings. Companies like Suntech Power have a number of BIPV products[204]. Photovoltaic glass, for instance, replaces a conventional windowpane, or, in the form of clear glass tiles or bricks, supersedes conventional architectural glass in awnings, skylights, and clerestory panels. Designed to be "see-through," completely transparent, it also generates electricity. Some PV roof and wall tiles look like today's tiles while absorbing those photons and turning them into power: others look a bit more like small PV panels (blue and glassy-seeming); they can easily be used to replace an entire roof. But the point is that they are integrated into a building's structure either during construction or as a retrofit.

Companies like First Solar are working on "thin film" photovoltaic technologies that you can literally build onto the wall or roof. Instead of aluminum siding, you can have "solar siding" that doesn't just sit there—it makes money for you. Instead of covering the roof with unsightly tar or a thick layer of silver paint, you can cover it with "solar bricks" that plug into the building's electricity panels. Watch those meters run backwards as they produce

> *"With Building-Integrated PV your walls, windows, roof, and bricks don't just sit there. They make money for you."*

more than you consume and the difference gets sold to the utility. With Building-Integrated PV, your walls, windows, roof, and bricks don't just sit there. They make money for you.

Figure 6.5. A side of solar panels with that building? (Photo: Tony Seba)

Today the efficiency of photovoltaic solar panels is 10-14%; that is, they convert about 10-14% of the sun's light-energy into electricity. In many areas of the country and the world, this efficiency is enough to pay for the system. Combining solar panels with concentrating solar power can raise the conversion efficiency to about 80%. That means that industrial-type technology that combines heat and power (CHP) could be used for homes and businesses.

What's the market opportunity for commercial scale solar? How much money can vendors and installers make as solar technologies become part of the fabric of the world's commercial buildings? This is a market that's at least as large as residential scale solar. Today SolarCity serves both markets and its business is just about evenly divided. Extrapolating that to 2050, we're looking at 1 terawatt of installed solar capacity in the commercial market. Assume again that the whole product will go down to $2-$3 per watt—and we're looking at a $2-$3 trillion market opportunity.

> *"We're looking at a $2-$3 trillion market opportunity in commercial scale solar."*

Solar Air Conditioning

One of the most interesting attractions in the desert heat of Dubai is the indoor ski run at the Mall of The Emirates. For $60 you can escape the desert heat for the day and cool down while schussing the run's 1,200-foot-long, 203-foot-deep drop. Complete with pine trees! Ski Dubai consists of 6,000 tons of snow made from desalinated water run through massive chillers (for how these work, see Chapter 4).[205]

Air conditioners have changed how Americans—and, increasingly, the relatively well-off in less affluent parts of the world—perceive the summer heat. Like the automobile and the washer and dryer, air conditioners have gone from a luxury to a middle-class "necessity" in less than two generations. Going to the movies for respite from the summer heat won't do anymore.

Figure 6.6. Indoor skiing at the mall in Dubai. (Photo: Tony Seba)

We love air conditioners. In 2006 the global market for air conditioners was 65 million units—with nearly all markets growing. China came from nearly no sales a couple of decades ago to 20 million units—the world's largest market. The US and Japanese markets remained stable at about 13 million and 7.5 million units, while the European almost doubled that year to 5 million units[206]. Home air conditioners, though, are not cheap to purchase. Central air conditioners, increasingly a feature of American homes, cost anywhere from $3,000 to $8,000, including installation, according to ConsumerSearch.com.[207]

In addition, air conditioners are energy hogs. As energy-hoggish as it is to burn oil to produce snow in the desert, the Mall of The Emirates with its 400-plus air-conditioned shops and entertainment centers needs 52 MW of capacity, of which Ski Dubai is said to use only (!) 4 MW[208]. A/Cs likewise consume hundreds of dollars every year in home energy bills here in the USA; how many hundreds depends on the home's location. When it's really hot, these electricity hogs can easily disrupt the whole energy infrastructure, bringing on brownouts and black-outs.

What we need is a product that generates cold air directly from solar heat when it's needed the most. The hotter it gets, the more cold air the sun will generate. So here's a market ready to be disrupted by a solar-energy air conditioner product. There are already scaled solar A/C units out there, like those produced by Denver's Coolerado Inc. [sic]. Employing no CFC refrigerants, these machines also use up to 90% less electricity than traditional units of the same volume, they're way quieter, and—yes—their cooling capacity increases as the air temperature does. Given the huge installed base of traditional A/C units, initially it makes sense for solar panels to drive them, but eventually the A/C design has to change so that it's a simpler, integrated whole product.

I'll say it again: *whole product.* The iPod succeeded when Apple brought out a whole product that seamlessly integrated the mp3 player (iPod), the PC music player (iTunes), and the music store (the iTunes store). Dozens of other mp3-player providers thought that the player was what the users were buying. In fact, as Apple understood before anyone else in the market did, they were buying a portable music-listening experience. Similarly, A/C buyers are not buying air conditioners. They're buying the ability to live in comfortable temperatures during hot summer days.

The market size is huge. Here's a simple calculation. Allowing for different sizes of A/Cs (from apartment units to central home units) let's assume the price is about $1,000. We saw that in 2006, 65 million units were sold. That makes a $65 billion market per year. *Over the forty years to 2050, that's a $2.6 trillion opportunity.*

> "Solar air conditioning is a $2.6 trillion market opportunity."

Here's another multi-trillion dollar market opportunity that would also save the grid from increasingly frequent brownouts and blackouts and save the planet from damaging pollution. Solar air conditioning is, conceptually speaking, a no-brainer. Where the brains come in—and the trillions come out—is making a whole product to drive down the cost curve so far that old-school, grid-powered A/C can't compete.

Photovoltaics are about to emerge from the "grid parity" ghetto because cleantech entrepreneurs are using their brains to change both the technology and the conversation about it. In October 2009, those entrepreneurs got a boost from the President, who stood in front of banks of PV panels at Florida Power and Light's 180-acre solar farm in Arcadia, Florida to announce the release of 3.4 billion in stimulus matching funds for clean-energy and smart- grid development[209]. Maybe the media frame around solar energy is finally going to break open.

"If we could ever competitively, at a cheap rate,
get freshwater from salt water, that would be
in the long-range interest of humanity and would
dwarf any other scientific accomplishments."
—*John F. Kennedy, 1961*

"Water is bottled electricity."
—*Bob Carr, Premier, New South Wales, Australia*

"One of the many things I learned as president was the
centrality of water in the social, political and economic
affairs of the country, the continent and the world."
—*Nelson Mandela, 2002*

CHAPTER 7

OPPORTUNITY V— BOTTLED ELECTRICITY: SOLAR CLEAN WATER

On April 27, 2009, I was in Houston, the energy capital of America, on a fundraising trip. Our afternoon meeting with a venture capitalist and the chairman and senior executives of an oil services company headquartered there was as intense and full of ups and downs as a fundraising meeting can be. After three and a half hours I concluded we were going in circles. I took my marker, wrote on my notepad "We're done—let's wrap it up," and flashed the pad to my CEO next to me.

We soon called it a meeting and went out to dinner at the city's "happening" restaurant for oil executives, Caffé Annie. No sooner had I bit into my Bronzino than the lights went out. The restaurant staff seemed to be ready for the occasion. In less than a minute, every table had candles and conversation volume went back up. It was raining outside, sometimes heavily, but no one seemed to be concerned about it. Power came back within a few minutes and then it was on and off intermittently for the rest of the evening. Our hotel proved to be no different. There was no power. There was no Internet. Worst of all, there was no running water.

I thought about the irony that America's energy hub had a Third-World grid. But that did not surprise me any more. My home town, San Francisco, was no better. Initially I felt uncomfortable in my hotel room without electric light, television, or Internet access. No Facebook or email for a whole evening! How did we ever communicate before the net? Then I thought about the upside: I would get an extra hour or two of sleep that evening.

Human beings lived for millennia without the comforts of the modern world. Many of these comforts have been directly and indirectly made possible by cheap energy from the steam and then diesel engine, by coal-fired electricity, and by motor transportation.

I thought about the relationship between energy and water.

We simply cannot live without water. Our bodies are two-thirds water and our brains are three-fourths water. Our blood plasma consists of 92% water. Dehydration can be lethal very quickly. Humans can go days (or weeks) without any food but can die within just two days for lack of water. A loss of just 2.5% of our body weight through water-loss can bring a loss of 25% of body efficiency[210]. Luckily, I had two extra bottles of water stashed in my hotel room.

In the modern world energy and water have a tight relationship—one that we don't always think about until we run out of one or the other. You need water to create electricity. You need energy to pump, clean, and transport water. That evening Houston (or at least the Galleria area of Houston) had no energy and no drinking water.

I wondered how many steps ahead of policy-makers T. Boone Pickens was.

There Will Be Peak Water

T. Boone Pickens is the quintessential twentieth-century billionaire oilman—with a twist. A wildcatter by age 26, he would later build an "oil company" whose business model was not drilling, distributing, or selling oil. Mesa Oil grew by using Wall Street financial engineering to raid and acquire much larger oil companies. During the 1980s he bought big chunks of big oil companies and then went after their CEOs and boards with a gusto that inspired Hollywood scriptwriters for years to come. He was seldom interested in owning, much less running, those companies. What he really cared about was turning a profit by selling his oil-company shares at a much higher price.

Cornering the Water Market?

Yet while much of the energy conversation in politics and the media was focused on "peak oil" and while crude was reaching the stratospheric price of $147 per barrel, Pickens was quietly (or not so quietly) amassing control over what in his opinion would soon become a more precious commodity: water. Pickens plans to pump water from the Texas corner of the Ogallala Aquifer.

The Ogallala is one of the largest and most plentiful underground freshwater "oceans" in the world. It runs the length of the North American continent from South Dakota to Texas—a total of 174,000 square miles (450,000 km²) or about 20% larger than all of Germany. It is what makes the US Midwest the agriculture capital of the world: 30% of all the irrigation water in the United States is pumped from this "High Plain Aquifer."[211] It also provides the drinking water for 82% of the people who live within its boundaries.

The Industrial Revolution was made possible by cheap and plentiful water as much as by cheap energy. Industrial users for much of the nineteenth and twentieth centuries used energy and created pollution without paying the real (external) costs of extracting, using, and polluting water. They used rivers, lakes and aquifers as both sources of "free" clean water and as sinks for waste and pollution. Many years of water use and misuse later, we're facing a situation in which most rivers and lakes are dirty, aquifers are at all-time low levels or brackish—and extraction and consumption are at all-time highs.

According to the Appalachia Center for the Economy and the Environment, "over 500 streams are impaired by acid mine drainage in West Virginia alone."[212] These polluted rivers may never be sources of freshwater again. This puts pressure on other sources to provide water for human consumption as well as for agricultural and industrial use. According to the World Bank, 90% of China's city groundwater and 75% of its rivers and lakes are polluted[213].

The Ogallala Aquifer may dry up within our lifetimes: some estimates give it 25 more years. In some areas, the water table has been measured to drop 1.5 meters (5 feet) every year. Altogether, the Ogallala is probably being depleted at a rate of about 12 cubic km (420,000 million cubic feet or 9.7 million acre feet) annually, which is equivalent to 18 Colorado Rivers pouring out to the sea every year[214].

This depletion has made some farmers wary of pumping more water, but it has also made many others like T. Boone Pickens want to pump it out even faster—and transport it to sell to thirsty cities like Dallas hundreds of miles away.

Water and Energy

Water and energy are so closely linked that no study of energy can be complete without looking at water. "Water and energy are the two most fundamental ingredients of modern civilization."[215] To cite just one statistic: according to the California Energy Commission, fully 19% of all the electricity used in the state of California is used in moving and pumping water.[216] Water is also essential for food production. About 80% of all the fresh water in the world is used for agriculture. In the United States, agriculture consumes 85% of the clean water.[217]

But the world is running out of cheap (or "free") ready sources of freshwater. Needless to say, countries with access to abundant freshwater need to do a better job managing our sources, distribution, conservation, and re-use of water. Israel, for instance, reuses 70% of its wastewater. No other country is even close to that figure.

Since about 80% of all freshwater in the world is used for agriculture, better irrigation systems as well as a switch to products with lower water content are essential long-term strategies. However, in large, less temperate parts of the world, increasing the water supply has been and will be done mostly through desalination.

Water from the Sun

The Atacama desert is one of the driest places on the planet. Located at altitudes of up to 6,885 metres (22,590 feet) in Northern Chile, this region has had virtually no rainfall in recent times. The Atacama is so dry that NASA uses it to test instruments for future Mars missions[218].

A land with no water or vegetation is usually unfit for human habitation. However, the Atacama's mineral resource wealth has made it a target for mining booms (and busts) since it was first visited by Europeans in the late 1500s. The incredibly arid conditions made resource extraction difficult and costly, since every drop of water used in mining as well as for drinking and cooking by miners had to be transported in. But in 1874 J. Harding and C. Wilson built the the first commercial solar still: a 4,700-m^2 device that relied on solar energy to produce 24,000 liters (6,000 gallons) of freshwater per day to quench the thirst of hundreds of Atacama nitrate miners[219]. The Atacama, like many deserts, can be made habitable by a combination of water and energy. In this case, solar energy.

A solar still is a simple device that can convert saline, brackish, or polluted water into distilled water. Like many simple and brilliant inventions, the solar still recreates the way Nature does things: in this instance, the way Nature evaporates water into the clouds. This is far from a new idea. Aristotle suggested just such a method of evaporating seawater to turn it into drinking water in the fourth century BC. Today there are a few still installations in several countries, including Australia, Greece, Spain, and Tunisia.

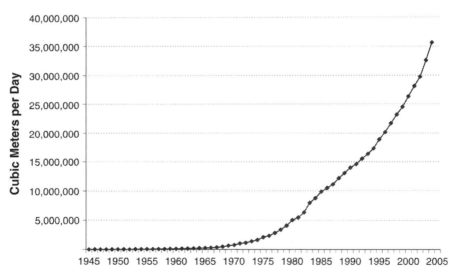

Figure 7.1. Cumulative Worldwide Installed Desalination Capacity
(Source and copyright: Pacific Institute[220])

However, since the middle of the twentieth century, the world has shifted to large-scale industrial desalination plants—most of them powered by fossil fuels. In 1945 the world had one working desalination plant, with an installed capacity of 325 cubic meters per day (m^3/d) or just under 86,000 gallons per day, according to the Pacific Institute, a California-based water think-tank. Sixty years later, in 2004, there were 10,402 desalination plants with an installed capacity of more than 35,627,374 cubic meters per day (m^3/d), or more than 100,000 times the capacity of that one 1945 plant.

The Looming Water Crisis and Desalination

According to the United Nations World Water Assessment Programme, "urgent action is needed if we are to avoid a global water crisis." But many places around the world are already in the midst of a water crisis. South Australia is going through a seven-year drought that is the worst water crisis in its recorded history. The causes are a combination of water mismanagement, climate change, agricultural abuse, and plain old lack of rain. Australian rice production fell from 1.64 million metric tons (MT) in 2001 to 19,000 MT in 2008, a drop of almost 99 percent[221]. Allocations of water to farmers have plunged as much as 95%. Adelaide is probably the first major city in the industrialized world to live in a permanent state of water crisis[222].

It takes 3,000 liters (792.5 gallons) of water to grow 1 kg (2.2 lbs) of rice, according to the Water Footprint Network.[223] Why an area that is marginally fertile like the South Australia Murray-Darling Basin was cultivating a water-thirsty grain like rice defies logic. But then again, "water management" seems to be an oxymoron. Water is not managed rationally. It will likely not be managed rationally anytime soon. What is more probable is that the governments of the world will increase the supply of clean water—by desalinating seawater.

Much of the San Francisco Bay Area gets its freshwater from the Hetch-Hetchy reservoir which is 160 miles (258 Km) away. Hetch-Hetchy was mostly built in the 1920s and is in serious need of repair and earthquake-proofing. Luckily, the reservoir is high in the Sierra Nevada and its water flows to us via gravity.

Southern California, by contrast, draws more than 4.4 million acre-feet (5.4 billion m³) per year from the Colorado River. The waters of this mighty river are in such demand by 7 different states that oftentimes it runs dry before it reaches the Pacific Ocean[224]. Increased population and agricultural and industrial growth in all these states means that the Colorado's water level is decreasing—and that struggles over its water are increasing.

Yet California, which is also in the midst of a water crisis, produced 2.3 metric tons of rice in 2004[225]. Rational water management? Not in the Golden State. Have we not learned from Australia? Despite water's supreme importance to human life, industry, agriculture, and even power generation, the state does not collect water information consistently or reliably. "There is no comprehensive groundwater monitoring program in California—and available information is often of dubious quality," according to the Natural Resources Defense Council (NRDC)[226].

On May 14, 2009, the San Diego Regional Water Quality Control Board announced that it had approved a $320-million desalination plant that will provide 50,000 gallons (200,000 liters) of clean water per day when completed in 2012[227]. In a state known for its sometimes acrimonious opposition to desalination plants (on environmental grounds) the decision to build the San Diego plant was unanimous. As of mid-2009 there were 20 more desalination plants waiting approval in California.

Clean Water, Dirty Power

Part of the opposition to desalination plants is that they produce two main types of environmental pollution. The first type is though the power generation itself. Desalination plants follow the traditional energy pattern: most of the energy comes from burning fossil fuels and thereby emitting CO_2 and other forms of pollution into the environment.

Desalinating water is so energy-intensive that every desalination-plant investment has to be coupled with parallel investments in power plants. According to the World Bank, "the typical ratio of power to water was 50MW: 22,500 m³/day water." [228] Following that ratio, the San Diego desalination plan would need the equivalent of a brand new 444-MW power plant to provide the energy for cleaning the saltwater.

Burning coal to clean water seems dysfunctional, to put it mildly. According to the Union of Concerned Scientists, the "typical" 500-MW coal plant generates 193,000 tons of sludge, 125,000 tons of ash, and 10,500 tons of nitrous oxide (NO_2)— the equivalent of half a million old cars on the road[229]. All of that garbage goes on or in the ground somewhere. If it is buried it may end up seeping into the groundwater, which gets polluted with toxic waste, including mercury and arsenic. That of course would decrease the supply of clean water and spur the development of more desalination plants. Dysfunctional indeed.

Clean water needs clean energy. Burning fossil fuels to clean the water is unsustainable and unaffordable in the long term.

Conventional Desalination Plant

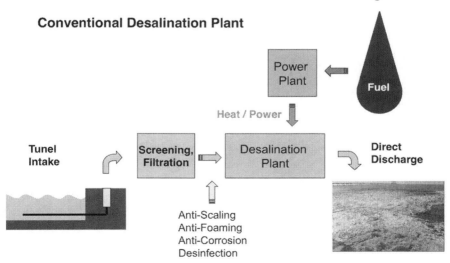

Figure 7.2. Conventional desalination plant (Source: "AQUA-CSP"[230])

The second type of desalination pollution comes from discharging the brine back into the sea. The San Diego desalination plant will take in 100,000 gallons (400,000 liters) of seawater to produce 50,000 gallons (200,000 liters) of clean water. That means that 50,000 gallons of water with twice the salinity of the original seawater will be dumped back in the ocean—every day. Raising the salinity around the outflow zone can affect marine flora and fauna and alter the near-offshore ecosystem.

Although many if not most desalination plants have been built without much concern for the environment, newer ones might be more conscious due to pressure from citizen groups. The desalination plant in Perth, for instance, has been monitoring and releasing data on salinity around the plant. The good news seems to be that ocean salinity returns to normal about 500 meters (5/16 of a mile) from the brine discharge units[231].

Whatever the environmental concerns, what seems certain is that the governments of the world are increasing the supply of desalinated water. There were 13,080 desalination plants around the world in 2008, according to the International Desalination Association. The plants had a production capacity of up to 55.6 million cubic meters of clean water per day[232]. This capacity is expected to *double* by 2015—just 7 years away.

The sun has a special relationship with the need for water. A hotter and sunnier climate increases the likelihood of water evaporation and, in its extreme forms, of desertification.

Yet whereas in the past the lack of water was a natural deterrent to population growth in the deserts, modern energy-dependent technologies have made it possible to have large settlements, industry, and even agriculture there.

Energy + $ + Water = Desert Metropolis

In 1953, Dubai was a small trading village in the Arabian desert. Its population was 20,000 and all its freshwater came from wells. The city did not build its first concrete building until 1956—with imported cement[233].

When I went to Dubai in the fall of 2008, I saw more cranes than I had seen anywhere except maybe Shanghai. Locals call Dubai "a vast construction site." This city boasted the world's largest saltwater port, the planet's tallest building, and its two largest shopping malls. Aspiring to be one of the world's top tourist destinations, Dubai was also building the largest airport, and the largest entertainment and leisure center (Dubailand!)

Dubai when I visited had nearly 1.5 million inhabitants—a 7,500% growth over just half a century. Most of the water to quench this population's thirst, mix all the concrete, and process its industry's heat came from desalination plants. In 2008, Dubai consumed 414 million cubic meters of water, of which just 18.5 million came from wells[234]. All but 5% of the freshwater in Dubai was desalinated.

Dubai as it is today clearly could not exist without this massive desalination capacity. Its natural freshwater could only support a small percentage of its population and economy. Furthermore, Dubai planned to increase its desalination capacity by 250% in just 4 years—at a capital cost of almost $20 billion[235].

The combination of large oil production, lack of natural freshwater aquifers, fast commercial and industrial growth, and outsize aspirations make the Middle East the world's largest desalination market—employing about 50% of total global desalination capacity. Saudi Arabia alone boasts about 25% of that capacity. Sixty per cent of freshwater in Persian Gulf countries comes from desalination plants.

Yet it's worth remembering that you don't have to be in the middle east to need desalination for freshwater. The Mediterranean island nation of Malta spends 22% of its power consumption to desalinate water[236]. I'll have more to say about desalination elsewhere in the world later.

Countries in the Middle East and North Africa (MENA) have a few things in common: little to no rainfall, high rates of evaporation of whatever rainfall they do get, high population growth, increasing urbanization, and increase in consumption patterns for personal, industrial, and agricultural purposes. This has led to massive "water deficits."

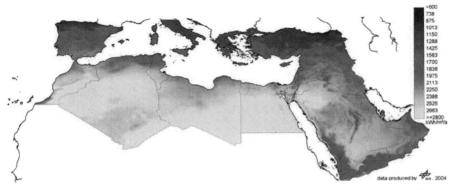

Figure 7.3. Solar energy radiation in Southern Europe, North Africa, and the Middle East. Lighter yellow indicates higher solar energy.
(Source: "AQUA-CSP"[237])

And MENA countries have something else in common: some of the most powerful direct solar radiation on earth.

Water is Not an Equal-Opportunity Employer

Most of the world's water is actually saltwater. Ninety eight percent (98%) of the water on the planet is in the oceans. Only about 2% of the planet's water is considered "fresh" or drinkable. However, 80% of that water is locked up in ice caps and glaciers[238]. That means that only about 0.4% of the world's water is actually fresh and available. Ninety percent of this water (0.36% of the planet's total) is found in aquifers and wells. Only about 0.036% of the planet's water is available in the form of rivers and lakes.

A quick look at a global water map (fig. 7.4) shows one of the basic facts about freshwater: it is unevenly distributed. Many (but not all) areas of North America, Europe, China, Southeast Asia, and South America show little or no water scarcity, while much of the rest of the world is either experiencing physical water scarcity or approaching it.

The International Water Management Institute (IWMI) is a Sri Lanka-based nonprofit scientific organization that has studied water issues around the globe for decades. IWMI specializes in water management and its implications for human existence. Every year they map the world on the basis of "water budgets"— who has or (does not have) enough water to grow food, sustain people's livelihoods, and preserve the environment.

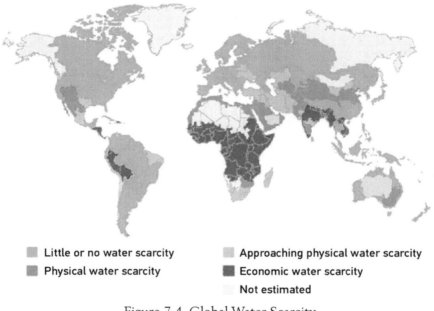

Little or no water scarcity   Approaching physical water scarcity
Physical water scarcity   Economic water scarcity
                                 Not estimated

Figure 7.4. Global Water Scarcity.
(Source: IWMI Annual Report 2006/2007[239])

Figure 7.4 is the IWMI's Global Water Scarcity map. The darker "red" areas have water scarcity relative to their population needs. The "pink" areas are on their way to experiencing water scarcity. Interestingly and usefully, the IWMI has a classification for "Economic" water scarcity—these areas may have enough water, but their population cannot afford to buy it!

The first time I looked at the IWMI map, I thought I was looking at a global solar radiation map. That's because the areas of the map with higher scarcity of water correspond so closely to the areas of the world with higher direct solar radiation. I have examined several different versions of global solar radiation maps, and in every case the relationship is virtually one-to-one.

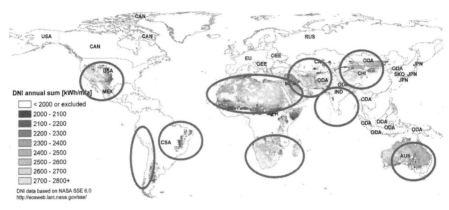

Figure 7.5. Global Direct Normal Incidence (DNI) solar radiation map.
(Source: NASA)

NASA's Direct Normal Incidence (DNI) solar radiation map highlights the most powerful sunshine in the world. These are areas where the sun's rays go through the least atmosphere or clouds that would weaken or deflect them.

High DNI is directly correlated to the best areas to build solar thermal plants such as power-tower and parabolic trough installations. As I saw from the maps, high DNI is also directly correlated with lack of freshwater. *The areas that are best suited for solar energy production are also the ones that need to desalinate water the most.*

Has anyone put these two facts together? Should we not be using solar energy to clean water in areas like North Africa and the Middle East?

"Solar energy received on each square kilometer of desert land is sufficient to desalinate 165,000 m³ per day or 60 million m^3 per year," writes Dr. Franz Trieb, who is responsible for a ground-breaking study on the use of Concentrating Solar Power for desalination[240]. (1 square km equals about 0.4 square miles.)

> *"Solar energy on 1 square km. of desert land is sufficient to desalinate 165,000 m^3 per day."*

Bottled Electricity

As I said at the beginning of this chapter, water desalination is an energy-intensive process. It's yet another example of a twentieth-century industry enabled by abundant and cheap energy.

According to *The Economist*, it takes anywhere from 3.7 kWh to 8 kWh of energy to produce a cubic meter (m^3) of water. The energy efficiency depends on the technology uses (reverse osmosis, multi-stage flashing, multiple effect distillation) and when the plants were built. Generally speaking, older desalination plants are closer to the high-consumption end (8kWh/m^3) and newer ones closer to the lower end (3.7 kWh/m^3).

At an energy price of 10 ¢/kWh, this means desalination costs anywhere from 37 cents to 80 cents per cubic meter of water. This also means that the energy consumption for the 2008 capacity of 55 million m3/day was somewhere between 205 GWh and 444 GWh—or $20.5 to $44.4 million dollars each day.

That's $7.5 billion to $16.5 billion in energy demand per year just to desalinate water.

Moreover, that 10 ¢/kWh doesn't tell the whole story. Countries with newer plants and abundant fossil fuel resources like the United Arab Emirates can afford both to invest in newer, larger desalination plants and to run them with their own oil resources. In conversations with officials in the UAE I learned that when they do the cost accounting for the energy, they don't use the market price of oil but the incremental cost of extracting it. This makes a huge difference.

In a place like Abu Dhabi the incremental cost of oil extraction is probably less than $10 per barrel. Under that type of accounting, the cost of the power to desalinate the water is probably closer to 2 ¢/kWh. At that cost, Dubai's almost 400 million m³ of desalinated water would cost just $8 million per year in power costs. At 2 ¢/kWh you can also afford to run an indoor ski lift at the local mall when the summer heat is raging outside.

By contrast, Hawaii's cost of electricity in 2007 was generally around 30 ¢/kWh because the state needs to buy oil in the open market (say at $80 per barrel) and its utilities use that fuel cost to price the electricity to the consumer. The same water volume, using the same fuel volume, would cost 15 times as much in Hawaii.

Countries that have older, smaller, less efficient desalination plants and need to import the fuel to power them have double trouble. The first problem is that they are hostages to world fossil-fuel prices. When a barrel of oil costs more than $80 (or $140) the cost of energy could rise above 30 ¢/kWh, making the water a very expensive commodity indeed. The second problem is that these countries may lack the cash to buy this fuel.

Certain commodity prices tend to rise together: when oil is expensive, corn and wheat tend to rise also, because of the petroleum inputs to modern grain production. When commodity prices rise, poor countries like Sudan or Algeria, with no traditional (fossil) energy resources of their own and low cash reserves, have to choose between buying staples like wheat to feed the population and buying fuel to run their electric power stations and desalination plants.

What these countries *do* have a lot of is deserts, with high direct normal insolation (DNI) that European countries would love to have. Luckily for these oil-poor desert countries, the future of desalination lies in Concentrating Solar Power.

Solar thermal energy is the best long-term way to desalinate water. This is the case for several reasons.

The first reason is that there's a high correlation between lack of water and high solar radiation. The more sun, the drier the land becomes, and the more groundwater evaporates. This sounds almost too commonsensical. What may sound less so is that the hotter it gets, the more *sub-surface* water evaporates.

There simply is not much water either above or below ground. But precisely because of all that water-evaporating solar heat, there's no need to pay for fuel to power desalination. Once the solar power plant is installed, the nation's government knows that it can keep producing the water for the same price for the rest of the plant's useful life.

The second reason is that CSP is radically more efficient at desalination than any other form of power. As I explained in Chapter 3, a CSP plant converts water into steam that is used to run a turbine and generate electricity. Any CSP technology converts about 25% of the solar thermal energy into electricity. The rest is released in the form of heat. However, when electricity generation is combined with a desalination process, the CSP plant can use an additional 50% of the otherwise wasted thermal energy to desalinate the water. This way a full 75% to 85% of the solar energy is used productively[241].

Combined Heat & Power

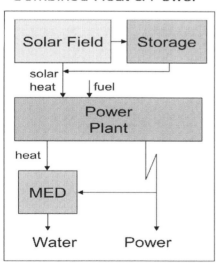

Figure 7.6. Desalination using concentrating solar power (CSP) and multiple-effect distillation (MED). (Source: "AQUA -CSP", DLR)

This efficiency is unparalleled among power plant technologies. According to the United States Energy Information Administration (EIA), nuclear plants have a conversion efficiency of 32%-33%[242]. Coal-to-electricity efficiency is also on the order of 30%[243].

The third reason that CSP is the best desalination technology is that a combined desalination/power plant can generate electricity for the grid when it is needed the most, usually for peaking power needs. During peaking power periods, both the demand for and the price of electricity shoot up to four times "normal." So while the conversation about "grid parity" I discussed in Chapter 6 focuses on a static price for coal, natural gas, or nuclear-generated power, the truth is that that on summer afternoons, when the sun is at its hottest, prices are at their hottest too. More solar energy, so more CSP wattage generated, resulting in surplus power. During those times, the CSP plant can deliver that extra power to the grid while still producing freshwater.

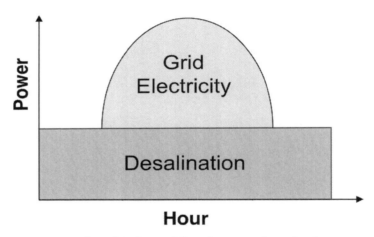

Figure 7.7. Combined Solar and Desalination plant desalinates water all day and night while sending electricity to the grid as needed. (Source: "AQUA-CSP")

Desalination plants need somewhere between 3.7 kWh and 8 kWh to produce one cubic meter of water. Given an average power cost of 6kWh per m³, they use 333.6 million kWh/day (333.6 GWh/day) or a capacity of 17 GW (at 20 hours of desalination per day.) That's huge by any standard. And the need is vital and growing every year.

This is why I believe that solar water desalination address-es one of the world's most important unmet needs—clean fresh water in dry countries—and at the same time represents one of the largest global energy market opportunities for the foresee-able future.

Off-Grid Clean Water

Much of the world is off *all* the grids: they have no ac-cess to electricity, telephone landlines, clean water, or sanitation. Some grim statistics about the direct consequences:

- Over one billion people on this planet have no access to safe drinking water.

- Water-borne diseases account for 80% of infections in the developing world.

- Nearly 4 billion cases of diarrhea occur each year.

- 200 million people in 74 countries are infected with the parasitic disease schistosomiasis[244], which causes a vicious spectrum of symptoms from impaired growth and devel-opment in children to organ damage, chronic fatigue, and increased vulnerability to HIV infection.

- Some 2.2 million people die every year because of unsafe drinking water—90% of them children[245].

But the human consequences of living without electricity or a ready supply of clean freshwater go far beyond disease. In Sub-Saharan Africa and in many other areas around the world, women and girls have to walk up to seven miles daily to get clean water for their families. Think about it: they spend up to two hours each day to just get the water that most of us just open a faucet to pour. That time helps prevent most of them from get-ting an education, better jobs, or economic or social mobility[246].

What's more, the practical demand for women and girls to use their days in this way reinforces outdated patriarchal traditions that oppose anything other than a domestic, uneducated role for them. Water is, literally, life. Lack of water means lack of a better life and livelihood, especially for women..

"Most women in the world spend their time collecting water, frequently from rivers, streams, or ponds. Basically open or polluted sources," says MIT Senior Lecturer Susan Murcott, a water expert who teaches in the Department of Civil and Environmental Engineering. "They are forced to drink polluted water and serve it to their families." Prof. Murcott invented the Kanchan™, a low-end water filter that removes arsenic and microbial contamination from drinking water[247]. She has put her creativity where her concern is.

> "Most women in the world spend their time collecting water, frequently from streams or ponds."

Appropriate Technology: Solar Water Purification for Pennies

Many if not most of the more than two billion humans who will be added to the planet's population over the next few decades will live in poorer countries and will—unless we make big changes—have no more access to clean water than they will have to electricity. Solar energy provides an opportunity to develop products and services that can meet the needs and improve the lives of those billions and the ones already here. Let me show you an example.

The sun's ultraviolet (UV) radiation is another characteristic of sunlight besides heat that can be harmful (that's why we use sun protection lotion), but when used properly, UV can literally be a "gift from the heavens." UV rays are amongst nature's most efficient sterilizers. The 1903 Nobel Prize for Medicine was awarded to Neils Finsen for his use of UV against tuberculosis[248]. UV kills and disrupts the reproductive abilities of bacteria, pathogens, viruses, and molds. Using short-wave UV rays for this purpose has been accepted practice in hospitals and sterile work facilities since the mid-twentieth century[249].

Now a Swedish company has come up with a simple concept to provide clean water to the world's poor. Solvatten is a briefcase-like product that cleans water by exposing it to the sun[250]: Each side of this "water briefcase" can hold about 5 liters (11 gallons) of water that is sterilized when exposed to the sun for about 2-3 hours on a sunny day (5-6 hours on cloudy days.)

The Solvatten purifier takes advantage of the UV rays to kill most harmful bacteria in polluted water. According to the company, water samples with more than 200,000 E. coli per 100 ml have successfully been treated to 1 E. coli per 100 ml, which is the World Health Organization's (WHO) minimum acceptable safe drinking water guideline.

There is yet another benefit to using the sun to clean water directly. One very common way that people make water safer to drink is by boiling it. It takes about 1 kg (2.2 pounds) of biomass (like firewood) to boil 1 liter (1 quart) of water. Assuming a family uses the solar-energy method to purify their water twice a day for 300 days, it would save 6,000 Kg (13,200 pounds) of firewood (or coal or other type of fuel) per year. This saves on deforestation, as the families chop down fewer trees for firewood, and on CO_2 pollution, since the family won't burn the wood they would have chopped. Alternatively, this would save a poor family the cash they would spend to buy the firewood or coal. (This assumes of course that the family can afford to buy the biomass in the first place.) Since the Solvatten water purifier costs about $60, it would cost a family about *one cent per liter of water* (3.8¢/gallon) if they use it for a year.

This is also one of those markets where an entrepreneur can do good while doing well. An inexpensive product like the Solvatten or Dr. Murcott's filter provides poor people access to clean water. Because these products need no fuel other than the sun (which is free and clean) they create no dependency on fossil fuels, they engender no pollution, and they could save nearly two million children's lives every year.

At $60 per water purifier and, say, 250 million families—growing to half a billion over the next few decades—this would make a market of $12.5 billion, growing to $25 billion per year. That's $0.75 trillion over the forty years to 2050.

> "At $60 per water purifier...that's a $0.75 trillion market."

Millions of Water Refugees?

Dubai without desalination technology could only support about 5% of its current population, commerce, and industry. What if Dubai ran out of fossil fuels to power its desalination plants and to pay for buying new ones? What if Dubai could only provide water to 75,000 of its people?

The potential tragedy of a city of two million about to run out of water is in fact playing out in Yemen, which is near Dubai on the Arabian peninsula. Sana'a today is the capital of Yemen, but it is also one of the region's oldest standing cities. A "World Heritage Site," Sana'a has been inhabited for about 2,500 years. Throughout the centuries it has served as a capital of the pre-Islamic Hymiarite Arab and then Sassanid Persian kingdoms and, as of the sixth century AD, of the Ethiopian viceroys in the region. It became part of the Ottoman Empire in the sixteenth century. The city boasts more than 100 mosques, and the world's oldest Quran was found there in 1972[251].

The city of Sana'a, like its cousin Dubai, grew fast throughout the twentieth century. As recently as 1931 it had a population of only 31,000 people—which grew to about 1.9 million by 2005. This growth mirrored Dubai's during roughly the same period.

Yemen has oil, and like Dubai's, it is running out. Yemen's oil reserves are expected to be depleted by 2020 or so. Dubai has invested in diversifying itself away from oil dependency. Luckily for Dubai, it is part of the United Arab Emirates. When the financial markets collapsed in late 2008 and early 2009, the real-estate market, the biggest driver of economic activity in Dubai, crashed with them. Fellow Emirate Abu Dhabi, which has plenty of oil left in the ground, came to the rescue and bailed Dubai out.

Fig 7.8. Yemen. (Source: CIA Factbook)

Despite its oil, Yemen is a relatively poor country, placing 88th in the world in terms of per-capita GDP, according to the *CIA Factbook*. It also has 0 (that's *zero*) km² of surface water. Unlike Dubai, when Yemen exhausts its oil, it will not have a sibling Emirate like Abu Dhabi to bail it out.

Sana'a is expected to run out of water by 2020. So by 2020, Yemen will have no oil and no freshwater. By then the city will likely have 2.5 million inhabitants but only enough water to support the most basic necessities of just 400,000 of them. At that point, Yemen will have basically two choices:

1. Relocate 2.1 million people out of Sana'a, or

2. Build desalination plants on the coast and pump the freshwater to the ancient city.

Let's be clear, though: whichever option Yemen chooses, it will still have to build desalination plants to sustain its population. The country will have next to no freshwater left. Like the oil, the aquifer that currently provides most of the region's freshwater is being quickly depleted.

Further complicating this picture is that Sana'a is located 209 km (130 miles) from the Red Sea and at 2,500 meters (8,200 feet) above sea level. This means that the desalinated water will have to be pumped both far and high to get it to this city. Not only is Yemen projected to run out of oil by 2020; it will also run out of natural gas by 2030. Therefore using fossil fuels to power the desalination plants or to pump the water to Sana'a is not viable.

On the other hand, moving 2.1 million people and resettling them would be a massive human, social, and logistical undertaking. Yemen would have to build a whole new large city or several smaller cities from scratch—including housing, schools, industry, roads, telecommunications, and energy infrastructure. That's just the beginning. The financial costs would also be large—a minimum of $35 billion[252].

But Yemen has one of the best solar resources on earth. The superior alternative by far would be to build solar plants to both desalinate the water and generate power to pump it up to Sana'a. What would it take to do this?

Forty square kilometers (15.4 square miles) of Concentrating Solar Power (CSP) plants combined with solar desalination would do it. The capital cost? Six billion dollars—about $3,000 per Sana'a resident for a lifetime of freshwater.

The right solution is clear, clean, and relatively inexpensive. The cost of another humanitarian disaster in a relatively unstable region of the world would be too costly (in human, military, and financial terms) to bear. The Yemen government and the world have the opportunity to create wealth, grow the economy, and save Yemen and the Arabian peninsula from a massive humanitarian crisis.

MENA Water Opportunity

Yemen's water shortage is not unique. In a way, Sana'a is a microcosm of the water crisis hitting the planet. From Cairo to Mumbai to Beijing, millions of people are facing a daily water deficit that has only been getting worse. There are already more than 300 million people in China who don't have access to safe drinking water[253]. According to the World Bank there will be 30 million environmental refugees in China due to water stress by 2020 if present trends are not reversed[254]. The water deficit in the Middle East and North Africa (MENA) is already massive. Wells and aquifers are already being used far beyond sustainable levels, which is worsening the situation and getting these regions closer to disastrous scenarios like Sana'a in ten years. Sana'a is just one of many areas that will have to build large-scale water desalination facilities.

Growth in population, economy, industry, and agriculture are predictably going to increase demand for water. Climate change may also do its part. The higher heat not only increases surface water evaporation but also contributes to underground water loss. The only viable choice that MENA and climatically similar countries have is to produce freshwater from desalination. And—at the risk of sounding like a scratched CD here—the only viable way to power desalination plants in most of these regions is with solar energy.

Let me repeat an amazing statistic I cited earlier. According to "Concentrating Solar Power for Water Desalination," a report by Franz Trieb of the German Aerospace Center (DLR), a CSP plant the size of Lake Nasser (which powers the 2.1 GW Aswan hydro plant) could "harvest an amount of energy equivalent to the present Middle East oil production."[255]

The multi-year DLR report also states that solar energy is produced today at the equivalent of oil prices close to $50 per barrel. Solar energy is projected to be produced at the equivalent of $20 per barrel in 2020 and $15 after that. Oil peaked at $147 in mid-2008 and has been in the $60s and $70s as of this writing.

Oil prices have also trended up for decades—a fact that will not change any time soon, if ever. Most countries in MENA cannot afford to buy oil. But even if they could, it would make no sense to do it when solar energy is projected to drop to the $15 per barrel level—and never go up again!

The DLR report researched the freshwater needs of Middle Eastern and North African countries through 2050. According to this study, the MENA region had a yearly freshwater deficit of 48.9 billion cubic meters per year (Bm^3/y) in 2000. *This is the equivalent of the whole yearly flow of the Nile river.* By 2050 the potable-water deficit is projected to triple to 150.4 Bm^3/y—equivalent to the yearly water flow of *three* Nile rivers. This number also assumes that the region will lower its per-capita consumption of water through better water management and will increase its production of clean water from wastewater sixteenfold to 64 Bm^3/y (up from just 4 Bm^3/y in 2000.)

What will it take to build this desalination capacity using solar energy? Using less than 0.3% of the entire desert area of the MENA region, enough electricity and desalinated seawater can be produced to meet the growing needs of MENA countries *and of Europe*.

So what's the market opportunity for building this desalination infrastructure? It will of course depend on what technologies are used. For current cost reference I looked at the Ashkelon desalination plant in Israel. This is a seawater reverse osmosis (SWRO) desalination facility. It's not exactly a solar MED plant but nonetheless a real reference point. This plant cost $250 million dollars and produces 100 million m^3 of clean water per year.[256] So the capital cost of the Ashkelon plant is $2.5 per m^3 of yearly production capacity. This does not include the power needed to run the plant.

The MENA area alone will need 150 Bm^3/y by 2050. At $2.5 capital cost per cubic meter of yearly production, MENA will have to invest $375 billion to just keep up with freshwater demand from desalination.

To meet its anticipated freshwater needs, MENA requires just about half of the world's desalination infrastructure according to the DLR report. By that simple yardstick, the world will have to invest $750 billion in desalination plants by 2050. Fuel not included!

"Solar water desalination may be a $750-billion market opportunity."

If MENA countries choose the fossil fuel route or the nuclear route, the investment in separate power plants and the fuel to run them will be enormous. Most of these countries (like Yemen) that won't have the oil or gas will simply not be able to do it. This will precipitate the humanitarian crisis of Sana'a and of dozens or hundreds of cities and villages around the region.

However, if these countries instead choose to invest in combined solar power and desalination, they will not have to invest in separate power plants—thus saving hundreds of billions in capital costs. What's more, the savings in long-term fuel costs would add to hundreds of billions in O&M cash-flow savings.

Think again of those 2-3 billion new human beings due to arrive on earth by 2050. We'll need to grow food, manufacture industrial goods, and provide drinking water for those nine billion people—water, water, and more water. Providing freshwater to a rising population is one of the biggest humanitarian and economic challenges of the twenty-first century. And nothing can clean water the way the sun can.

"Your theory is crazy—but not crazy enough to be true."
—Niels Bohr

"Everything that can be invented has been invented."
—Charles H. Duell, Commissioner,
U.S. Office of Patents, 1899

"All of us will live on in the future we make."
—Senator Edward M. Kennedy

CHAPTER 8

OPPORTUNITY VI— ENERGY IN A BOX: BATTERIES & ENERGY STORAGE

On the morning of November 2, 2008, the Red Eléctrica de España (REE or Electrical Grid of Spain) ordered a full or partial shutdown of 2,800 MW of wind production. Energy production in Spain had exceeded demand and wind electricity was the culprit—by about the size of three nuclear plants. An orderly slowdown was necessary to prevent the generating systems from overloading the transmission grid and risking the stability of the whole system[257].

"Excess energy production" is a phrase we do not often hear—especially excess of the clean variety. All this excess production of electricity would have burned no carbon dioxide, sent no nasty mercury into our rivers and atmosphere, and generated no radioactive uranium or plutonium that would stay with us for 100,000 years. It sounds like a dream come true for clean energy advocates. We should have such problems in the United States!

But why did the REE order the slowdown? Energy economists would say that the reason was the arduous and always tricky task of matching demand and supply of electricity. Dig a little deeper, though, and you might find out it was the lack of energy storage. Insufficient cost-effective electricity storage cost Spain millions of dollars that day. This lack is a huge pain to wind operators all over the world.

Wind is—proverbially—volatile and needs a sophisticated grid to handle it. As an energy source it can go from almost no production one day to tremendous production the next. According to the REE, wind production was 43% of total electricity production in the whole of Spain at 4:47 am on November 24th, 2008 while less than three days later (November 27th, 2008 at 4:22 pm) that number went down to 1.15%.[258]

The ability to store energy when it is produced and release it when it is needed is one of the unmet challenges of the electricity revolution—not today's renewable-energy revolution, but the original revolution that gave us the national grid starting a century ago. To emphasize a crucial point: the problem of energy storage is neither new nor specific to clean energy. Energy storage is one of the great unsolved, waste-producing, and hush-hush challenges of the fossil-fuel (and nuclear) era as well.

Energy storage in all forms, especially electricity storage, may well provide some of the largest market opportunities in energy during the twenty-first century. Electricity storage shows several of the necessary attributes for a big new market winner to emerge: there's huge customer pain, no clear market leader, and no market-ready technology breakthrough ready to dominate the twenty-first century.

"Electricity storage shows several of the necessary attributes for a big new market winner to emerge."

Interestingly, solar thermal or Concentrating Solar Power (CSP) is the probably the only form of energy generation that has "solved" the energy storage problem. As I've mentioned already in my discussions of Solar Millenium and Andasol and Industrial Scale Solar CSP is using the most cost-effective and environmentally safe energy storage solution on the market today. It's almost time to discuss that technology in more detail.

But first, a word about waste.

Waste in the Dark: Conventional Power's Dirtiest Little Secret

June 24, 2009 was one of the longest days of the summer in the northern hemisphere. It was just three days after summer solstice—which is both the longest day of the year and officially the first day of summer. That day, sunrise in San Francisco was at 5:48 am. and sunset was at 8:35 pm. For electric utilities, that is also the longest day of the year.

Most of the energy we consume follows the sun. From the time we wake up and turn on the lights, boil water for coffee, take a hot shower, and drive off to our offices, schools, or factories, our energy demand goes up and down with the sun's path across the sky.

The California Independent Systems Operator (CAISO) is the organization charged with operating most of the state's high-voltage wholesale transmission grid. Figure 8.1 is CAISO's electricity demand curve in California on June 24, 2009. Notice that demand hits bottom at just above 22,000 MW between 2:30 am. and about 5:00 am. and then steadily rises until it peaks at exactly 35,040 MW between 4:00 and 5:00 pm. June 24 was a Wednesday, so factories and offices were open. However, schools were out for summer break, so their energy demand does not show in the graph.

Figure 8.1. California electricity demand, June 24, 2009.
(Source and copyright: California ISO[259])

The system had forecast a peak demand of 36,024 MW, which was almost 1 MW more than the actual peak demand. The available unused capacity was about 2,500 MW higher than the forecast peak, so there was plenty of spare capacity to meet that peak demand. Notice that from about 11:00 pm. to 5:00 am. or so there is a dramatic difference between consumption (the bottom dark red line) and available production (the top jagged green line.) This means that up to a third of energy production is literally wasted. Specifically, the graph shows up to 9,000-10,000 MW of waste the night of June 24.

A coal-fired power plant cannot be turned on and off like a light switch. It takes days for such a plant to power (heat) up and to power (cool) down. That's why coal plants are designed with a capacity that matches peak daytime usage: that is, they produce at a rate that matches the maximum expected daytime consumption of energy. At night, most offices, factories, and schools are closed, so their power consumption goes down dramatically. At home, we turn off the TVs, PCs, and lights and go to bed.

However, power plants keep burning coal whether or not there is demand for the energy produced. While most of us sleep at night, coal plants keep spewing all the carbon into the air, all the coal ash into the ground, and all the mercury down the rivers—and the electricity they produce into a wasteland. Nearly everything a coal plant does at night is waste or wasted.

Nuclear plants are much the same. They take days to power on or off, so they're basically on all the time. They keep burning fuel day and night, and they need millions of gallons of water to cool them even when there's no use for the electricity they generate. And all that time they are turning their uranium fuel slugs into plutonium and their reactor walls and parts into other radioactive isotopes, all of which has to be stashed somewhere very secure for millennia. Waste, waste, and more waste.

For nearly a century the utilities have (unsuccessfully) worked to smooth out this discrepancy between electricity supply and demand. One strategy the power companies have traditionally followed is to try to pump up demand for night-time electricity. Because of the excess in energy supply in the evenings, the price of electricity is much cheaper then than during peak daytime usage.

This attempt at shifting human activities to the evening has had limited success. Some factories can indeed have two or three work shifts—mainly because they are capital-intensive (they have expensive equipment that should not sit idle), but also because they're energy-intensive. For instance, auto manufacturers invest billions in each assembly plant and want to use this machinery for as many hours during the day as possible. Auto manufacturing is also energy-intensive—and not as labor-intensive as it used to be. Still, despite more than a century of increasing industrialization, electricity usage, and ever more accurate resource planning, most human activity just refuses to move into the evening hours.

Another look at the CAISO curve (Fig. 8.1) reveals something else: the difference between real demand and forecasted demand. Sometimes this variation can be as large as 10 percent either way. This doesn't sound like much, but on June 24 it was as much as 2,000 MW. This is the equivalent of two nuclear or coal-fired plants that would need to be added or taken away on a moment's notice. But it can't be, because coal and nuclear plants can't be easily turned on and off.

Here's a scary statistic. If the whole world capacity of 14 TW of energy were utility-scale power plants (which it isn't) and we had 10% of them running because of discrepancies between real and forecasted demand, *we would have the equivalent of 1,400 coal or nuclear plants (1.4 TW) running constantly without contributing any power to the grid.* What solutions have the utilities come up with?

For one, natural gas plants can be turned on with 30-minute notice. That's one of the main reasons natural gas has grown its market share over the last few years—powering "peaking plants." Also, electricity can be imported from adjacent states—like Nevada, in this case. But if you've been to Las Vegas recently, you'll remember the intensely hot summers (and springs and falls). Nevada is probably going through its own summertime real-versus-forecasted issues. The point here is that even if you as a utility can in theory buy more power on the spot markets created by deregulation, the states (and utilities) closest to you are likely to have a demand curve that looks a lot like yours, following the sun. So the power may less readily available than you'd like—and certainly more expensive.

Another and ultimately much more promising way to smooth out the difference between demand and supply is by using energy storage. But what large-scale energy storage technologies are in use right now? Here's one you probably don't know about.

Pumped-Water Storage Hydroelectric Plants

The San Luis Reservoir is located near Gilroy, California, the self-described "Garlic Capital of the World." Actually, San Luis is the upper reservoir of two, and Forebay is the lower reservoir, in an unusual type of hydroelectric plant. Together the two reservoirs store energy in a technology called Pumped Hydro Storage (PHS).

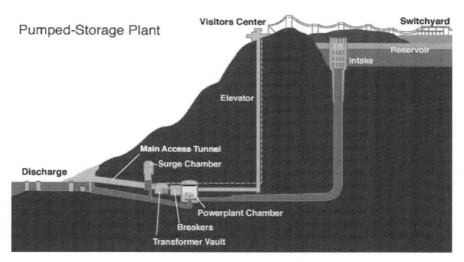

Figure 8.2. Pumped Hydro Storage (PHS) Plant (Source: TVA[260])

Here's how it works. During the evening, when there is excess electricity production and prices are low, the system pumps water from the lower reservoir to the upper reservoir. During the daytime at peak electricity demand, when energy prices are higher, the water in the upper reservoir is dropped again through pipes into a hydroelectric power plant, running a set of turbines that generate electricity sold at high prices. The San Luis pumped storage began operating in 1968 and uses eight turbines to generate a total of 424 MW of power. Its 2.52 billion cubic meters of water make it the largest off-stream reservoir in America. PHS is a real, operating form of high-capacity grid energy storage.

This is an ingenious solution that has been widely adopted around the world. In 1999, the European Union had about 32 GW of storage out of 188 GW of hydro power. The United States had 19.5 GW of PHS generating capacity[261]. The main problem with this type of PHS, though, is that "more energy is consumed in pumping than is generated."[262]

That is, it takes more energy to pump the water from the lower to the upper reservoir than is generated by the same water running a turbine. In fact San Luis, like all PHS installations, is a net consumer of electricity. In 2007, hydroelectric pumped storage consumed a net 7.0 GWh of energy, according to the U.S. Energy Information Agency[263].

Would you buy a battery that takes in more energy than it gives out? What's the point? As you have probably figured out by now, the point of PHS is to act as a "stabilizer" of the grid. As I explained in the previous section, you cannot just turn off a nuclear or coal power plant at night. So these plants keep producing electricity that, mostly, no one will buy. If some of this electricity were not used to pump water up from one reservoir to another, still more of it would be totally wasted in the evenings.

PHS also acts as an electricity-price arbitrage system. Literally and figuratively, PHS buys low and sells high. Even if it's a net waster of energy, it makes money by buying electricity to pump water at low prices and selling it at high peak demand prices.

Why don't we have more pumped-hydro storage? A big issue with PHS is similar to hydroelectric power in general: this is not a growth industry. It takes large areas to store the water and the best areas may already be taken. In fact, over the last decade 430 dams have been demolished in America[264]. Like computer mainframes, dams including PHS reservoirs had their day; but the greatest need now is for smaller, more distributed storage solutions. If we follow this metaphor through to complete realization, we will probably have medium-sized storage (like minicomputers) and then smaller, residential or personal distributed batteries (more like PCs.) An interesting point to remember in this analogy, though: *mainframe computers have not disappeared either.* They have changed and become specialized to certain niches, but they remain part of the data processing picture. So we will still need better, more efficient equivalents to PHS in the new, solar-based grid—better energy-storage "mainframes." The one we're already using stores energy not in cold water, but in very hot salt.

Solar Salt Batteries

Gemasolar, you may remember, is a solar power tower under development near Seville, Spain. When completed as planned in 2011 it will have a capacity of 17 MW and will have 15 hours of energy storage. *That is not a typo.* It will have a 15-hour "battery." So when it opens, Gemasolar will become the world's first 24/7 solar plant.

A round-the-clock solar plant dispels several myths. The first myth is that solar is a daytime-only technology. The second myth is that "renewables" lack energy storage. Solar has solved the energy storage challenge in an economical, elegant, and environmentally safe manner. The solution is called Molten Salt Energy Storage (MSES), also known as salt batteries. It was first developed not in Spain, but in the California desert in the early 1990s.

In 1992 the original Solar One, the plant that proved the solar power tower concept, was reborn as Solar Two. Located in Barstow, California, Solar Two had a major goal to add to Solar One: energy storage that would allow it to operate long after the sun went down[265] and also while desert clouds passed over. The energy storage ("battery") technology used molten salt as the transfer fluid. The chosen type of salt was a combination of sodium and potassium nitrate, which retains 99% of the heat for up to 24 hours. Another way to put this number: this battery loses just 1% of the heat energy per day. You can generate power whenever the demand happens—hours or days after you store the heat.

Potassium nitrate also happens to be environmentally safer and cheaper than most chemical-based battery alternatives.[266] In the Middle Ages, this ingredient was used to preserve food and it is still used in the production of corned beef[267]. Potassium nitrate is also used in toothpaste (for sensitive teeth) as well as in garden fertilizers. The fertilizer market is indeed the largest revenue generator for the few producers of this salt. So when energy providers tell you they are "clean," ask them whether they could please eat the stuff they store energy in.

"So when energy providers tell you they are "clean", ask them whether they could please the stuff they store energy in."

Solar Two operated between April 1996 and April 1999 (see chapter 10). This plant demonstrated the ability of solar to produce and dispatch electricity hours after sundown. Its molten-salt energy storage technology had a measured efficiency of 97%. The tech met all expectations, and a decade later it is still the most efficient form of energy storage in parabolic trough and solar power tower[268].

Spain's Gemasolar picked up where Solar Two left off. In fact, it was designed with basically the same solar power tower technology developed at Solar Two. For this reason Gemasolar was in fact born with the name "Solar Tres" (Solar Three), implying a sequential advance on, or at least a new version of, the California original. A Gemasolar/Solar Tres White Paper calls molten-salt technology *"the best developed central receiver system today"*.[269]

Solar salt batteries are a good market opportunity. Many of the large operating concentrating solar power plants in the United States have been "peaking" plants, which means that they'll have minimal storage. Nevada Solar One has just half an hour of storage. PS10 in Seville has one hour of steam-based thermal energy storage.

On hot sunny days, peak electricity demand and therefore peak price happen in the early evening. Meanwhile, the peak supply of solar energy happens in the early afternoon. To better match the supply of solar energy with market demand, solar power developers need to store the energy for about six or seven hours. This allows them to "time-shift" the production of electricity. Think of Tivo or DVR. As a TV consumer, you don't care when that show was broadcast. You only care that when you sit down in front of the tube it'll be there. It's not by coincidence that Solar Millennium's Andasol-1 (Spain) has seven hours of molten-salt storage and Abengoa Solar's Solana plant in Arizona will have seven hours too.

The offer of relatively cheap energy storage that allows energy producers to maximize the price they get for selling their electricity is one that's hard to resist. Molten-salt storage costs around $100/kWh (today); but wind cannot use thermal storage. It can only use electricity storage that is on the order of $1,000/kWh. Industry insiders believe that an electricity-storage technology breakthrough that delivers a 10-times improvement in cost/performance is unlikely to be commercially available within a decade. In the meantime there will be smaller incremental improvements to existing battery technologies.

Today, MSES requires industrial equipment and skilled operations and maintenance, so it is mainly cost-effective on an industrial and utility scale. For island-scale solar plants, salt batteries become an effective option for generating "baseload" electricity. Like Gemasolar, they would be able to provide electricity round the clock. It's likely that a transition would involve daytime solar-power generation combined with fossil fuels like diesel or natural gas as night-time and backup sources.

Molten salt storage is also fairly economical. At the CSP Summit in San Francisco on June 30 and July 1 2009, the numbers that company executives mentioned clustered around $85-$100 per kWh of storage. And as salt energy-storage product innovations make MSES easier to use and bring price cuts and easier installation and maintenance, the technology can open up larger market opportunities.

Looking at simple scenarios, assume that 1TW of utility- or industrial-scale solar CSP plants are built with five hours of storage each (to be able to time-shift). This would give us 5 TWh (5 billion kWh) of storage. Assume further that the price drops to $50 per kWh. We're looking at a market opportunity of $250 billion. Certainly if solar CSP grows to meet a larger portion of the 10-terawatt gap that the planet will face in four decades, and if more of it is used for baseload, always-on power plants, we're looking at markets several times larger. But what about smaller-scale energy storage?

> "We're looking at a market opportunity of $250 billion."

The key issue for scales below utility, industrial, and "big island" is storage for electricity itself—also known as *batteries*. There are many types of batteries at several scales: from lithium-ion batteries that power our personal computers to the use of large hydroelectric plants to pump water up in the evenings. The development of inexpensive and scalable energy-storage products is one of the areas of highest technological need and should prove to be one of the most intense development efforts over the next few decades. This opportunity will have room for several companies on the scale of GE, Google, or Intel.

Electricity storage at the points of production, transmission, distribution, and consumption will become an increasingly important part of the twenty-first century energy infrastructure. But that infrastructure is going to change too. As I've already noted, the architecture and technology of our national power grid is obsolete, and the actual physical plant is becoming decrepit. Let's talk about the grid and storage for a bit, because new battery technologies above the "flashlight" scale will be closely connected, both physically and developmentally with the creation of a twenty-first century grid.

The New Grid and "Cloud Storage"

Electricity generation during the last century has been based on a top-down, centralized model. The electricity is generated elsewhere—"out there" somewhere—and we consume it here. It is like the old mainframe model, where the data was processed in expensive centralized computers and the results delivered to us on the other side of glass walls by white-coated "priests," as they were known at IBM. The only form of grid storage so far also been in large installations "out there"—like PHS reservoirs or for that matter molten-salt storage.

As we move forward with rebuilding the electrical infrastructure, the concept of grid storage will change radically. It will likely be closer in concept to the contemporary PC-and-Internet data-storage or "cloud" model. Some of our data is stored locally on our PC hard drive, while the rest of it is stored (and partly processed) in the Internet "cloud" somewhere—that is, distributed across various drives and servers in huge data centers run by providers. If you use web email like Gmail, Hotmail, or Yahoo Mail, you're using cloud storage for that data. If you use both office email and personal email, you're using an even more distributed data-storage model, whereby some data is in your computer, some is at the company's data centers, and some in the cloud. There are redundancies all over the grid—so that a tree falling in Ohio won't leave half the nation without power.

In much the same way, energy storage will be more distributed. Even the concept of "grid storage" will itself morph to the point where large, centralized storage locations will be only a part of the distributed, decentralized "cloud" storage picture. But to accomplish that shift, we will have to crack the very hard nut of cost-effective small and medium scale electricity storage.

Electricity batteries currently cost \$1,000 to \$3,000 per kWh—an order of magnitude higher than the cost of MSES thermal batteries. This is why wind (or PV) electricity storage can be so expensive and why wind turbines typically go without.

Electricity storage is also what makes battery-powered cars so expensive.

Scalable Energy Storage: Multiple Market Opportunities

Wind energy has come down in price considerably as technology improves and adoption increases. The World Wind Energy Association predicted a 25% market growth to 152,000 MW in 2009 despite the worldwide recession. In many places around the world, though, wind turbines have had a major problem. Wind is not just unpredictable in general, but in particular it may blow strongly at night—precisely when we have excess capacity. Also, when wind does blow and spin the turbine, it may suddenly swamp the high-voltage transmission lines. Try stuffing more water in a pipe than its capacity. It just spills out, no matter how hard you try.

A major solution to these problems is *localized electricity storage*. Cost-efficient batteries would allow the turbine to generate electricity at maximum capacity and store it locally. The operator would then sell power to the grid when there is transmission capacity and when the price for electricity is highest. Wind energy is already as cheap as coal, with a LCOE under 5 ¢/kWh[270].

As I've explained, daytime electricity prices are much higher than at night—sometimes by as much as two to four times. Investing in a storage system that at least allows a wind turbine to time-shift from, say 4:00 am. generation to 6:00 pm. consumption could provide a great return on investment. A 5-MW turbine operating at 25% efficiency (six hours per day) with six hours of storage would need 30 MWh of batteries. At today's $1,000/kWh price, the battery alone would cost $30 million. What's the problem? A 5-MW turbine costs about $7.5

million—installed. There is no way to justify adding storage at current battery prices.

If you brought the battery prices down to $100 per kWh, the 30-MWh battery would cost $3 million. *Question:* How can you justify adding 40% to the price of the turbine? *Answer:* If it increases cash flow by 41%. At today's differential between peak-time and night-time electricity prices, it would be an investment well worth making. So this is a mid-size battery, the equivalent of a mini-computer (smaller than a mainframe but larger than a personal computer.) Who will be the Digital Equipment Corporation of electricity storage? What's their market opportunity?

The World Wind Energy Association has predicted 1.5 TW of capacity by 2020. Investors usually discount forecasts. Let's assume the capacity is a little smaller and that it takes longer to get there: about 1 TW by 2050. Let's further assume that these turbines will have batteries with an average of 5 hours of storage each. That's 5 TWh of storage capacity. Further assume that the cost of storage is $50 per kWh (less than one-twentieth of current prices.) Following these assumptions, the market opportunity for electricity storage for wind turbines would be about $250 billion.

> *"The energy-storage market opportunity just for large wind turbines would be $250 billion."*

This does *not* include the residential solar PV electricity storage market, which I'm going to talk about in just a moment.

The Electrification of Everything...

On July 6 2009, Best Buy announced it would start selling "Green Vehicles," which it defined as battery-electric-powered bicycles, scooters, motorcycles, and the like. It said it was going to sell the Segway personal transporter and the Brammo Enertia, an $11,195 futuristic electric motorcycle that "can travel 45 miles at speeds of up to 50 miles per hour and plugs into a standard outlet.[271]"

Best Buy is best known as a seller of large televisions, sound systems, and other electronic products. They sell pretty much anything that is used in a middle-class home and can be plugged into an electric outlet. I cannot imagine a Ford dealer selling a 42-inch LCD television. Does it make sense for Best Buy to get into the transportation business?

Well, when Honda Motors first entered the U.S. market, it did so with a scooter. Fifty years later it was the fourth-largest auto company in America, where it sold more cars than Ford[272]. Clearly, starting with a scooter can lead to domination in the auto industry. This begs the question: will the automobiles of the future be sold in a car dealership or an electronics store?

Let's take a step back. This book starts out from the primary-energy big picture *as it is today*. That picture includes petroleum used in transportation, natural gas used in fertilizer plants, biomass used in off-grid homes in poor countries, as well as nuclear and coal-fired plants to generate electricity for grid-connected homes, businesses, and industry.

Electricity is only a subset of the energy consumed in the world. However, electricity demand is still growing as a percentage of primary energy and it is expected to keep doing so for the foreseeable future. Total energy demand is expected to double over the next four decades, and the percentage share of electricity is going up as well. In 1940, just 10% of the energy consumed in America was in the form of electricity. By 1970, that figure had grown to 25%, and by 2003 it was 40%.[273]

Another way to measure the value of electricity is its importance to the economy. The percentage of Gross Domestic Product (GDP) that is directly dependent on electricity went from 20% in 1950 to 60% in 2008, according to GlobalSmartEnergy[274]. There is an almost linear relationship between electricity growth and GDP growth (Fig. 8.3).

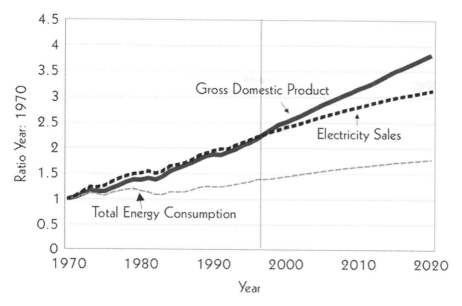

Figure 8.3. Electricity and Economic Growth. (Source USDOE[275])

The fact is that more and more of our world's appliances and tools are electric. Personal computers were virtually non-existent 30 years ago. Now they consume 2.5% of America's energy. Similar statistics can be cited for microwave ovens, espresso machines, and mobile phones. As American society became wealthier, we added a second and even a third television set in our homes. Now we're adding a second or third personal computer.

But it's not just the United States and the other G-8 nations that are undergoing this process. Rapidly industrializing countries like China and India are adding hundreds of millions of people to the middle class. China alone is said to have moved more than 300 million people from poverty to the middle class over the last generation—roughly equivalent to the entire population of the United States. This may well be one of the most important unsung humanitarian feats of the last century.

The new middle class in emerging nations, however, wants to follow our pattern and purchase new refrigerators, air conditioners, and computers that demand ever-increasing quantities of electric power. As we focus on energy efficiency, these products will consume less energy per unit. However, there will be more and more billions of them (whether they're iPods or mobile phones) where there were none before. My electric toothbrush may be more energy-efficient than the one I had three years ago, but it demands more electricity than brushing my teeth did ten years ago when I used a good old nonelectric toothbrush powered by my hand. Likewise for my iPod, iPhone, and laptop computer.

An electric toothbrush is one thing. A hybrid or battery-powered car is an altogether different electric animal. As battery-powered cars (Battery Electric Vehicles or BEVs) become mainstream, you would expect fossil fuel consumption to go down and electricity consumption to rise, right?

Not quite. BEVs will indeed increase electricity consumption. And as a product they are driving (no pun intended) the development of mid-range battery technologies, as we'll see. However, they could also do much more damage to the environment.

The Electric Car:
More Environmental Damage?

There are about 700 million cars in the world today. The International Monetary Fund (IMF) expects the number of cars to quadruple to 3 billion by 2050[276]. Most of these new cars will be produced and driven in rapidly industrializing countries like China and India. If these cars are gasoline-powered, the oil industry will have to double its production of gasoline (assuming that the mileage improves by 100% by then).

However, one of the emerging trends in the automotive industry is plug-in hybrid or battery-run vehicles (PIHV). In this scenario, most cars will be powered by batteries instead of gasoline. They will shed much of the engine block that converts gasoline power into mechanical power and transmits it to the drive-train. Batteries will power the car directly.

Many people take it as a given that because they don't use gasoline, plug-in cars are "green," better for the environment than their gasoline-powered cousins. The truth is more nuanced. Take China. Coal-fired power plants produce 80% of China's electricity[277]. Use this electricity to power your car and you're probably producing more environmentally damaging toxic and greenhouse-gas waste than if you used gasoline. It's not much different in the United States: about half of America's electricity comes from coal.

For plug-in battery or hybrid vehicles to really make an environmental difference, they need to be powered by clean energy sources. Furthermore, the build-outs of the clean-energy infrastructure and the battery-car infrastructure can benefit one another in many ways. Let's start with an examination of the economics of mid-size batteries right now, and right where they mostly are: in cars.

Tesla Batteries: Mid-Size Storage

The Tesla Roadster, a BEV, has a stack of lithium-ion batteries rated at 53 kWh (the equivalent of 8 gallons of gasoline). The average US household consumes 936 kWh per month or about 31 kWh per day[278], which means that the Tesla can store the equivalent of 40 hours of electricity for the average U.S. home.

If every home owned a Tesla battery, we could solve the energy storage problem, right? Not quite. A Tesla replacement battery reportedly costs more than $36,000[279]. This comes to about $680 per kWh of storage. This does not include the packaging, cooling, and safety systems, which would place it far above the $1,000 per kWh that seems to be the lithium-ion battery industry Holy Grail. At these prices, Li-ion batteries are not worth the investment for most of us.

The biggest difference between an electric car and one powered by a gasoline (or diesel) internal combustion engine is that the e-car is powered directly by an electric battery, while today's gas engine relies on the drive train components (engine, transmission, driveshaft, clutch, and so on) to convert fossil fuel or biofuel energy into mechanical power[280]. That much is obvious, but the difference has further crucial implications.

Here's one: the last gasoline-powered internal-combustion engine vehicle (ICEV) will officially be built when the cost of an electric battery falls to $3,600. That is, when an electric battery equivalent to today's Tesla (53 kWh) which can move a Tesla Roadster 244 miles (392 km) falls to about 10% of the price of today's Tesla batteries, or in the $3,600 range. That is when the whole clunky, hard-to-maintain, expensive-to-run transmission apparatus of today's ICEV will be more expensive to make than the simpler battery-electric vehicle (BEV). This calculus doesn't even include the cost of fuel, which as I previously mentioned is an order of magnitude cheaper for BEVs, or the environmental or maintenance costs of the hundreds of parts in today's ICEV (including all the chips now required to regulate a baroquely complicated energy conversion process to any kind of efficiency at all).

But the demise of the internal combustion engine (ICEV) will happen well before that point in history. Today's ICEV is inefficient, heavy, and costly to maintain. Here's why:

A battery is many times more efficient than an internal combustion engine. And that efficiency both makes for and exploits other efficiencies, all of which drive down the cost of the BEV.

- Today's cars use only about 20% of the energy in the gasoline—the other 80% literally goes down the tailpipe[281]. This calculus is flipped with electricity storage. An electric battery-engine uses about 80% of its energy and wastes only 20%.

- Because the electric car dispenses with the drive train altogether, it is much lighter. It can achieve a higher power-to-weight ratio and is therefore even more fuel-efficient. This is why France's TGV high-speed train, which achieves speeds of 200 miles per hour (320 Km/h), is electric[282].

- As I've mentioned elsewhere, clean energy will soon be much cheaper than dirty energy. Today's utility-scale CSP plants generate power at the equivalent of oil at $50 per barrel. Solar is headed to the equivalent of $20 or less within a decade. Oil, on the other hand, peaked at $147 per barrel during 2008, and after dropping for about a year is back to the $70-80 per-barrel level and is again headed up to triple digits.

How many of the 3 billion cars running around 2050 will be electric? Basic economics would say that when car batteries fall sufficiently in price, most of them will. This will be like the transition from horse-drawn carriages to the automobile a century ago. Resistance will be futile.

Let's assume for market-size determination that car batteries will store about 50 kWh of energy (today's Tesla stores 53 kWh.) Furthermore, let's assume that the price of that battery will have fallen to $50 per kWh or about $2,500 per car. If only a billion cars are primarily electric battery-driven, we're still looking at a $2.5 trillion market opportunity. That's with 33% market penetration.

> "The automotive battery (electricity storage) market opportunity would be $2.5 trillion. That's with just 33% market penetration."

What kind of power source are the other two billion cars going to use? Assuming that these cars are "city cars," a.k.a. neighborhood electric vehicles—small or low-end cars—they will have, at a minimum, a small (10-20 kWh) battery capable of short-distance city driving (48 km or 30 miles). At about $50 per kWh, that's $500-1,000 for each of two billion small or low-end cars. Do the numbers and you'll see a new opportunity: the low-end battery/electricity storage market: $1-$2 trillion.

Personal Energy Storage Systems

When the first microcomputers (as personal computers were then called) hit the market three decades ago, they were ridiculously underpowered and expensive by today's standards. Many thought that they were interesting toys for computer and math geeks, but the prevailing wisdom voiced by industry insiders like Ken Olsen, the CEO of Digital Equipment Corporation, one the most successful computer companies at the time, was that "there's no reason anyone would want a computer at their home."

PCs quickly came down in price, an ecosystem of software and hardware developers invested in making them even more useful, and the rest, as they say, is history. Silicon Valley was born and with it trillions of dollars in wealth, millions of high-paying jobs, and new industries that very few would have foreseen back then.

Solar photovoltaic has been going down a price-efficiency curve that is quite similar to the PC's. Every year, PV's cost goes significantly down and its efficiency and reliability go up. It has been doing this for three decades and, just as PCs did before, PV will continue on this curve for decades. PV, like the PC, is a "disruptive" technology par excellence!

As PV adoption numbers grow, an ecosystem of hardware and software products will develop to support and make the most of the power generated from the sun. One of the most important products (again) will be energy storage. I foresee several reasons why personal power storage systems will be widely adopted with PV systems and will be as much part of a PV system as hard-drive data storage or an Internet connection are today:

- If a PV system is off-grid, the user will have to store power when it's generated (during the day) and time-shift it to use it whenever it's needed (partly during the day and partly during the evening.) The same logic applies in the case of village- and island-scale solar installations—only they will need much larger energy-storage systems.

- In markets where the grid is not stable or demand is outstripping supply, there are frequent brownouts and blackouts. This is the case in numerous developing and fast-growing countries. India, which has a 25% energy shortfall, has frequent rolling blackouts[283]. It is common for 44% of the rural households who do have grid access to lose power for up to 12 hours at a time[284].

- Your electric or hybrid vehicle uses electricity at a price, so storing it when it's cheap to use later would lower your overall cost. This would complement the automotive energy storage opportunity beautifully. You'll be able to generate (using PV panels) your own power or buy it on the market when it's cheap and store it so you can transfer it to your car at home. If the expectation of one to three billion electric car owners becomes anywhere near a reality, this use alone would provide for another multi-trillion dollar market opportunity.

- Finally, as the smart grid is built, it is very likely that an eBay-like energy trading market will emerge (more on this in the next chapter.)

Today the PV power that is not used at home is sold to the utility at the price set by the utility, as the electric-meter needle moves "backwards." As we can already see in markets like New Zealand, relatively small electricity generators can sell to end users using a service called Powershop[285]. (More about Powershop and its potential in the next chapter.) As this concept grows popular around the world, the personal storage system (PSS) will become a business tool just like the PC is today.

For this residential and business market to materialize, we'll need a Tesla-like battery priced more like a personal computer or flat-panel LCD TV. Given the typical downward cost curve of photovoltaics and high-technology products, we can reasonably expect this to happen. When I graduated from the

Stanford Graduate School of Business in 1994, a flat-panel LCD
TV cost about $14,000—about the price of a new car. Only a
few well-off early technology adopters could afford to purchase
such a device. Today, higher-quality LCD and plasma TVs can be
found for under $1,000 and are flying off the shelves despite the
global recession. Today I saw a Best Buy flyer advertising a 19-
inch LCD High Definition TV for $309!

At some point over the next ten
or fifteen years, the electric-battery
price curve will hit a point at which
many solar PV panel users could buy
a battery to hold several hours-worth
of electricity in their homes and businesses.

> *"You're looking at a trillion-dollar market for personal energy storage systems."*

Like the PC market today, this has the potential to become a multi-trillion dollar field. Take a billion PC consumers
or battery-car owners willing to buy a $1,000 personal energy
storage battery (holding 10 or 20 kWh) and you're looking at a
one-trillion dollar market for personal energy storage systems.
Consumers in those markets would have both the need and the
financial incentive to own such equipment.

When the price of a decent personal or domestic electricity storage system hits the $300-
$400 mark, it can become as popu-
lar as the mobile phone. According
to the International Telecommunications Union, there were 4.1 billion
mobile phone subscribers in the
world at the end of 2008[286]. Suddenly you have an extra three billion
consumers who could possibly afford this battery—and another trillion-dollar market.

> *"When the price of a decent electricity storage system hits $300-400, it can become as popular as the cell phone. Suddenly you have another trillion-dollar opportunity."*

Just as mobile phone services generate more revenues
than the phones themselves, and just as software and information services generate more than sales of personal computers, the

market for "electricity management" services that will likely be added to the energy storage systems will be eventually in the trillions and will come to overshadow the storage-system business.

Personal computers were not adopted only at home. They were adopted in the business market in a big way, because they made workers more efficient, which increased profits. Even the simplest word-processing software on a PC was orders of magnitude superior to a typewriter. Why? One reason was that PCs let you store draft documents and edit them later as well as recycle keystrokes in updated versions. Efficient electrical storage allows the same kind of latitude with energy use.

Anyone living in Northern California during the summer of 2001 will remember the rolling blackouts in the heart of Silicon Valley. Businesses today can't afford poor-quality power. Downtime costs enterprises billions of dollars a year: a single hour of downtime costs an airline reservation system $60,000, a semiconductor manufacturer $2,000,000, and a credit-card operator $2,580,000[287]. (Need I remind the reader that both Intel and Visa are based in Silicon Valley?) The less reliable the grid and the quality (wattage) of the electricity it delivers, the more businesses will want to invest in energy storage to keep their operations running while the utility gets its act together.

The residential and commercial personal energy storage markets would therefore mirror each other just as they have done in PCs and as they seem to be doing in PV. Solar City, the fastest-growing PV energy-systems integrator in California (which I featured in chapter 6), does roughly half its business in the commercial market and the other half in residential.

Along these lines, an interesting market opportunity will be in the supply chain of energy storage and electric cars. Whereas the mainframe (and the minicomputer) were sold directly by manufacturers, the personal computer opened up new retail distribution channels. Companies like CompUSA and later Best Buy and Apple with its Stores created multi-billion dollar businesses selling computers, software, and services. Best Buy is already getting ahead of the curve selling electric battery automobiles. Tesla sells its $100,000 cars online. Stay tuned for more channel disruption—and opportunities.

Have we exhausted the trillion-dollar market possibilities? Not quite. The energy-storage opportunity is tied in with another I'll introduce in the next chapter: the smart grid. But first, a word of caution to technology entrepreneurs.

Selden vs. Benz: A Cautionary Tale of Technology Innovation and Business

In January 1886, German inventor Karl Benz was granted a patent in Europe for a four-stroke engine automobile. His company, Benz & Cie, built a production "Motorwagon" in July and sold 25 units over the following seven years. Three decades later Benz merged with Daimler and as Daimler-Benz created the Mercedes Benz, one of the most enduring product lines in one of the most important industries of the twentieth century[288].

Not long after the release of the automobile, the horse-drawn carriage industry was well on its way to being relegated to the museum. The motor-car architecture with its internal combustion engine powered by gasoline had a performance for the price that was far superior to the existing horse-carriage architecture. The car could go faster, farther, and longer. It carried more weight, required less maintenance (no horses), and it produced no manure. (It may seem quaint now, but the sheer quantity of excrement deposited in the streets of large cities through most of the nineteenth century by horses drawing carts, carriages, cabs, and omnibuses was a serious sanitation issue.)

There was nothing that carriage manufacturers could do to compete with the new automobile architecture, no matter how hard they tried. Increasing the number of horses per carriage wouldn't help. Building carriages with cheaper materials or with metal alloy wouldn't help. Building dog-carts as smaller, cheaper alternatives wouldn't have helped. Outsourcing production to China would not have helped either, even if it had been feasible.

The automobile of the late 1890s and early 1900s was an example of "radical innovation." This type of innovation brings a new product to market with a price/performance that is at least an order of magnitude greater than the established product—which is soon made obsolete.

This brings up two noteworthy points in the energy storage market. The first point is that *energy storage is an industry in severe need of radical innovations*. The companies that invent and successfully bring to market a "battery," based on a radical new electricity-storage technology, that offers a price/performance 10 times better than existing products stand to become the new Edison Electric or Daimler-Benz of the twenty-first century.

The second point I want to make is that *successfully bringing the technology to market is as important as inventing the technology itself*—maybe more. While Karl Benz is generally credited with being the inventor of the automobile, many others invented and were even awarded patents for similar technologies. In 1895, the U.S. Patent Office awarded patent number 549160 to George Selden, a lawyer from Rochester, NY. Mr. Selden had invented his "horseless carriage" in 1878 and had applied for a patent the following year; but then he put in a series of addendums to his original application that delayed the U.S.P.T.O. decision for 16 years. George Selden had officially invented the automobile[289]. However, while he was the proud owner of one of the most valuable patents in history, Selden was not successful in bringing a product to market. Enter Herr Benz on the main stage of technology history; exit Dr. Selden.

Today there are many organizations working on "next-gen" energy-storage technologies. Research Universities like MIT, large companies like IBM, and small companies and entrepreneurs are furiously trying to develop a radical battery that will bring an order of magnitude greater energy density for less than we pay for lithium-ion batteries today.

One key runner in this race is good old Big Blue. IBM is re-defining itself as an energy technology company. It has invested billions in developing products and services for intelligent networks and grids of all kinds: energy, water, and car transportation networks. IBM is also working on battery technology that aims to store ten times more energy than today's top lithium-ion batteries. "High-density, scalable energy storage technologies are emerging as the greatest game-changer for this new era of renewable energy sources and smarter grids," says Sharon Nunes, VP of IBM's Big Green Innovations organization[290].

Is the future Edison of electricity storage going to come from a lab at IBM, Intel, or GE? Or is it going to come from a small team of scientists and engineers working in a tiny boot-strapped workshop, like the Palo Alto garage where David Pack-ard and Bill Hewlett got their start? As we'll see in Chapter 10, the archetypal "two visionaries in a garage change the world" story may—perhaps—be passé in the rapidly maturing IT industry, but in clean energy it most certainly is not. However it comes about, though, cost-efficient energy storage offers more amazing opportunities.

"Electricity flow is cash flow"
—*Alex Nigg, Venture Capitalist*

"Clean affordable energy is going to happen globally.
The US is either going to lead or be left behind."
—*Jeffrey Immelt, CEO, General Electric*

"The map is not the territory."
—*Alfred Korzybski, founder of General Semantics*

CHAPTER 9

OPPORTUNITY VII—INTERNET TIMES TEN: THE SMART TRANSMISSION GRID

Gee Perry lives with his wife Christie and their six-year old daughter Hannah in a two-bedroom house in the Johnsonville neighborhood just north of Wellington, the capital of New Zealand. A network engineer by training, Mr. Perry delighted in telling me that he had just sold a TV monitor for $2 on TradeMe (a New Zealand website that is roughly equivalent to eBay). He was even more delighted to tell me that for the last six months he has been saving about $NZ 20 (about $12) in electricity costs per week by using an Internet-based electricity retailer called Powershop.

Powershop is a unit of Meridian Energy, an electricity generator and retailer based in Wellington, New Zealand. "The vision of Powershop is to be like eBay for electricity," says CEO Ari Sargent. "Any electricity generator in New Zealand, including Meridian's competitors, can offer their own brands of electricity at different prices and different times." Besides eBay, there's a bit of iTunes Store in Powershop too—since anybody can offer their own content online—and nothing really gets "shipped."

Many countries require their electric utilities to buy the clean power generated by residential or commercial solar installations and then resell it to consumers. Powershop goes beyond that. In the Powershop model, I could build a small 1-MW solar plant and offer the "SebaSolar" brand on Powershop, where I could sell at prices that I set—not the utility. This would probably provide New Zealanders with the most choices any electricity user has anywhere in the world. Kiwi electricity users could choose between, for instance, 300 units (kWh) of "NeoGeo" for 9 cents/unit, 400 units of "SebaSolar" for 10 cents/unit, Or 300 units of "WindyWelly" for 6 cents/unit. Eventually anyone should be able to sell power to anyone else. Just as iTunes transformed the world of music, this could be a transformational technology in the power industry.

Powershop's revenue model is more in tune with an Internet company than with the energy industry: to take a percent of each transaction. They don't charge "connection fees" like many utilities (including cable companies and telephone companies), since that would raise barriers to consumer adoption. eBay doesn't produce, transport, or sell anything. The success of this company came from enabling everyone to be a seller or a buyer of nearly anything.

Mr. Perry uses Powershop two to five times per week to check on his power consumption and look for special deals. "Why would you want to pay more for the very same electricity?" He asked me rhetorically. "Besides, Christie and I have a new baby on the way. We could use the extra money!"

New Zealand, a country the size of California with a population smaller than that of the San Francisco Bay Area, has created a relatively open, competitive power market that offers consumers choice and some of the lowest electricity rates in the developed world.

That's smart.

The California Grid

The afternoon of February 17, 2009 began like any other Tuesday in the winter trimester at Stanford. I was in my home office getting ready to teach "partnership strategy" using the case of a Silicon Valley company. One of the questions I always ask my executive students as they craft strategy is: "does location matter?" The San Francisco Bay Area is home to Google, Intel, Apple, Cisco, HP, Genentech, Oracle, Salesforce.com, Applied Materials, Facebook, and many of the world's technology powerhouses. It is also home to Stanford University and University of California at Berkeley.

I had just downloaded that evening's class lecture Power-Point file from the iMac desktop to the PC laptop. I felt lucky to live in San Francisco. Even on such a cold, windswept, rainy day there was nowhere else I'd rather be. As I was getting ready to print out a teaching "cheat sheet" with an outline and key points for the case study, the electric power went out. The printer, the Internet router, the Mac, the speakers, the lights, and everything else without a built-in battery died. I found out how useless my computer "power backup" was. Not only did it not protect the computers or the backup disk, but its high-pitched beep was so loud and annoying that I had to switch it off.

This was not the first time in my experience that San Francisco had lost power during a rainy day. I could not help but be struck by the irony that the world's high-tech hub—like Houston, the nation's energy hub—had such a Third-World electric transmission and distribution infrastructure. Just in California, businesses lose up to $17 billion per year due to power interruptions[291]. But the problem is not just in the Golden State.

Figure 9.1. Distribution lines in San Francisco, USA. (Photo: Tony Seba)

On August 13, 2003, a tree fell on a transmission line in Ohio. Within hours, most of the U.S. Northeast went dark. More than 50 million people from New York to Boston to Detroit were without power for up to two days. The blackout cost 11 lives and an estimated 50 billion dollars[292]. Due to transmission grid problems, what should have been a small local annoyance (a fallen tree) ballooned out of control and the whole United States Northeast went dark.

Blackouts are not the only grid problem that costs us money. American businesses lose $135 billion per year due to power interruptions. The grid is the circulatory system for a modern society's technological body. America has postponed investments in the grid just as many of us keep postponing going to the gym. The blackouts, brownouts and related problems are increasing signals that the system is diseased.

The United States grid has 200,000 miles of high voltage transmission lines (the highways of electricity) and 5.5 million miles of distribution lines (the streets) that deliver electricity to homes, schools and businesses[293]. This grid is without a doubt one of the twentieth century's top engineering and technological achievements. Its contribution to economic growth and social cohesion in America has few parallels.

America's grid, however, was built in the early to mid-twentieth century to power light-bulbs, washing machines, and transistor radios. It was not designed to support today's airports, information-based military, or Wal-Mart sized computer data centers, let alone semiconductor fabrication facilities or millions of plug-in car batteries.

Our grid was also not built for "wholesale" power transactions. In the past, most utilities generated what they thought their market needed. If they came up short, they would buy "wholesale" power from others—mainly from other utilities. Over the last few years the electricity trade has grown, as generators and even intermediaries have joined utilities in the exchange of power. Between 2000 and 2005, wholesale trade grew by 300%[294].

We have under-invested in the grid since the 1970s. We are like trust-fund kids living off of their parents' investments. We believed Wall Street's promise of never-ending asset growth. However, unless we invest in the grid, our kids will inherit a crumbling infrastructure. "The average transformer in America is 42 years old," says Marie Hattar, a smart-grid vice president at Cisco Systems. "Their expected life is 40 years." So the average transformer in America is living on borrowed time.

You can find the same story with every important piece of hardware that dots the American electricity grid landscape. According to the Department of Energy:

- 70% of transmission lines are at least 25 years old;
- 60% of circuit breakers are at least 30 years old.

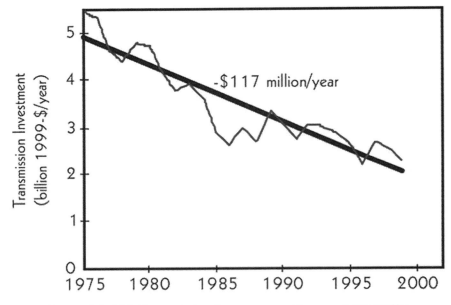

Figure 9.2. U.S. Transmission Investments. (Source: USDOE[295])

While electricity demand and GDP have more than doubled since 1975, investments in transmission have decreased on average $117 million each year since 1975—to less than half what they were then (fig 9.2).

The U.S. Northeast blackout was like a massive heart attack. Furthermore, the conditions that caused the August 2003 blackout remain in place, according to Eric Lerner . If America is to remain a leading economic power of the twenty-first century, we will have to bring the grid back to life and invest to upgrade it to world-class levels.

How much? The total amount of capital spending for transmission and distribution of electricity by electric power utilities around the world is currently estimated to be in the range of \$85-\$100 billion[297]. That's just to keep up with current demand. Assume that the capital investment will just grow with the most conservative demand growth of 1.75% over the next 40 years (mirroring the growth from 14 TW to 30 TW). That means that the world will invest \$5.5 trillion in the power grid—just to keep up with demand. We may have to spend much more if we actually want to modernize it and stay a step ahead of demand growth.

> "Capital investment in the power grid (transmission and distribution) is expected to be \$5.5 trillion."

The International Energy Agency (IEA) believes that spending will come faster. According to the IEA the world will have to spend \$11 trillion in energy infrastructure between now and 2030—of which half (\$5.5 trillion) could go to transmission, according to the IEA. "Updating and upgrading the grid will cost nearly \$1 trillion through 2030 in North America alone."[298]

Fig. 9.3. High-voltage transmission lines to Dubai. (Photo: Tony Seba)

And this doesn't just mean replacing old, decaying transformers, breakers, and lines. The old grid was based on a centralized local-monopoly model, in which utilities could plan generation and transmission capacity. But the world is moving to a more decentralized power generation model in which anyone can be a producer as well as consumer of electricity. But in this model, just as in the old one, what links all consumers to all producers is the grid. With all these new producers, that's a lot of linkage—and current—to manage.

Lack of centralized planning means a higher likelihood of congestion on the grid. Imagine car traffic on the notoriously congested Highway 101 between San Francisco and San Jose slowing to an intermittent but permanent crawl. It's not just the drivers on 101 who are affected. Many drivers going from San Francisco to San Jose need to be routed to Highway 280, which runs a few miles west parallel to the 101. Then the 280 gets clogged as well. So do feeder streets all the way along both routes as they back up. So do local surface streets that savvy drivers use to get around the mess.

If traffic congestion gets bad enough, these two cities are to a significant extent cut off from each other. Shoppers don't travel between the two cities if they can help it; businesses based at one end stop trying to sell at the other end because of chronic distribution headaches. This means that what was in effect one large market (the whole Peninsula from San Francisco to San Jose) is effectively cut into two markets, north and south, both of which become less efficient as they have diminished competition.

So it is with electricity transmission. What grid congestion can do is to effectively sever one larger wholesale market into two or more smaller markets. Users in the smaller markets only have access to power generators in their geography, not to potentially lower-cost generators elsewhere. Each smaller market clears prices at different points and volumes—which makes them less efficient.

The *theoretical* solution to this problem has been provided by MIT Professor Paul L. Joskow: "successful wholesale markets require 'over-investment' in capacity—compared with a perfectly coordinated, centrally planned strawman—to create truly competitive market.[299]" Joskow goes on to say: "[U]nregulated wholesale electricity markets work best when transmission congestion and constraints do not place significant limitations on the number of generators which can compete to serve demand and provide reliability to the network at specific locations."

In other words, we have to invest trillions to bring the transmission grid up to new technology and reliability standards as well as adequate network topology (the big map of where all the lines go) and to accommodate expected growth in electricity demand. Then we need to add more capacity so as to minimize congestion and create successful electricity markets.

The Electricity Backbone

Part of what makes New Zealand an interesting case study for twenty-first century energy transformation is that it has already dealt with many of the issues that much of the rest of the world is just now confronting. As I've mentioned in earlier chapters, most of the country's electricity production comes from hydroelectric plants in the South Island. Most of the population and energy consumption is in the North Island. To connect the two islands, the country has built long-distance transmission lines that go under water.

China's Three Gorges Dam is the largest hydroelectric power plant in the world, with a generation capacity of 18.2 GW. As is the case with many utility-scale hydroelectric, solar, or wind plants, power is generated far from the population and industrial centers that consume it. This hydro plant is 975 km (609 miles) from the bustling population center of Shanghai and 890 Km (556 miles) from the industrial center of Changzhou.

In the early 1990s China did not have a grid to speak of, so the decision to build the transmission lines from the Three Gorges Dam was made both without the encumbrances of "legacy" hardware and software infrastructure and with the intent to build a national transmission grid for the future. The builders of these lines and of the nascent China power grid chose a technology called HVDC, which stands for High Voltage Direct Current. That's the same one the consortium that is building the giant CSP plants in the North African desert will be using to carry all that solar electricity to gray-skied, energy-deprived Northern Europe. When Brazil built the then largest hydroelectric dam in the world at Itaipu, it too built an HVDC transmission line across the country to carry the power. New Zealand's latest underwater transmission backbone is also an HVDC line.

Why did these countries choose HVDC? For a couple of reasons.

The first reason is that for long-distance transmission, HVDC has lower energy losses than anything else in the market. It loses about 3% per 1,000 km (620 miles). The distance from Phoenix, Arizona to New York City is about 3,400 km (2,100 miles). If a plant was built near Phoenix to send all its power over a dedicated line to New York, it would lose about 10.2% of that power. By contrast, losses in high-voltage AC systems come to between 15% per 1,000 km (for 380 kV) and 8% per 1,000 km (for 750 kV[300]). From Phoenix to New York, this would mean a transmission loss of up to 51%.

This is important because the average annual solar radiation in one place is twice that in the other: as I mentioned earlier, a given solar plant built near Phoenix would yield twice the output of an identical one built in New York. Even after taking a 10.2% shave (2,100 miles ÷ 620 miles x 3% loss) the Phoenix plant would be 90% more productive. Efficient, clean energy generation and use require efficient long-distance transmission.

Another reason for HVDC is that it needs far narrower right-of-way than the alternatives. Right-of-way is the long strip of land that needs to be established (purchased or "eminentdomained") to build transmission lines, train lines, or roads on. Even small savings in right-of-way add up because they are multiplied by the whole length of the transmission lines. A savings of 1 meter (3.3 feet) in width over 1,000 km (620 miles) of length would save 1,000 km² (386 square miles) of land—which is a lot of forest, farmland, or desert.

What's the savings in right-of-way for HDVC? According to the German Aerospace Center (DLR), HDVC is up to four times more space-efficient than the equivalent AC lines[301]. Given the NIMBY ("Not In My Backyard") attitude that prevents the rapid approvals of transmission grid projects, a 75% savings in land rights could go a long way to helping accelerate this process.

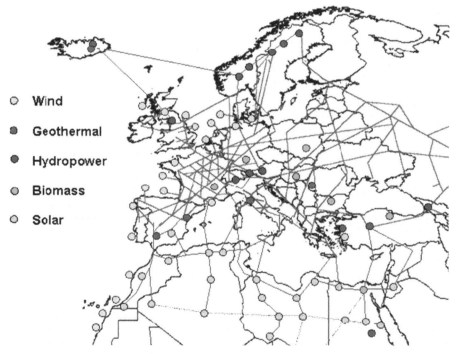

Figure 9.4. Visions of the Trans-Mediterranean grid with HDVC lines transmitting solar electricity from the Sahara to Europe. (Source TRANS-MED Final Report[302])

The Cisco of the Smart-Grid Market Opportunity

On April 21, 2009, Florida Power & Light and Miami-Dade County announced the $200-million Wireless Smart Grid Initiative, a plan to add "smart meters" to one million homes and buildings in the county[303]. Should the plan prove successful, FPL said it would extend the program to all its 4.5 million customers.

That FPL is an early adopter of smart grid technology should be no surprise. You may remember (from Chapter 1) that FPL has been operating some of the SEGS (Solar Energy Generating Systems) plants that have been generating electricity in California since the 1980s.

The companies who were part of that announcement include some of today's industrial powerhouses like GE and Cisco Systems. GE, the descendant of the original Edison General Electric, was one of the most successful companies of the twentieth century and has been in the electricity business for a century. Cisco Systems is the networking company whose computers power much of the plumbing of the Internet.

2009 felt like the "year of the smart grid" in Silicon Valley venture-capital circles. While I was on a fundraising tour, we consistently heard that investors were looking for smart-grid opportunities. It seemed that not a week went by without an announcement of a multi-hundred-million dollar smart-grid project. On July 13, Baltimore Gas & Electric (BGE) announced a $500 million smart-grid project in the Maryland area[304] BGE said that the use of smart meters and other devices could save consumers up to $2.6 billion in electricity and gas bills.

Despite that—or maybe because of that—many questioned whether the smart grid was overblown. The Obama administration had budgeted more than $3.9 billion for smart grid development as part of the economic stimulus package. Were the utilities announcing smart grid projects just to get a piece of that cash? What kind of a market opportunity does the smart grid represent? Is it a long-term as well as short-term opportunity? On October 27, President Obama visited a solar PV manufacturing plant and announced that the administration would indeed be handing out $3.4 billion for smart-grid infrastructure development, specifically to help advance renewable energy. So it's more than time to take the smart grid seriously—and learn more about what it is.

The Smart Grid: Layers of Opportunity

The smart grid is an end-to-end data network and intelligence overlay running on top of the power grid. According to Greentech Media's David Leeds, the smart grid is comprised of three layers[305]:

- Electricity/Power Layer
- Data Network Layer
- Application Layer

Each smart-grid layer presents a set of market opportunities. Executives are excited. GE's CEO Jeff Immelt says: "If the top 50-100 cities adopt the smart grid, then it's a $3-$5 billion [a year] revenue opportunity for us."[306] "Within three or four years, GE is poised to reap as much as $4 billion a year in revenue from smart grid technologies", said John Krenicki, vice chairman and chief executive of GE's Energy Infrastructure unit[307].

That's $120-$200 billion revenue opportunity for GE alone between now and 2050. So GE wants to be the... well, the General Electric of the (power layer) smart grid.

Cisco CEO John Chambers says that "this [smart grid] is an instant replay of the Internet. Instead of moving around data, voice, and videos, and zeros and ones; you move electricity around."[308] Marie Hattar, VP of Cisco's Network Systems and Security Solutions group, believes that the smart grid will be

10 to 100 times larger than the Internet because "every home and business has electricity, and potentially every device in every home and business will participate in this network."[309]

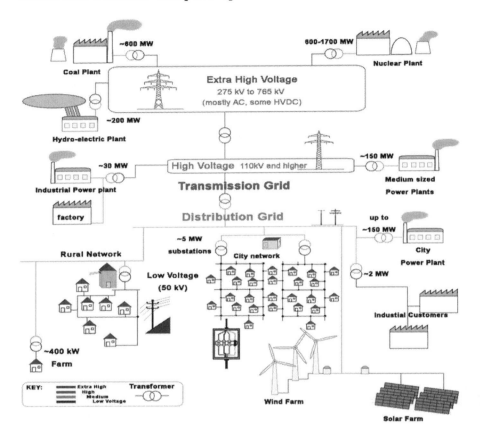

Figure 9.5. Opportunity: Adding intelligence to every device in every residence, business, factory, battery, generation plant, generation source, and transmission and distribution pole. (Graphic source: Wikipedia)

The idea is that there will be a parallel network (the "Energy Internet") running on top of the electricity infrastructure. This network will run from the power producers through the transmission and distribution lines to every manufacturing plant, business, and home that receives electricity.

Every home appliance could be potentially connected to this network: air conditioner, washer-dryer, television, refrigerator—and of course computers. The home could have a "router" that would gather the home electricity data and relay it to the grid.

Today electrons "download" instantly, but the data about those electrons only "uploads" every month. The smart grid network would allow both electrons and data to move in both directions in real time. The torrent of real-time energy-flow data coming from billions of devices in homes and businesses running through millions of transformers over hundreds of thousands of miles of transmission and distribution lines is hard to comprehend. This is several orders of magnitude larger than the existing Internet. Hundreds of Wal-Mart-size data centers will have to be built around the world just to keep up with this data. "We expect Smart Grid to be a $20 billion-per year market," says Cisco's Ms. Hattar.

Could Cisco actually be a little conservative in that estimate? Let's walk through a thought exercise. Cisco had 2008 revenues of $39.5 billion, according to Morningstar, an investment research provider. If the smart-grid data network is potentially ten times the size of the existing Internet, then it stands to reason that the revenue potential is much more than that $39.5 billion/year—which is already almost double Ms. Hattar's actually rather cautious figure.

Assuming we ramp up from zero spending in 2008 to $40 billion in 2050, we're looking at an $800 billion revenue opportunity. Cisco has about 80% market share of the Internet. Assuming the same market share of the new energy internet, then we're talking about a $1 trillion revenue opportunity. So it's clear why Cisco wants to be the Cisco of the data network layer of the smart grid. While a company (probably very) like GE would participate in developing the power layer, Cisco would compete to build the data network layer.

"The network layer of the smart grid (the "Energy Internet") could be a trillion-dollar revenue opportunity."

The third layer of the smart grid would then provide entrepreneurs with a platform on which to develop a whole new set of applications and intelligence and service businesses. Thinking back to the build-out of the existing Internet, we see that many, if not most, of the opportunities came not from building the network, but from services and applications built on top of it. Companies like Google, eBay, Apple, Intuit, and Facebook created multi-billion dollar businesses in that way.

So conceptually, the smart-grid application layer brings at least as many opportunities, if not even more opportunities, than the power and data layers.

Looking for Smart-Grid Application Opportunities

In the early 1980s, as I mentioned in previous chapters, there were *microcomputers*. They performed many of the basic functions done by mainframe computers, but they were relatively isolated and relatively simple: word processing and business number-crunching, mostly, the core functions of the home or office PC to this day. As time went on, microcomputers got faster and more powerful and became Personal Computers. A few adventurous businesses started connecting them into small departmental networks which then connected to other departmental networks with "inter-networking" routers. These campus networks or intranets then connected to the larger networks via the newborn Internet. Over two decades the humble microcomputer went from an underpowered toy to the most important single machine in the vast worldwide network called the Internet.

We have been conceiving and designing a smart grid that resembles the Internet in scale and scope—only bigger. This smart grid will have to deal with the complexities of matching millions of power customers who own billions of devices getting their energy from millions of generators, with the inflow and outflow of millions of energy storage devices, and millions of other devices (transformers and the like) across the transmission and distribution lines.

But most of the world is made up of small towns or villages, the majority of which are *not* connected to a national or even a regional grid. India alone has more than 500,000 villages that are not grid-linked. They probably have a diesel-powered generator, maybe solar and/or wind generation, and maybe a biomass burner. They have a few dozen homes and businesses. Is there a smart grid model for them?

I see the *smart microgrid* as an early example of a successful application that works with the network and power layers of the smart grid. A smart microgrid allows a village or relatively small population or business center to manage energy supply, storage, and demand in an intelligent way. Just as solar is enabling the democratization of energy, the emerging smart microgrid can help to enable a smart, efficient transition to village-scale solar.

For an example of a microgrid I spoke with Alexis Ringwald, a cofounder at Mountain-View-based Valence Energy. Ms. Ringwald, I think, has a great story to tell. While some of her classmates at Yale's Environmental Management program were getting ready for jobs at Wall Street, she had set her sights halfway around the world: at India. Armed with a Fulbright Scholarship, she crisscrossed the Indian subcontinent researching renewable energy finance and climate change at The Energy Resource Institute (TERI.) In her free time, Ms. Ringwald helped organize a tour to travel 2,400 miles across India in solar electric cars to document the best solutions to climate change. On her return to the U.S., she followed her entrepreneurial heart, and together with Kailash Joshi, Raju Indukuri, and James Bickford she started Valence Energy to develop smart microgrids with an eye to the Indian market.

Ms. Ringwald told me about a Valence project to be launched in India at the end of 2009.

Palm Meadows is a new neighborhood being developed in Hyderabad with 330 new smart-meter-enabled premium homes. The development will be connected to the grid, and will have

83 kW-worth of solar photovoltaic panels and a 2-MW diesel generator.

"Our software will choose between solar, diesel, and the grid. We will emphasize solar energy and use the grid to complement it. The software can also enable demand response, which means that when the grid goes down (which it does a lot in India) it will automatically turn on the diesel generator and also switch off nonessential loads." Valence will let users know exactly what they're paying for electricity as well as how much carbon dioxide they are producing.

Just as there were local area networks and then wide area networks, and then everything was connected to the larger Internet, the development of smart microgrids can happen in parallel with that of the smart "macrogrid" or "Intergrid." In the meantime, users in islands or villages have access to the benefits of a centrally managed power station, with its possible efficiencies and economies of scale and its stable power supply—without having to depend on a national or regional transmission grid. "There are 400 million people in India without access to modern energy services," says Ms. Ringwald. "For them it makes sense to use rural smart microgrids."

Closer to home as well as in developing nations like India, this technology can also be applied to a university campus or business campus. Many campuses are in fact like villages, with their own primary or backup power generation equipment, energy storage, and specific usage patterns to manage. And it can also be applied to military installations. Military bases are self-sufficient, relatively isolated communities that often look like small cities. They need reliable energy services and cannot afford to lose power when the grid fails. Many military installations have their own electric generation facility and may also connect to the grid to complement this power. (Which is why, as I mentioned earlier, they are excellent candidates for "island-scale solar" too.)

The adoption of solar energy happens in parallel and more or less simultaneously at the levels of individual home, neighborhood, and village. Smart microgrids can help the transition by automatically managing energy sources: give priority to solar or wind sources and use backup fossil-fuel generation when and if needed. They could turn air conditioners off when users are not home and back on a few minutes before they return, or sell excess power back to the grid at certain prices.

The possibilities are endless. Here are a few more.

Application-Layer Opportunity 1— The eBay of the Smart Grid

Today's grid is built on the basis of a centralized planning for generation and storage. As in any Soviet-style, top-down, centralized planning structure, it doesn't provide for much in the way of flexibility, consumer input, or market-driven innovations.

As we discussed in the last chapter, the smart grid provides a more distributed and two-way approach. Periodical publishing is a good analogy here. In the old days, news and commentary came via newspapers and magazines produced at centralized locations and distributed to readers. You were either a publisher or a reader. The web turned that model on its head: now anyone can be a publisher, whether the "publication" is as potentially elaborate as a blog or as simple as a Facebook page. In the old days you had to travel physically to a market or a store to buy stuff, or set up your own physical shop and supply chain if you wanted to sell it. Now anyone can be a seller and a buyer on eBay. The smart grid should provide the opportunity for consumers of energy to be producers and sellers too.

New Zealand's Powershop provides users with a Weekend Plan option whereby they can use power from different sources on weekdays from the ones they use on weekends. Future smart-grid-connected consumers will probably be able to buy energy from different providers on a daily or hourly basis. They will prioritize their preferences and let the smart-grid devices take care of the rest.

Same thing for energy storage. Some of my data is stored on my Mac or a backup drive, while other data is in the Internet "cloud." I could rent energy storage on the smart grid "cloud" and have inventory "out there" as well as in my business or home. I could use an application to consume, add to, or sell from that inventory.

Just as eBay or Apple's iTunes enabled thousands of people to get into new businesses, the smart grid should allow many to participate in the energy market by producing, storing, and selling energy—and the energy-generation scalability that in turn permits them to produce their own power will come overwhelmingly from solar.

Application-Layer Opportunity 2— The SAP of the Smart Grid

The national average "load factor" is about 55%. Put another way: electricity assets in the industry are used just above half the time. The rest of the time their production capacity is wasted, as I discussed in the previous chapter. Today's obsolescent electricity-asset infrastructure comprises trillions of dollars in capital and hundreds of millions in fuel that ratepayers are paying for but not consuming.

Much of American (and world) industry has gone through a wrenching capacity-utilization improvement over the last few decades. Companies like Wal-Mart, Dell, and Southwest Airlines have redefined and dominated their industries by improving their asset utilization. Wal-Mart's inventory control system, for instance, is tightly linked with the factories and distribution systems of its main suppliers. This way, the supplier's factories are turning out and resupplying product almost immediately as Wal-Mart stores sell it. What this means for a Wal-Mart supplier is that it will not produce inventory that may go unsold. So both Wal-Mart and its suppliers use their assets (factories, inventory, people) more efficiently— which in the end means lower prices for the end consumer (and/or more profits for the supplier and Wal-Mart). Furthermore, since the supplier can anticipate demand, it can make better capital investment decisions. It can invest in equipment, warehouses, and raw materials and use them with a better demand-forecasting model.

This supply chain management (SCM) is a subset of what has come to be known as Enterprise Resource Management (ERP). Do the same thing for sales, marketing, finance, and other business processes and you have a more efficient company that uses its assets and resources without much waste.

There are, it's true, many drawbacks to a highly efficient, ERP-driven company. Such companies use their assets quite efficiently but may lose the creativity and nimbleness required to bring new products and services to market. Dell is a case study of a highly efficient company that forgot that the point of its existence was not to be efficient but to be customer-driven. However, utilities are far from being a Dell. There is a *lot* of waste in a system that only uses 55% of its assets efficiently. In the case of the energy industry this waste is not figurative. It's quite literal (as we saw in the energy storage chapter.) There's a lot of coal pollution literally going down the drain into our rivers and up the smokestack for nothing, because that electricity is not being consumed.

The SAP of the smart grid would help guide more appropriate capital investments for new capacity and would help manage the infrastructure we have more efficiently. The Internet has enabled the development of software industries based on Enterprise Resource Planning (ERP). Germany's SAP has created a multibillion-dollar-a-year franchise developing this market. There are trillions in energy infrastructure assets waiting for the SAP of the smart grid to make efficient.

Application-Layer Opportunity 3—
The Oracle of the Smart Grid

As I've already mentioned in connection with Cisco's early interest in this market, the smart grid will probably be one of the biggest data generators of all time. This data will need to be moved stored across the world in real time. Even more important, we will need to make sense of this data—also in real time.

Companies that can help us analyze, simplify, and act on all this energy data will have a chance at large market opportunities. Just like Intuit's Quicken helps us manage our finances today, there may be an opportunity for an energy Quicken that helps us keep track of our energy assets, income, and expenses. Grid operators, energy producers, utilities, policy makers, and consumers will all need different sets of tools to make demand, supply, trading, operations, maintenance and capital investment decisions.

Of course, we can get carried away with Internet analogies. For instance, can you think of a Facebook of the smart grid? A social network for smart meters? Probably not. (Although Singularity believers would beg to differ; they anticipate "social networks" for intelligent machines within this century.) But something like Oracle is a certainty because the smart grid cannot succeed without those data storage and processing applications.

On the other hand, there may be quite different opportunities emergent from the smart grid that we haven't even imagined yet. Nobody could have predicted the Facebook phenomenon when Netscape went public in 1996. That was barely over a dozen years ago! The automobile was not just a horseless carriage, television was not just radio plus pictures, the Internet was not just a faster way to send mail, and the web is not just interactive television and remote shopping. The "killer app" that transformed the Internet was the web browser. First popularized by Netscape, it changed the way that we consume and produce content, conduct commerce, communicate, and socialize. As those possibilities opened up, so did bandwidth, because tens of millions more users now had real interest in using the web—for shopping, for research, for viewing (and now sharing) pictures and video, and latterly for socializing.

We still don't know what the killer app for the smart grid will be. What we can probably say is that the smart grid will open up many large entrepreneurial opportunities—some hinted at here and some in heretofore unheard-of areas.

Smart Grid—Benefits and Challenges

There is no doubt that the smart grid will deliver benefits that far outweigh the costs of building it. Still there are a few challenges that stand in the way of building it and might forestall its wide adoption.

First, the benefits.

According to the Electric Power Research Institute (EPRI), the 20-year cost of building a smart grid in America would be about $165 billion, or $8.3 billion per year above the $18 billion per year that would be spent in a business-as-usual scenario[310]. The benefits of the smart grid would amount to $638-802 billion over the same 20 years. That would be a $4-5 return for each dollar invested.

Now, the challenge.

The EPRI study was published in 2004, yet deployments were slow to happen over the following few years—despite the magnitude of the market opportunity. What was the problem? Were venture capitalists too busy investing in web 2.0 companies instead of cleantech startups? Were the utilities too busy just coping with record fossil-fuel prices? Hard to say. But the nature of networks provides a plausible explanation for this apparent timidity on the part of the Valley's supposedly bold (and even sometimes foolhardy) VCs.

America's grid is a network with more than 3,100 utilities that serve more than 130 million customers who paid $247 billion in electricity bills in 2003[311]. The key fact here is that it's a *network*—or in the U.S., actually three networks, but the principles still apply. Since the grid is a network, there are "network effects"— participants benefit when other members join and create value in the network. Think of the Internet, the telephone, or Facebook: the more members they have, the more people you can communicate with, the more developers will create applications to enhance that communication, the more members the larger and enhanced network will attract, and so on. In economics this is known as a "virtuous cycle."

The problem with networks, though, is that they need to achieve a "critical mass" before most people will join. The benefits do not necessarily accrue to those who take risks and invest early. (The fate of Netscape is a salutary lesson in this regard.) Someone needs to invest to kick-start the network and help it achieve critical mass. The Internet had the backing of the government for decades before it went mainstream. The phone network had a government-sanctioned monopoly for nearly a century, which let AT&T invest with the full knowledge that it would reap the benefits of those network effects.

What has finally (we hope) kick-started the smart grid in America? As I noted earlier, the Obama administration budgeted $3.9 billion for the smart grid in its stimulus bill, the American Recovery and Reinvestment Act, soon after it came to power[312]. In October 2009, as I've also noted, the President announced the upcoming disbursement of $3.4 billion of that promised sum. These funds will come in the form of matching grants, matching private investment dollar-for-dollar. The effect is a net $6.8 billion kick-start investment in smart grid development. That's an order of magnitude or two less than the amount we need to get the smart grid built out. But it may be enough to generate a critical mass of smart grid adopters and kick-start the network. Suppliers invest in product development, utilities adopt, consumers save, the economy grows—which enables the virtuous cycle of network growth. That's smart.

"Sometimes it falls upon a generation to be great.
You can be that generation."

—Nelson Mandela

"We must ensure that entrepreneurs and
inventors everywhere on the globe
have the chance to change the world."

—Al Gore

"The difference between what we do and
what we are capable of doing would suffice
to solve most of the world's problems"

—Mohandas Gandhi

CHAPTER 10

SOLAR ENTREPRENEURSHIP OUTSIDE THE GEARS: A LIVING CASE STUDY

Silicon Valley is the place where Hewlett and Packard, Jobs and Wozniak, and Brin and Page started business empires in their garages, back yards, or dorm rooms. The story, now repeated enough times in real life to be an archetype, is of two guys (or gals) going from eating pizza and corn chips for breakfast while building the "next big thing" to becoming multimillionaires or even multibillionaires. Who's going to start the HP, Cisco, Google, or Apple of the clean-energy era?

I want to share the story of two guys who actually launched their venture in a garage, and who I believe have the potential to make a huge impact in solar energy—and therefore in all energy markets. I was the first executive hired by the two garage-guy corporate founders soon after they came up with their invention. As their Vice President of Corporate Development I participated in the journey from laboratory to beta product, including business planning, strategy making, fundraising, and flying around the world to meet with plant developers, policymakers, and dozens of investors. It also started me in a new direction in my work as entrepreneur, advisor, educator and speaker on technology strategy. While this is still early in the story, I think it's a great case study in successful innovation. Their approach to finding an opportunity is one I would like to share with cleantech entrepreneurs. Actually, I want to share it with all entrepreneurs.

Two guys (or gals) in a garage can make a big difference in energy. Join me as I talk about the entrepreneurial journey of Pete Childers and Jonathan Blitz.

Seeing the Light

Jonathan Blitz is a former criminal defense attorney who regularly trolled the littered backstreets of Durham, North Carolina, for "grease"—waste oil from fryers and the like—to fuel his smelly, tricked-out Ford F150 diesel truck. In the summer of 2003, Blitz had modified his truck to run on cooking oil. He had driven it more than 60,000 miles on vegetable grease by the time his wife introduced him to Pete Childers in 2006. In his free time, Blitz worked in ceramics and high-temperature materials technology. He loved to work on everything from kilns to welding to piping and heating and cooling systems. Blitz would spend weekends converting not just his Ford truck but also his kilns and heating systems to work on biofuels instead of diesel or fuel oil.

Childers, who grew up in the Chicago neighborhood of Hyde Park two blocks from the home of US President Barack Obama, studied Artificial Intelligence, cognitive science, and computing at Yale and then Duke University. He worked in educational services before being hired by a fast-growth high-technology company that was competing head-on with the most successful software company of all time: Microsoft. He was the Vice President of Learning and Online Strategy at Red Hat Software's training and certification division, which he built from scratch, turning it into the highest-revenue and highest-margin line of business for the company. Childers told me how in 2005, sitting in his executive corner office at the company's brand-new headquarters in NCSU's Centennial Park, he thought about the achievements of America's information and communications industries over the last three decades: personal computers, the Internet, and mobile phones, to name three. Then he thought about the fact that the infrastructure underlying all those achievements was broken. He realized that everything behind that electrical outlet on the wall relied on technologies, architectures, and business models that went back to the nineteenth century.

Childers recounts that his concern about the ability of our power infrastructure to support our present and future technology achievements quickly grew into existential angst as he started connecting the dots of what lay behind that plug on the wall: waste, environmental degradation, and century-old thinking and business philosophies. Childers could have worked as a highly-paid technology executive for the rest of his career. Having realized that America was facing an imminent energy crisis that could take the rest of our technological achievements down with it, he decided he had to do something about it.

Not long after being introduced by their wives, Childers and Blitz realized they shared a passion for clean energy and a desire to rid the world of fossil fuels. Soon after they met, they started looking for an opportunity to develop an alternative to fossil fuels.

They decided to work on biofuels; more specifically, they wanted to develop bio-oil from algae. Since Blitz had already been working on biofuels for several years, the two used his garage as a lab, studying algae as a possible source of alternative fuels. Blitz built a "photo-bioreactor" and "brewed" various biofuels to test processes and yields. He bought algae strains from the University of Texas online algae store and cultured a high-lipid strain in a sterile propagation system. Blitz told me he designed and fabricated the bioreactor from plastic sheeting, a pump, and PVC plumbing parts.

But the algae research kept bumping up against the fact that, as Blitz put it, "the energy going into making biofuels was larger than the energy the biofuels could produce. He realized it was a dead-end technology. "I had a second law of thermodynamics epiphany: that you're using this biological system to gather solar energy into a chemical fuel at 2% efficiency, spending additional energy and other resources like water and feedstock to process that fuel, and then you're burning that fuel in a combustion system that's only 20% efficient if you're lucky. Why go through all that trouble when you can use a direct solar thermal system to get an order of magnitude more energy on a net basis?"

Blitz also did the numbers and realized that it would take cultivating fuel crops on the majority of U.S. farmlands to substitute biofuels for current American gasoline consumption. That sounded like more imports and more carbon dioxide to him— the opposite of what he wanted.

Blitz and Childers then pored over wind, photovoltaic, and geothermal power reports. They soon came to the conclusion that they would need hundreds of millions of dollars and a large team of researchers to make a substantial impact in any of these areas. They decided to stay away from those markets. Then they saw the pie chart that would change their lives (Fig 10.1).

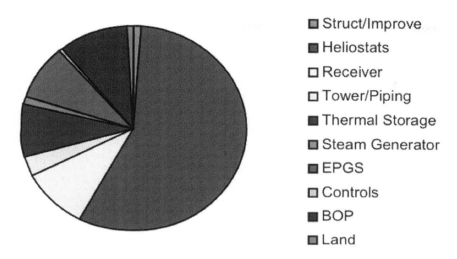

Figure 10.1. Cost of Building a 100 MW solar power tower plant.
(Source: Sandia National Laboratories: see below.)

They were reading the 2007 Sandia *Heliostat Cost Reduction Study*[313] and the National Renewable Energy Labs (NREL)-commissioned studies by Sargent and Lundy[314] (2003, 2005). These studies said that heliostats—the mirrors mounted on tracking systems that are essential to power-tower CSP—represented the largest cost of building a concentrating solar power tower plant. In fact, they represented 55% of the cost of building such a plant.

When one component dominates the cost structure the way heliostats dominate that pie chart, it calls for management and engineering attention. Cutting any other slice of this pie chart would make a small difference in the overall cost of building the plant. The cost of heliostats, moreover, has a huge impact on the number that matters the most: the levelized cost of electricity or LCOE.

If heliostats cost the plant developer $300 per square meter, they could produce electricity at a cost of 12 cents per kilowatt hour (¢/kWh). My October 2009 Pacific Gas and Electric (PG&E) bill had a charge of $0.11550 (between 11 and 12 cents) per kWh. If the numbers in Fig 10.1 are correct, then

PG&E could not possibly make a profit if it had to pay $300/m²
for its heliostats to build a solar plant. They have to be able to
produce at a LCOE lower than 11.55 ¢/kWh. However, if they
were able to cut the cost to $200/m², they could produce at
8.7 ¢/kWh and make a small margin. Cut it further, to $100/m²,
and they could make more than 100% markup on the electricity.
How could an electric utility turn down that opportunity?

Heliostat Cost ($/m²)	LCOE (¢/kWh)
$300	12.0 ¢/kWh
$200	8.7 ¢/kWh
$150	7.3 ¢/kWh
$100	5.9 ¢/kWh
$80	5.4 ¢/kWh

Figure 10.2. How heliostat cost (per square meter) affects the cost of
producing electricity (Source: Sandia National Laboratories[315])

Reducing the cost of heliostats, Childers and Blitz realized,
was thus essential for making CSP financially viable and competitive with fossil fuels. They could not believe that this problem had not been solved by the major power developers. They
did some market research to find out if the problem had indeed
been solved, contacting solar development companies and their
suppliers to find out what heliostat providers were charging for
their products.

No one would say. It looked as though heliostat prices
were an industry secret. Blitz and Childers were intrigued and
decided to look at the heliostat problem more closely. Before I
tell the rest of their story, though, here's the strange, century-
long story of the heliostat.

A Short History of Sun-Seeking

"A heliostat (from helios, the Greek word for sun, and stat, as in stationary) is a device that tracks the movement of the sun."[316] So says Wikipedia. A heliostat is basically a mirror mounted on a stationary, articulated orientation system. It swivels horizontally and vertically to track the sun throughout the day, redirecting the sunlight along a fixed axis towards a stationary target or receiver.

Figure 10.3. Solar Two Power Tower plant, Barstow, CA.
(Graphic source: Wikipedia[317])

A solar power tower plant, like the one shown in Fig. 10.3, has hundreds or thousands of large heliostats that track the sun and position themselves at the exact angle to reflect the sunlight at the receiver on top of the tower.

Heliostats can be any size. The heliostats that eSolar uses in its 5-MW plant in Lancaster, CA, are about 1.2 m² (12.9 ft²) which means they are 1.1 meters (3.6 ft) on each side. Brightsource uses 14.4 m² (155 ft²)[318]. They are one or two orders of magnitude smaller than the heliostats for the power plants that proved the technology, such as Solar Two in Barstow, California; the largest commercial installations such as PS10 and PS20 in Seville use heliostats that are 120 m² (10 m by 12 m).

Lest anyone think we're dealing with new technology here, we can find many early versions of heliostats in America and Europe. The 1901 edition of *The World's Work* has a chapter entitled "Harnessing the Sun," which describes a type of heliostat then operating in California. This "Solar Motor," as it was called, promised to "pump water, grind grain, and saw lumber and run electric cars."[319] Electric cars? Run by solar energy? What a detour we seem to have taken!

An early photograph (Fig. 10.4) captures this heliostat in operation at the Ostrich Farm in Pasadena, California. It looked like a large inverted umbrella hollowed out in the center. At about 12 meters (35 feet) tall, the Solar Motor consisted of 1,800 glass mirrors sized between 7.5 cm (3 inches) and 60 cm (2 feet) on a side (the mirrors needed to get narrower the deeper their ring in the inverted cone as its circumference narrowed also). Remarkably, the chapter about it explained how could generate "steam and power" and could lift fourteen hundred gallons a minute.

Figure 10.4. A 1901 Heliostat or "Solar Motor"
(Graphic Source: The World's Work[320])

This heliostat was run by a fifteen-horsepower (11 kW) engine "Supporting the upper part of the umbrella...the solar motor is automatically balanced, the weight resting on roller bearings." The author complains that "coal is exceedingly expensive and there is little wood to be had." Soon, however, the discovery and exploitation of vast tracts of oil and coal drove prices down and thereby also drove solar research, development, and commercialization to a grinding halt. Not much happened in heliostat development over the next eight decades.

Oil Shock and Energy Independence

After the second "oil shock" of the 1970s sent oil prices skyrocketing yet again, the Carter administration created the Solar Energies Research Institute to invest in the development of solar energy and approved a budget of $3 billion[321]. The Solar One pilot plant was commissioned by the U.S. Department of Energy (DOE) and was completed in 1981. It had a capacity of 10 MW and generated electricity until 1986. It was located in the Mojave Desert town of Daggett, 10 miles east of Barstow, California.

The DOE budgeted $7.3 million for heliostat design and invited several giant multibillion dollar companies, including Boeing, McDonnell Douglas, Westinghouse, and Honeywell, to submit their designs. The winning heliostat was a pedestal-mounted architecture developed by McDonnell Douglas. The heliostat field at Solar One consisted of 1,818 mirrors, each 40 m² (430 ft²) with a total area of 72,650 m² (782,000 ft²). The U.S. represented 80 percent of the world's solar power market at the time[322]. Then the Reagan administration slashed funding, and Solar One closed shop in 1986 when the funds for solar energy development dried up.

The original design used water as the heat transfer medium in the tower receiver. With all those heliostats focusing on the receiver atop the tower, the water was heated to up to 950 degrees F (500°C). This superheated steam was then used to run a turbine and generate electricity. Some of it was stored in a tank to generate electricity later, thus smoothing electricity generation. Solar One proved that solar power tower worked.

PS10 in Seville picked up where Solar One (and later Solar Two) left off. PS10 uses 74,800 m² of mirrors compared to
Solar Two's 72,650 and has a generation capacity of 11 MW versus Solar Two's 10 MW. One major difference is that PS10 uses
fewer but larger mirrors. PS10's mirrors are 120 m² each, three
times the size of Solar Two's 40-m² ones.

Figure 10.5. Abengoa Solar's PS10 heliostat field outside Seville.
(Photo: Tony Seba)

Having been designed and built by an aerospace company
like McDonnell Douglas, the heliostats worked as expected. The
goal was for the heliostat field in Solar Two to be available 90%
of the time; in practice, typical heliostat availability fluctuated
between 88% and 94%[323]. MDD's heliostats were "rocket science" precision instruments that followed the sun like computer-
controlled clockwork.

However, space-rocket technology is expensive. While
they worked relatively well, heliostats still represented more
than 50% of the cost of building solar power-tower plants. Low-
ering their cost was essential to making solar electricity more
adoptable.

Sandia National Laboratories, a U.S. government organization, commissioned a study to investigate ways to cut the cost
of producing heliostats. Appropriately titled *Heliostat Cost Reduction Study* and funded by the U.S. DOE, the report included
interviews with more than "30 heliostat and manufacturing ex-
perts from the United States, Europe, and Australia."[324]

The *Study's* conclusions present a plethora of recommen-
dations that could help cut the cost of heliostats. The recommen-
dations include: increasing the size of heliostats (to make them
cheaper on a per-meter basis), outsourcing their production to
China (to take advantage of lower labor costs), and increasing
volume (to take advantage of manufacturing scale). These are all
more or less commonsense conclusions, if a lot harder to implement than to arrive at. But as we are about to see, cost-cutting
innovations often come out of the blue.

Architectural Innovation

Most innovation takes place within existing product cat-
egories, architectures, or frameworks. An innovation may give
your car 10% better mileage, make your personal computer 10%
faster, or your refrigerator 5% more efficient. These innovations
may be the result of customer input. For instance, if a large customer wanted a faster Internet connection, it would let Cisco
know—and Cisco in turn would build a router that was 10%
faster. Innovations may also be the result of competitive pres-
sures. BMW would have to employ a lighter metal alloy that
allowed its cars to get better mileage if Mercedes Benz or Lexus
did the same.

But there is a more radical kind of innovation than these
sorts of increments, important though they are. *Architectural innovation*, a phrase coined by Rebecca Henderson of MIT and Kim
Clark of Harvard[325], involves radically improving a component of
a product or changing the product's basic design to the point that
you make the existing product and its business obsolete.

Digital cameras are an architectural innovation par excellence. Companies like Kodak and Fuji built multibillion-dollar companies and business ecosystems around photochemical film photography. However, digital technologies transformed photography mainly by replacing a key component: the film. Digital cameras don't use it. So no investment in improving film technology could help Kodak or Fuji. Nanofabrication of films would not help. Manufacturing films in China or producing a higher quantity to cut costs would not help either. Since film was Kodak's and Fuji's cash cow, replacing it totally upset their business models. The film development business and infrastructure were made obsolete by the digital camera, just as the carriage-building business and its infrastructure (livery stables, buggy whips, wheelwright and blacksmith shops, etc.) were made obsolete by the automobile.

For most of the last few decades, the companies and research laboratories dedicated to improving the price/performance of the heliostat did it within the confines of the existing architecture: things like outsourcing, size changes, and new metals. Different companies claimed varying degrees of success; but no one shattered the price performance of heliostats to make solar power tower competitive with fossil-fuel electricity.

California startup eSolar, which has raised nearly $200 million to develop solar power tower plants, got around the high price of the drive by making heliostats smaller[326]. This meant that they could use cheaper "toy" drives instead of the big, expensive "truck transmission" drives needed to drive a heliostat that measures 120 m^2 (1,292 ft^2) and weighs several tons. They claim to have invested millions developing software to achieve the precision that could be achieved through hardware before. Sounds good.

Lancaster, California outside Los Angeles was the site of eSolar's first power-tower plant, a 5-MW plant with 24,000 heliostats. To compare numbers, Abengoa Solar's PS10 uses 1/38th that number of heliostats (a total of 624) but has more than twice the generating capacity (11 MW). The big difference is PS10's heliostat size—each heliostat is 120 m², 100 times bigger than the ones used at Lancaster.

The problem with working within an existing architectural framework is that at some point the whole thing falls apart under its own weight. Microsoft Windows, for instance, has become so complex that many feel it has become unworkable. No matter how much memory I might add to my PC, it is slow, has untold security holes, and crashes every day—losing versions of this book with it. Microsoft spends tens of millions to plug the holes, prevent the crashes, and manage the complexity of many layers of operating system. At some point the best thing to do is start over. (Or, in Microsoft's case, they spend hundreds of millions of dollars to convince us that everything is actually fine.)

Conceptually (and physically) managing complexity in CSP can be a problem too, if you are using smaller heliostats. In February 2009, eSolar announced it had won approval for a 245-MW plant with Southern California Edison. If they used the same-sized heliostats as at their Lancaster plant, they would need more than a million of them.

Then again, companies like Microsoft, Google, and Yahoo manage hundreds of thousands of cheap computers in their data centers. These companies have written complex software algorithms to allow data processing and storage to be allocated to many computers simultaneously, so that if any one of them crashes, no data will be lost. For these companies, it may be cheaper to swap out and throw away a malfunctioning computer than to fix it. Could the same ever be true of heliostats? And can the equivalent kind of redundancy and therefore very robust, reliable system performance be developed for them?

Presumably eSolar has invested heavily in developing the software and hardware that control the movements of tens of thousands of heliostats in the desert. To scale to millions of heliostats, the company will need to do in the hot, dusty, stormy desert what Google does in cool, controlled data-center environments. If eSolar pulls off managing their millions of small heliostats under those conditions, they will have a technology advantage over their competitors. But if they don't succeed, the heliostat field turns into Windows Vista: so complex it's unmanageable, it crashes all the time, and it sucks the profits it generates into maintaining the system—or into telling the world it's all fine.

Innovating Outside the Gears

The size of the heliostat field in terms of *total mirror area* can be a constant even when the size of the individual mirrors changes. For instance, you could choose to have 75,000 m² of mirrors: that could be 750 heliostats of 100 square meters each, or 75,000 heliostats of one square meter each. But managing complexity gets exponentially more difficult when you increase the numbers. Managing 375,000 heliostats is more than ten times more difficult than managing 37,500.

The key question then is: how do you innovate so you can have larger and fewer heliostats that cost less on a per-square-meter basis? How do you get to 7,500 heliostats (not half a million) that cost less than $150/m²—so you can bring the cost of electricity down to fossil-fuel levels?

As they set about to improve the heliostat, Peter Childers and Jonathan Blitz focused on redesigning its most expensive component: *the drive.* Heliostats need to reflect the sunlight and point it at the receiver at the top of the tower. For this reason, they are set in rings around the tower (Fig. 10.3.) The inner ring can be about 100 meters (110 yards) from the receiver, while the outer rings can be up to a kilometer (850 meters—½ mile) away. Just as a military sharpshooter needs higher-precision optical instruments the further away from the target he or she is, an outer-ring heliostat needs higher accuracy or some of the precious reflected sunlight will miss the tower. Simple geometry: the wider the radius, the smaller the margin of error and the greater the precision required.

Heliostats at large scale solar plant may require a precision of 1 milliradian (mrad). Here's a quick geometry refresher: there are 360 degrees in a circle. The sun moves 180 degrees from sun-up to sunset in about 12 hours (actually it's the earth that rotates on its axis—but who's paying attention?) In the fields of gunnery and tracking, one degree (or even one second) of arc may not be accurate enough, so they use the radian as a unit. There are about 6,400 radians in a circle (instead of 360 degrees.) One milliradian is about 5.6 hundreds of a degree[327].

Now consider that deserts can be very windy even under normal circumstances. So heliostats must achieve the needed accuracy under winds of up to 20 mph (32 kmph). Higher winds will trigger alert conditions, and the heliostats may need to "stow away": that is, lie flat so the winds don't damage them. Furthermore, the structure that holds the mirror can measure up to 12 × 12 meters (144 m²) and weigh up to two metric tons. This is about the size of one side of a tennis court and the weight of BMW's largest sedans.[328])

One of the reasons heliostat drives are so expensive is that they have intricate gear-work: dozens or hundreds of gears. Think of a Rolex made by the truck division of Volvo: intricate, precise, and heavy-duty at the same time. John O'Donnell, a co-founder of solar thermal plant developer Ausra, summed up the challenge of heliostat designs for me. "Two words," Mr. O'Donnell said. "Torque and stiffness." You have to move a two-ton stiff armature of up to 144 m² under 30-mph winds while not bending the load and maintaining 1 milliradian precision. "Meet the challenge and you win the prize," he said.

The New Design Challenge

Most of the power producers who are developing new utility-scale solar plants in America work on a Power Purchase Agreement (PPA) with the utility in question. As I've explained previously, this means they get a fixed price for the electricity they produce for the duration of the 20-year or 30-year contract.

Because solar fuel is free, the LCOE consists of operations and maintenance (O&M) costs plus interest on the capital. Assuming the interest rate is fixed, the LCOE is also fixed for the duration of the contract. Say the heliostat cost $300/m² and the LCOE is 12 ¢/kWh. Assume also that the price at which the utility will buy the power from the developer is 15 ¢/kWh. This is a nice 3 ¢/kWh profit—for decades.

The main way for the power producer to increase profits is to cut costs. Assuming that the table in Figure 10.1 is right, if you lower the heliostat cost to $100, LCOE would drop to 5.9 ¢/kWh. That's a difference of 15-5.9 ¢/kWh or *9.1 ¢/kWh*. So profits essentially triple. (In Europe power producers mostly work with Feed-In Tariffs, but the analysis would lead to the same results.)

Achieving cost reductions, as I've recounted, was paramount to the founding design team of Childers and Blitz. So they thought of a simple, cheap, and effective way to achieve a large production price crunch on the heliostats. According to their engineering and manufacturing calculations, the final design they came up with could cut the price of the drive by about 80%. Since the drive was up to 50% of the cost of the heliostat, this new drive allowed them to lower the cost of the heliostat by up to a third. Follow this logic and you discover that the capital costs (and maintenance costs) of a power-tower plant drop by 20%, and the cost of electricity therefore drops by at least 20%. With this kind of payoff it's likely that large industrial power developers would sit down and listen. Even to a small startup.

The USS Solution: Riding on Air

How did USS think they could achieve this cost reduction? Air. Cells of compressed-air bags are capable of so much lift that they have been used to lift earthquake-collapsed building debris, re-rail railroad and mining cars as well as recover overturned highway trucks—objects weighing tens of tons. Could airbags work not just to lift a large flat heavy object but to move it precisely?

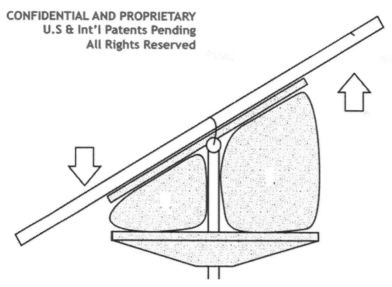

Figure 10.6. Conceptual design of USS heliostat drives.
(Source: Utility Scale Solar, Inc.)

Figure 10.6 is a conceptual design of what Childers and Blitz created. There are two "fluid cells" that inflate and deflate to lift a static object up or down. (As a reminder: in physics and engineering, a "fluid" can be any liquid or gas, including air: remember the "heat transfer fluid" in water-based CSP systems, which changes from liquid to gas and back again?) This basic two-cell system would move the object on one axis: that is, it could follow the sun East-West. Most photovoltaic panels that do have tracking only track on one axis. Furthermore, parabolic troughs, the most popular form of concentrating solar thermal power (described earlier in this book) only need single-axis tracking. But as I've explained, heliostats for power tower need double-axis tracking.

If instead of two bags you were to use multiple bags, you could move the flat surface in two dimensions at once (Fig. 10.7). Maybe even three!

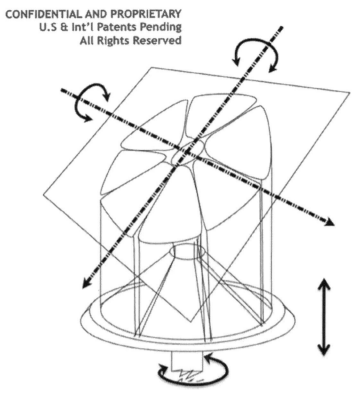

Figure 10.7. Conceptual design of USS heliostat 2-axis drives.
(Source: Utility Scale Solar, Inc.)

Childers and Blitz needed to test their invention by building a proof of concept device—on the cheap. They bought hoses,
air bags, and an air pump at the nearest Home Depot and built the
"proof of concept" over a weekend in Blitz's backyard in North
Carolina. Manipulating the air pump manually to fill and empty
the bags, they saw what air was capable of. The concept worked.

The two men quickly incorporated a company and called
it Utility Scale Solar (USS), Inc. They also filed for U.S. and International patents, after raising the first million dollars in angel
investor money and hiring a team of a half-dozen engineers to
develop a real product. The goal was to replace expensive-to-
build, hard-to-install, and hard-to-operate gear-based precision
drives with an inexpensive, easy-to-install, easy-to-operate drive.

The key question was: could you build an instrument with the required high levels of stiffness, torque, and precision from non-precision, low-cost, off-the-shelf parts?

The answer, it seems, was yes. The USS technical team invented and patented the "pipe-in-drum" drive with two airbags that achieved the high torque and precision required by industrial strength solar plants. Figure 10.8 shows an advanced rendition of the heliostat with two drives: one for azimuth or "east-to-west" movement and the second for elevation or "up-and-down" movement.

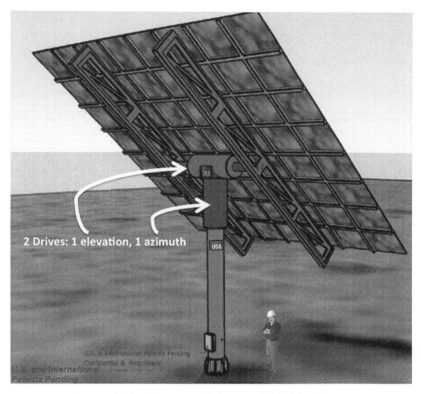

Figure 10.8. Conceptual design of USS heliostat.
(Source: Utility Scale Solar, Inc.)

So USS substituted air for precision gears. Five moving parts instead of dozens or hundreds of moving parts. Air power instead of gasoline or diesel power. How can gear motors compete with air? Just as digital cameras were a totally new architecture for picture-taking, the USS team believe their new drive has the potential to create a new architecture for heliostats.

If that turns out to be the case, then you probably do not want to be the Kodak or Fuji of solar power-power—financially and technologically committed to a design architecture that has suddenly and irremediably become obsolete.

As this book went to press the product has been produced in prototypes that have been tested for smooth motion, torque, range of motion, submilliradian accuracy, and control under robotic guidance, all using just air. Company engineers even came up with software to run the heliostat's guidance mechanisms. (Remember that Childers had studied Artificial Intelligence?)

USS promises to single-handedly lower the cost of producing solar electricity in CSP plants by up to a third with their heliostat. In the process they could help make solar power tower become competitive with fossil fuels—certainly competitive with gas in the short term and competitive with coal in a few years. Power developers benefit by increasing their margins, utilities benefit by cutting the costs for the next solar power plant, consumers benefit by getting clean energy at a lower price.

A potential investor told me: "It sounds too good to be true. You have to launch and test the product to prove these claims." Apparently, some people who ought to know better from the history of tech innovation find it hard to believe that you can disrupt an industry with something as common as air. It's sad to see that so many investors have forgotten the "venture" part of venture capital.

The Market Opportunity

The USS team started the company to design a new type of drive that would lower the cost of solar energy. The big opportunity that attracted the founding team was in solar power-tower CSP.

Chapter 3 ("Desert Power") of this book posits that the installed base of utility-scale solar could scale to terawatts (trillions of watts.) Today, solar power-tower plants cost anywhere from $4 to $6 per watt—of which the cost of heliostats comprise up to 50%. So the revenue opportunity for heliostat makers would be anywhere from $1-$2 per watt.

To put that $1-$2/watt margin in perspective: today there are more than 6 GW (six billion watts) of solar power tower capacity announced in America alone. Take the low end, one dollar revenue opportunity per watt, and you have a heliostat market opportunity in the $5 billion range. That's a pretty good market opportunity for a startup company.

It gets better. If we assume, as we did in Chapter 3, that solar is developed on a utility scale to the terawatt level by 2050, then you have a *trillion*-dollar opportunity. Just think: every mirror in the desert will have to track the sun. Each 1 TW of utility-scale solar power-tower infrastructure means $1 trillion worth of heliostats. USS saw a larger market opportunity than solar power tower.

All forms of Concentrating Solar Power (CSP) like power tower, parabolic trough, linear Fresnel, and Stirling engines have to track the sun. Concentrating Photovoltaic (CPV) also needs to track the sun with high accuracy. Photovoltaic panels can generate *up to 40% more power* if they track the sun (as opposed to just sitting there on a rooftop.)

While each one of these markets has different needs, and each requires a different type of sun-following technology, tracking seems to be a constant. Tracking seems also to be a "boring" area of solar tech—like wheels for cars or routers for the Internet. An essential part of the infrastructure, but one that not many investors and entrepreneurs outside the industry pay attention to.

Like the whole clean energy and solar energy market, this is an evolving story, one that will be fascinating to watch. Having been part of the USS team from the "aha!" moment to the launch of the beta version of the "Megahelion" heliostat described above, I can say for sure that two entrepreneurs in a garage can make a huge difference in solar and clean energy—just as earlier such pairs, right here just south of San Francisco, revolutionized computer hardware and software.

The USS team, by all appearances, has met the product design challenge. They are helping to open the door to a new and better world.

ABOUT THE AUTHOR

Tony Seba is currently a lecturer in clean energy, entrepreneurship, finance and technology strategy at Stanford University. His courses include "Clean Energy—Market and Investment Opportunities" and "Strategic Marketing of High Tech and Cleantech." Mr. Seba is also an internationally known keynote speaker on the future of energy, entrepreneurship, innovation, and cleantech and high-tech market opportunities.

Mr. Seba is an entrepreneur and executive with more than 20 years of experience in fast-growth high-tech and cleantech businesses. As the Vice President of Corporate Development at Utility Scale Solar, Inc, he helped the company grow from "two guys in a garage" through business development, fundraising, strategic partnerships, and product launch. Previously, as PrintNation.com's founder, President, and CEO, Mr. Seba raised more than $31 million in VC funding, and established the company as the undisputed leader in its market segment, listed in the *Upside* Hot 100 and the *Forbes*.com B2B "Best of the Web." As Director of Strategic Planning at RSA Data Security, he helped the company successfully enter new technology markets and guided its $200-million merger with Security Dynamics.

Mr. Seba's leadership has been recognized in publications such as *Investors Business Daily, Business Week, Upside,* and *Success.* Mr Seba was cited as one of Bridgegate's 20 "difference makers" in Southern California. He has served on many boards of directors and advisory boards. He holds a BS in Computer Science and Engineering from Massachusetts Institute of Technology (MIT) and an MBA from the Stanford University Graduate School of Business.

ENDNOTES

1   "Perspectives for Concentrating Solar Power in Coastal Areas of Mediterranean Sea,"

2   2007 Residential electricity consumption in San Francisco county: 1.451 TWh. Source: The California Energy Commission, Energy Consumption Data Management System: http://ecdms.energy. ca.gov/elecbycounty.asp#results

3   "Solar Trough Systems," SunLab Snapshot, U.S. Department of Energy DOC/GO-10097-395, April 1998, www.nrel.gov/docs/ legosti/fy98/22589.pdf

4   Gene Berdichevsky et al., "The Tesla Roadster Battery System," August 16, 2006, in http://www.teslamotors.com/learn_more/ white_papers.php

5   "Average Retail Price of Electricity," Energy Information Agency, at http://www.eia.doe.gov/aer/txt/ptb0810.html

6   "Goldman Sachs subsidiary buys Mojave solar plants," February 27, 2009, http://www.sustainablebusiness.com/index.cfm/go/news. display/id/17753

7   "Green-tech VC jumps nearly 40 percent in 2008," CNET, January 9, 2009, http://news.cnet.com/8301-11128_3-10132411-54.html

8   "Arizona to Build 280 MW solar power Plant in Arizona," Cleantech Group, February 21 2008, http://cleantech.com/news/2488/ abengoa-to-build-280-mw-solar-power-plant-in-arizona

9   "Environmental Impact of Coal Power," Union of Concerned Scientists, http://www.ucsusa.org/clean_energy/coalvswind/c02c. html

10 Picture original in "Egyptian Gazette" in *The Power of Light*, Frank Kryza, McGraw-Hill, 2003

11 "The Dow Jones Industrial Average History" originally published in *The Dow Jones Averages 1885–1995*, edited by Phyllis S. Pierce with a foreword by John A. Prestbo, Editor, Dow Jones Indexes, in www. djindexes.com/mdsidx/downloads/DJIA_Hist_Comp.pdf

12 *Social Trends in America, vol. 1, Employment Trends*: Data Presentation, http://social.jrank.org/pages/849/Employment-Trends-Data-Presentation.html

13   "Utility Scale Solar Heating Up," *Energy and Capital*, July 3, 2009, http://www.energyandcapital.com/articles/utility-scale-solar-heating-up/905 accessed July 9, 2009

14   "Tennessee Ash Flood Larger Than Initial Estimate," *New York Times*, December 26, 2008, in http://www.nytimes.com/2008/12/27/us/27sludge.html

15   "Mercury Found in Every Fish Tested, Scientists say," *New York Times*, August 19, 2009, http://www.nytimes.com/2009/08/20/science/earth/20brfs-MERCURYFOUND_BRF.html?_r=1

16   International Energy Agency, June 6, 2008, at http://www.iea.org/Textbase/press/pressdetail.asp?PRESS_REL_ID=263

17   Ted Turner and T. Boone Pickens, "New Priorities for our Energy Future," *The Wall Street Journal*, August 16, 2009, http://online.wsj.com/article/SB10001424052970203863204574348432504983734.html

18   "Assessment of Parabolic Trough and Power Tower Technology and Performance Forecasts," Sargent & Lundy, 2003

19   Frank Van Mierlo, Wikipedia http://en.wikipedia.org/wiki/File:World_Energy_consumption.png

20   http://www.nytimes.com/2008/11/25/world/25climate.html?pagewanted=2&hp

21   Daniel Nocera, "On the Future of Global Energy," *Daedalus*, 22 Sept 2006, American Academy of Sciences

22   Daniel Nocera, "On the Future of Global Energy," *Daedalus*, 22 Sept 2006, American Academy of Sciences

23   "U.S. Dependence on Oil in 2008: Facts, Figures, and Context," Andrew Grove, Robert Burgelman, and Debra Schifrin, Stanford Graduate School of Business, Research Paper No. 1997, August 2008

24   "U.S. Dependence on Oil in 2008: Facts, Figures, and Context," Andrew Grove, Robert Burgelman, and Debra Schifrin, Stanford Graduate School of Business, Research Paper No. 1997, August 2008

25   "The Top 10 Highest Paid CEOs of 2008: Pay Hits the Gas Pedal as the Economy Hits the Brakes," *The Corporate Library*, 2009, at http://www.corporatelibrary.com

26   Central Intelligence Agency, *The World Factbook 2008*, https://www.cia.gov/library/publications/the-world-factbook/rankorder/2038rank.html

27   "The Truth About America's Energy: Big Oil Stockpiles Supplies and Pockets Profits," *A Special Report by the Committee on Natural*

Resources Majority Staff," U.S. House of Representatives, Committee on Natural Resources, Rep Nick J. Hall – Chairman, June 2008

28   ABB website: http://www.abb.com/cawp/seitp202/82b4ae72c448bd ab4825704200020779.aspx

29   "Top Ten Utility Solar Integration Rankings," Solar Electric Power Association (SEPA), Report #05-09

30   "Wood Pellets Catch Fire as Renewable Energy Source," *The Wall Street Journal*, July 7, 2009

31   "Wood Pellets Catch Fire as Renewable Energy Source," *The Wall Street Journal*, July 7, 2009

32   "Wind Power in Denmark," Wikipedia, http://en.wikipedia.org/wiki/ Wind_power_in_Denmark

33   World Wind Energy Report 2008, February 2009, by World Wind Energy Association, Bonn, Germany, at www.wwindea.org

34   "Wind versus biofuels for addressing climate, health, and energy," Professor Mark Z. Jacobson, Department of Civil and Environmental Engineering, Stanford University, Jan 31, 2007

35   *World Wind Energy Report 2008*, February 2009, by World Wind Energy Association, Bonn, Germany, at www.wwindea.org

36   "Basic Principles of Wind Energy Evaluation," American Wind Energy Association, http://www.awea.org/faq/basicwr.html

37   "Liberty Wind Brochure," Clipper Windpower Corp., at http://www. clipperwind.com/productline.html

38   Geothermal Energy in Iceland, Wikipedia, http://en.wikipedia.org/ wiki/Geothermal_power_in_Iceland

39   "The Geysers," Calpine Corp, at http://www.geysers.com/

40   *The Future of Geothermal Energy*, Massachusetts Institute of Technology, 2006, ISBN: 0-615-13438-6

41   "Geothermal FAQs," U.S. Department of Energy, http://www1.eere. energy.gov/geothermal/faqs.html

42   "Geothermal FAQs," U.S. Department of Energy, http://www1.eere. energy.gov/geothermal/faqs.html

43   "Geothermal Power—A Hot Way to Produce Electricity," Alameda Municipal Power, http://www.alamedamp.com/electricity/geothermal. html

44   *The Future of Geothermal Energy*, Massachusetts Institute of Technology, 2006, ISBN: 0-615-13438-6

45   Nathan Lewis, "Challenges for Global Energy" KITP Public Lectures, http://online.itp.ucsb.edu/plecture/lewis/rm/flash.html

46   "Hydropower—A Key to Prosperity in a Growing World,"
     International Energy Agency brochure

47   "Hydro-Electric Power's Dirty Secrets Revealed," *New Scientist*,
     February 24, 2005, http://www.newscientist.com/article/dn7046

48   Kaua'i Island Utility Cooperative Renewable Energy Technology
     Assessments, Black & Veatch, March 2005

49   "Levelized Cost of New Generating Technologies," Energy
     Information Administration, Annual Energy Outlook 2009 (revised),
     April 2009, SR-OIAF/2009-03

50   "The World Commission on Dams Framework – An Introduction,"
     International Rivers, Feb 29, 2008, at http://www.internationalrivers.
     org/en/way-forward/world-commission-dams/world-commission-
     dams-framework-brief-introduction

51   "Hydroelectric Power Water Use," United States Geological Services
     (USGS) at http://ga.water.usgs.gov/edu/wuhy.html

52   "Hydroelectric Power Water Use," United States Geological Services
     (USGS) at http://ga.water.usgs.gov/edu/wuhy.html

53   Timothy Searchinger et al, "Use of U.S. Croplands for Biofuels
     Increases Greenhouse Gases Through Emissions from Land-Use
     Change," *Science Magazine*, February 2008, in http://www.sciencemag.
     org/cgi/content/abstract/1151861

54   "Energy versus Water – Solving Both Crises Together," *Scientific
     American*, October 2008, http://www.sciam.com/article.cfm?id=the-
     future-of-fuel&page=3

55   "Review of Solutions to Global Warming, Air Pollution, and Energy
     Security," Prof. Mark Jacobson, The Energy Seminar, Stanford
     University, October 1, 2008

56   David Pimentel and Tad W. Patzek, "Ethanol Production Using Corn,
     Switchgrass, and Wood; Biodiesel Production Using Soybean and
     Sunflower," *Natural Resources Research*, Vol 14, No. 1, March 2005,
     No. 1, @2005 DOI: 10:1007/s11053.005-4679-8

57   Marc Jaboson, "Review of Solutions to Global Warming, Air Pollution,
     and Energy Security" The Energy Seminar, Stanford University,
     October 1, 2008

58   Winnie Gerbens-Leenesa,1, Arjen Y. Hoekstraa, and Theo H. van
     der Meer, "The Water Footprint of Bioenergy," Department of
     Water Engineering and Management and Laboratory of Thermal
     Engineering, University of Twente, Enschede, The Netherlands April
     2, 2009

59   "Fulcrum BioEnergy Squeezes Fuel from Garbage," VentureBeat,
       Sept 3, 2009, http://green.venturebeat.com/2009/09/03/fulcrum-
       bioenergy-squeezes-fuel-from-garbage/

60   Energy Information Administration, Petroleum Basic Statistics—2008,
       http://www.eia.doe.gov/basics/quickoil.html

61   "Ford Nucleon," Wikipedia, The Free Encyclopedia., retrieved Aug 19,
       2009, at http://en.wikipedia.org/wiki/Ford_Nucleon

62   "New Wave of Nuclear Plants Faces High Costs," *The Wall
       Street Journal*, May 12, 2008, http://online.wsj.com/article/
       SB121055252677483933.html?mod=hpp_us_whats_
       news#articleTabs%3Darticle

63   Professor Stephen Ansolabehere et al, *The Future of Nuclear Energy*,
       Massachusetts Institute of Technology, 2003. ISBN 0-615-12420-8

64   Craig Severance, "Business Risks and Costs of Nuclear Plants", January
       2, 2009, Grand Junction, Colorado

65   Seabrook Station Nuclear Power Plant. (2008, December 11). In
       Wikipedia, The Free Encyclopedia. Retrieved February 24, 2009,
       from http://en.wikipedia.org/w/index.php?title=Seabrook_Station_
       Nuclear_Power_Plant&oldid=257213510

66   "New Wave of Nuclear Plants Faces High Costs," *The Wall
       Street Journal*, May 12, 2008, http://online.wsj.com/article/
       SB121055252677483933.html?mod=hpp_us_whats_
       news#articleTabs%3Darticle

67   "Business Risks and Costs of New Nuclear Power," Craig Severance,
       Grand Junction, Colorado

68   "Progress Energy Florida Projects a 31% increase in 2009," *Tampa Bay
       Business Journal*, August 28, 2009, http://tampabay.bizjournals.com/
       tampabay/stories/2008/08/25/daily64.html

69   Joe Romn, "The Self-Limiting Future of Nuclear Power," Center For
       American Progress, June 2008

70   "21st Anniversary of the Chernobyl Disaster," History of the
       Chernobyl Disaster, accessed July 17, 2009, http://www.chernobyl.
       org.uk/chernobyl.html

71   "Tenessee Ash Flood Larger Than Initial Estimate," *The New York
       Times*, December 26, 2008, http://www.nytimes.com/2008/12/27/
       us/27sludge.html?_r=1&scp=1&sq=fly%20ash&st=cse

72   "Coal Ash Revives Issue of Its Hazards," *The New York Times*,
       December 24, 2008, http://www.nytimes.com/2008/12/25/
       us/25sludge.html?_r=1&th&emc=th

73   Union of Concerned Scientists, http://www.ucsusa.org/clean_energy/
      coalvswind/c02d.html

74   "Coal Ash is more Radioactive than Nuclear Waste," *Scientific
      American*, December 13, 2007, at http://www.sciam.com/article.
      cfm?id=coal-ash-is-more-radioactive-than-nuclear-waste

75   "The Illusion of Clean Coal, *The Economist*, March 5 2009, http://
      www.economist.com/opinion/displaystory.cfm?story_id=13235041

76   "Solar Energy: A New Dawning, Silicon Valley Rising," *Nature –
      International Journal of Science*, September 6, 2006, http://www.
      nature.com/nature/journal/v443/n7107/full/443019a.html

77   Franz Trieb et al, "AQUA-CSP—Concentrating Solar Power for Water
      Desalination," Final Report, German Aerospace Center, DLR, Institute
      of Technical Thermodynamics, Stuttgart, Germany, November 2007

78   "The Truth About America's Energy: Big Oil Stockpiles Supplies
      and Pockets Profits," *A Special Report by the Committee on Natural
      Resources Majority Staff*," U.S. House of Representatives, Committee
      on Natural Resources, Rep Nick J. Hall – Chairman, June 2008

79   "Archivo General de Indias," Dec 16, 2008, in Wikipedia: http://
      en.wikipedia.org/wiki/Archivo_general_de_indias

80   "El Sistema Eléctrico Español – Avance del Informe 2008," Red
      Eléctrica de España, December 19, 2008 (p.5)

81   "20 20 by 2020 – Europe's Climate Change Opportunity,"
      Commission of the European Communities, Brussels, January 23,
      2008

82   "Power in the Desert: Solar Towers Will Harness Sunshine of
      Southern Spain, *The Guardian* (UK), November 24, 2008, http://
      www.guardian.co.uk/environment/2008/nov/24/andalucia-spain-
      renewable-energy-technology

83   "Spain leads global solar production targeting 25GW by 2020:
      Report," *Platt's Electric Power News*, April 29, 2009, in http://www.
      platts.com/Electric%20Power/News/8525919.xml?src=Electric%20
      Powerrssheadlines1

84   Donald Worster, "Environmental History: The view and the Grand
      Canyon," http://www.nps.gov/history/history/hisnps/NPSHistory/
      environmentalhistory.htm

85   "Solar Thermal Projects Gather Steam – and Opposition," *The Los
      Angeles Times*, Dec 3, 2008, in http://www.latimes.com/business/la-fi-
      bigsolar3-2008dec03,0,4276063,full.story

86   "World's Biggest Solar Power Farm To Be Set Up In Kutch Desert,"
      The Times of India, Aug 5, 2009, at http://epaper.timesofindia.com/

Repository/ml.asp?Ref=VE9JQS8yMDA5LzA4LzA1I0FyMDAxMD
A=&Mode=HTML&Locale=english-skin-custom

87   Greg Kolb et al, "Heliostat Cost Reduction Study," Sandia National
      Laboratories, Report SAND2007-3293, June 2007

88   Source: Brightsource website: http://www.brightsourceenergy.com/
      technology/faqs

89   "Carnot cycle." Wikipedia, http://en.wikipedia.org/wiki/Carnot_cycle

90   "Holy Desertec: $555B Solar Saharan Project Finds a Dozen Backers,"
      Earth2Tec, July 13, 2009, http://earth2tech.com/2009/07/13/holy-
      desertec-555b-solar-saharan-project-finds-a-dozen-backers/

91   "Red Paper – An Overview of the Desertec Concept," Desertec
      Foundation,

92   "National Solar Plan," Government of India, Final Draft, April 29,
      2009

93   Craig Severance, "Business Risks and Costs of Nuclear Plants," January
      2, 2009, Grand Junction, Colorado

94   "The Writing on The Wall," The Economist, May 7, 2009, http://
      www.economist.com/world/unitedstates/displaystory.cfm?story_
      id=13611471

95   "The Clean Energy Scam," Michael Grunwald, Time Magazine,
      May 27, 2008, http://www.time.com/time/magazine/
      article/0,9171,1725975-2,00.html

96   "Citing Need for Assessments, U.S. Freezes Solar Energy Projects",
      The New York Times, June 27, 2008, http://www.nytimes.
      com/2008/06/27/us/27solar.html?_r=1,

97   "The Truth About America's Energy: Big Oil Stockpiles Supplies
      and Pockets Profits," A Special Report by the Committee on Natural
      Resources Majority Staff, U.S. House of Representatives, Committee
      on Natural Resources, Rep Nick J. Hall – Chairman, June 2008

98   "BLM to Continue Accepting Solar Energy Applications," Bureau of
      Land Management Press Release, July 2, 2008, http://www.blm.gov/
      wo/st/en/info/newsroom/2008/July/NR_07_02_2008.html

99   "AT&T: Our History," December 16, 2008, in http://www.att.jobs/
      history.aspx

100   Brighsource website, accessed July 30, 2009, http://www.
      brightsourceenergy.com/projects

101   "Monday, June 12 Proves Strongest Day Yet for Yahoo! Fifa World
      Cup Site Visitation with 226 Million Page Views and More Than 5
      Million Visitors Worldwide," Comscore Press Release, at http://www.
      comscore.com/press/release.asp?press=915

102   "Google's Data Center Spend and Save," Manish Vachharajani, *The Fastlane*, http://blog.manish.vachharajani.com/2008/11/googles-datacenter-spend-and-save.html

103   "Data Center Power Consumption by the Numbers," Greentech Media, June 2008, http://greenlight.greentechmedia.com/2008/06/26/data-center-power-consumption-by-the-numbers-341/

104   "Data Center Energy Forecast Report – 2008," Silicon Valley Leadership Group, July 29, 2008, http://svlg.net/campaigns/datacenter/

105   "List of Countries by GDP (nominal)," in Wikipedia, The Free Encyclopedia, December 6, 2009, in http://en.wikipedia.org/wiki/List_of_countries_by_GDP_(nominal)

106   "Reduce energy consumption—IBM Software for a Greener World," International Business Machine, October 2008 http://www-01.ibm.com/software/info/getcatalog/index.html?src=itke_TIC

107   "Green Grid Metrics – Describing Data Center Power Efficiencies," Feb 20, 2007, The Green Grid, http://www.thegreengrid.org/gg_content/

108   "Basic Research Needs for Solar Energy Utilization – Report of the Basic Energy Sciences Workshop on Solar Energy Utilization—April 18-21, 2005," Office of Science, U.S. Department of Energy, revisions Sept 2005.

109   "Basic Research Needs for Solar Energy Utilization – Report of the Basic Energy Sciences Workshop on Solar Energy Utilization—April 18-21, 2005," Office of Science, U.S. Department of Energy, revisions Sept 2005.

110   "Save Energy Now in Your Process Heating Systems," *Best Practices: Process Heating*, U.S. Department of Energy, Industrial Technologies Program, DOE/GO-102006-2274, January 2006 , DOE/GO-102006-2274

111   Frito-Lay's company website: http://www. Frito-Lay.com/our-planet/snacks-made-with-the-help-of-the-sun.html

112   Source: Frito-Lay's website at http://www. Frito-Lay.com/our-planet/snacks-made-with-the-help-of-the-sun.html

113   Industrial Technologies Program, Presentation to States Energy Advisory Board, U.S. Department of Energy, July 26 2006

114   "Energy Intensive Industries," U.S. Department of Energy, at http://www1.eere.energy.gov/industry/program_areas/industries.html

115   Industrial Technologies Program, Presentation to States Energy Advisory Board, U.S. Department of Energy, July 26 2006

116   "Solar Industrial Process Heat – State of the Art," European Solar
       Thermal Industry Federation, WP3, Task 3.5, Contract EIE/04/204/
       S07.38607

117   "Solar Industrial Process Heat – State of the Art," European Solar
       Thermal Industry Federation, WP3, Task 3.5, Contract EIE/04/204/
       S07.38607

118   "Understanding Electricity Prices in Ireland," 2008 Report, Sustainable
       Energy Ireland, Energy Policy Statistical Support Unit, Table 7, page
       15.

119   "Solar Industrial Process Heat – State of the Art," European Solar
       Thermal Industry Federation, WP3, Task 3.5, Contract EIE/04/204/
       S07.38607, Table 1, page 8

120   "Save Energy Now in Your Process Heating Systems," Best Practices:
       Process Heating, U.S. Department of Energy, Industrial Technologies
       Program, DOE/GO-102006-2274, January 2006 , DOE/GO-102006-
       2274

121   Figure from: "Improving Process Heating System Performance: a
       Sourcebook for Industry," U.S. Department of Energy, 2nd edition,
       2007.

122   "The Life and Influence of Frank Shuman," Profiles in Tacony History,
       in http://www.historictacony.org/hist_profiles/vol4.html

123   Picture from The Power of Light, Frank Kryza, McGraw-Hill, 2003

124   "Start Mission to Egypt," Michael Geyer, editor, International Energy
       Agency (IEA) Solar Power and Chemical Energy Systems, February
       1996

125   "Catching Some Rays," Amr A. Mohsen, Business Today Egypt,
       May 2005, at http://www.businesstodayegypt.com/article.
       aspx?ArticleID=4990

126

127   "Solar Heating and Cooling for a Sustainable Energy Future in
       Europe," European Solar Thermal Industry Federation, Sixth EU
       Framework Programme for Research and Technological Development,
       FP6 (Contract Number TREN/07/FP6EN/S07.68874/038604)

128   Franz Trieb et al, "AQUA-CSP—Concentrating Solar Power for Water
       Desalination," Final Report, German Aerospace Center, DLR, Institute
       of Technical Thermodynamics, Stuttgart, Germany, November 2007

129   "Assessment of Parabolic Trough and Power Tower Technology and
       Performance Forecasts," Sargent & Lundy, 2003

130 "Obama's Energy Policy Will Increase our Dependence on Foreign Oil," *American Thinker*, accessed July 17, 2009, http://www. americanthinker.com/2009/03/obamas_energy_policy_will_incr.html

131 "Data Center Power Consumption by the Numbers," *Greentech Media*, June 2008, http://greenlight.greentechmedia.com/2008/06/26/data-center-power-consumption-by-the-numbers-341/

132 "Learn more about YPG—Yuma Proving Ground," http://www.yuma. army.mil/chub_what.shtml accessed July 6, 2009

133 "Data Center Energy Forecast Report – 2008," Silicon Valley Leadership Group, July 29, 2008, http://svlg.net/campaigns/ datacenter/

134 Energy Information Administration – Official Statistics for the United States Government – Data for 2007 at http://tonto.eia.doe.gov/ask/ electricity_faqs.asp

135 "Marshall Islands," *National Geographic*, http://travel. nationalgeographic.com/places/countries/country_marshallislands. html

136 "Marshall Islands declares 'economic emergency' over energy crisis," AFP, July 3, 2008, http://afp.google.com/article/ ALeqM5ikBtl6qL61WolgUgiOLRl146WAbg

137 Arizona Public Service Company, Resource Alternative Planning, Stakeholder Meeting Report, March 7, 2008, Docket No. E-01345A-08-0010

138 "Southwest sees Fuel Hedges' Pesky Sides," *Business Week*, Oct 16, 2008, at http://bx.businessweek.com/airline-industry/ view?url=http%3A%2F%2Fc.moreover.com%2Fclick%2Fhere. pl%3Fr1647948122%26f%3D9791

139 Ten-day moving average. Dollars per barrel for NYMEX sweet light crude WTI. Source: Wikipedia, http://en.wikipedia.org/wiki/ File:WTI_price_96_09.svg, accessed July 2, 2009

140 "An Economic Assessment of Renewable Energy Options for Rural Electrification in Pacific Island Countries," Alison Woodruff, *SOPAC Technical Report* 397, February 2007

141 "Solar-charged LED light," Inventor of the Week, Lemelson-MIT Program, http://web.mit.edu/invent/iow/walsh.html

142 "American Lights up Lives with Solar Lamps," *Shenzhen Daily*, May 19, 2009, http://paper.sznews.com/szdaily/20090519/ca2913434.htm

143 "Average Electric Rates for Hawaiian Electric Co., Maui Electric Co. and Hawaii Electric Light Co.," Hawaiian Electric Company, http:// www.heco.com/portal/site/heco/menuitem.508576f78baa14340b4c0 610c510b1ca/?vgnextoid=692e5e658e0fc010VgnVCM1000008119f

ea9RCRD&vgnextchannel=10629349798b4110VgnVCM1000005c0
11bacRCRD&vgnextfmt=defau&vgnextrefresh=1&level=0&ct=article

144   Picture source: Wikipedia: http://en.wikipedia.org/wiki/
      File:EuroDishSBP_front.jpg

145   "US military energy consumption- facts and figures," Energy Bulletin,
      Sohbet Karbuz, May 21, 2007, http://www.energybulletin.net/
      node/29925

146   ARPANET, Wikipedia, http://en.wikipedia.org/wiki/ARPANET

147   Robert Redlinger, "Throwing Away the Crystal Ball—Thriving in an
      Uncertain Energy Future," Chevron Energy Solutions presentation,
      August 7, 2006

148   "Powering America's Defense: Energy and the Risks to National
      Security," Center for Naval Analyses (CNA) Military Advisory Board,
      May 2009, accessed at http://www.cna.org/nationalsecurity/energy/

149   "Obama Shines Light on Air Force's Super Solar Array," Wired, May
      27, 2009, http://www.wired.com/dangerroom/2009/05/obama-
      shines-light-on-air-forces-super-solar-array/

150   "Army Launches New Energy Initiatives, Test Projects," Army.
      Mil News Release, Oct 6 2008, http://www.army.mil/-
      newsreleases/2008/10/06/13073-army-launches-new-energy-
      initiatives-test-projects-at-posts/

151   "Lockheed, Starwood Team up to Provide Solar Thermal Power in
      Arizona," Cleantech Group, May 22, 2009, http://cleantech.com/
      news/4492/starwood-energy-lockheed-team-provi

152   Lockheed-Martin Corporation, 2008 Annual Report

153   "List of United States Military Bases," http://en.wikipedia.org/wiki/
      List_of_United_States_military_bases

154   "Base Structure Report – Fiscal Year 2008 Baseline," United States
      Department of Defense

155   "Fluor Wins contract for eSolar 46 MW CSP Plant,"
      RenewableEnergy.com, August 27, 2009, accessed from http://www.
      renewableenergyworld.com/rea/news/article/2009/08/fluor-wins-
      contract-for-46-mw-esolar-csp-plant

156   "Military Budget of The United States," in Wikipedia, http://
      en.wikipedia.org/wiki/Military_budget_of_the_United_States

157   Photo by: Michael Kaufman, Feb 9, 2008, Copyright permission:
      http://en.wikipedia.org/wiki/File:KKP_Auslauf.jpg

158   "District Heating". In Wikipedia, http://en.wikipedia.org/wiki/
      District_heating

159   "District Heating," University of Rochester Energy Library, accessed
       July 20, 2009 at http://www.energy.rochester.edu/dh/

160   "New York City steam system." Wikipedia, 11 Jul 2009, http://
       en.wikipedia.org/wiki/New_York_City_steam_system

161   Source: http://en.wikipedia.org/wiki/File:Steam_Rising_from_New_
       York_City_Streets.JPG

162   Patrick Lamers, "Strategies for the Deployment of District Cooling,"
       Euroheat & Power Conference June 5, 2008

163   "Cooling with Solar Heat – Growing Interest in Solar Air
       Conditioning," *The Solar Server*, Dec 2008, http://www.solarserver.de/
       solarmagazin/artikeljuni2002-e.html

164   "Thermally Activated Technologies: Absorption Heat Pumps,"
       Distributed Energy Resources, U.S. Department of Energy

165   "Thermally Activated Technologies: Absorption Heat Pumps,"
       Distributed Energy Resources, U.S. Department of Energy

166   "District Heating and Cooling – A Vision Towards 2020—2030—
       2050," *DHC+ Technology Platform*, May 2009, at www.dhcplus.eu

167   "Chiller Market Grows, Diversifies," *The ACHR News*, Feb 18, 2008,
       http://www.achrnews.com/Articles/Feature_Article/BNP_GUID_9-5-
       2006_A_10000000000000263347

168   "Electricity Rate Comparison State by State" for July 2008, Nebraska
       Energy Office, (updated Oct 2008) http://www.neo.ne.gov/
       statshtml/115.htm

169   "Average Electric Rates for Hawaiian Electric Co., Maui Electric Co.
       and Hawaii Electric Light Co.," Hawaiian Electric Company, http://
       www.heco.com/portal/site/heco/menuitem.508576f78baa14340b4c0
       610c510b1ca/?vgnextoid=692e5e658e0fc010VgnVCM1000008119f
       ea9RCRD&vgnextchannel=10629349798b4110VgnVCM1000005c0
       11bacRCRD&vgnextfmt=defau&vgnextrefresh=1&level=0&ct=article

170   Energy Information Administration – Official Energy Statistics from
       the U.S. Government, http://tonto.eia.doe.gov/state/state_energy_
       profiles.cfm?sid=HI

171   "Average Electric Rates for Hawaiian Electric Co., Maui Electric Co.
       and Hawaii Electric Light Co.," Hawaiian Electric Company, http://
       www.heco.com/portal/site/heco/menuitem.508576f78baa14340b4c0
       610c510b1ca/?vgnextoid=692e5e658e0fc010VgnVCM1000008119f
       ea9RCRD&vgnextchannel=10629349798b4110VgnVCM1000005c0
       11bacRCRD&vgnextfmt=defau&vgnextrefresh=1&level=0&ct=article

172   United Nations Education Scientific and Cultural Organization
       (UNESCO) World Water Assessment Programme http://www.unesco.
       org/water/wwap/facts_figures/water_energy.shtml

173   "China's Growing Cell Phone Market," *PC World*, May 29, 2009,
      at http://www.pcworld.com/article/132307/chinas_growing_cell_
      phone_market.html

174   "Banking for the Poor," Grameen Bank, http://www.grameen-info.org/
      index.php?option=com_content&task=view&id=177&Itemid=182

175   "Muhammad Yunnus: MicroCredit Missionary," *Business Week*,
      December 20, 2005, at http://www.nextbillion.net/news/microcredit-
      missionary

176   "Muhammad Yunnus: MicroCredit Missionary," *Business Week*,
      December 20, 2005, at http://www.nextbillion.net/news/microcredit-
      missionary

177   "The Nobel Peace Price for 2006" The Nobel Foundation. NobelPrize.
      com , http://nobelprize.org/nobel_prizes/peace/laureates/2006/press.
      html

178   Grameen Shakti, http://www.gshakti.org/chart/2.html

179   Grameen Shakti "At A Glance March 2009," http://www.gshakti.org/
      glance.html

180   "Grameen Shakti Brings Sustainable Development Closer to Reality
      in Bangladesh" , GreenBiz.com, January 21, 2009, http://www.
      greenbiz.com/blog/2009/01/21/grameen-shakti

181   Grameen Shakti "At A Glance March 2009," http://www.gshakti.org/
      glance.html

182   United Nations Education Scientific and Cultural Organization
      (UNESCO) World Water Assessment Programme http://www.unesco.
      org/water/wwap/facts_figures/water_energy.shtml

183   Grameen Shakti "At A Glance March 2009," http://www.gshakti.org/
      glance.html

184   "Zayed Future Energy Prize Recognizes Dipal C. Barua," Reuters,
      January 19, 2009, http://www.reuters.com/article/pressRelease/
      idUS154081+19-Jan-2009+PRN20090119

185   "GE Plunges into Solar Water Heater Market," *Contractor Magazine*,
      accessed July 16, 2009 at http://contractormag.com/green-
      contracting/ge_plunges_solar/

186   "90% Of Israeli Homes Have Solar Water Heaters," Environmental
      News Network, July 7, 2008, http://www.enn.com/energy/
      article/37584

187   "The Residential Water Heater Market 2006," *Kema Report* #E06-158,
      July13, 2006

188   "Mars Exploration Rover." Wikipedia,18 Jul 2009, http://en.wikipedia.
      org/wiki/Mars_Exploration_Rover

189   U.S. Department of Energy, "Light and the PV Cell," http://www1.
      eere.energy.gov/solar/printable_versions/pv_cell_light.html

190   U.S. Department of Energy, "Light and the PV Cell," http://www1.
      eere.energy.gov/solar/printable_versions/pv_cell_light.html

191   Tony Seba, *Winners Take All – 9 Fundamental Rules of High Tech
      Strategy*, 2006

192   "Lightening The Load," *The Wall Street Journal*, October 6, 2008,
      http://online.wsj.com/article/SB122305854616202945.html

193   "So Much for 'Energy Independence'," Robert Bryce, *The Wall Street
      Journal*, July 7, 2009

194   "The Economics of Climate Change," *Stern Review* http://webarchive.
      nationalarchives.gov.uk/+/http://www.hm-treasury.gov.uk/
      independent_reviews/stern_review_economics_climate_change/stern_
      review_report.cfm

195   "Global PV Market Perspective," *Solar&Energy*, June 1, 2009 (http://
      www.solarnenergy.com/eng/intro/)

196   "Photovoltaics." Wikipedia, accessed 31 Jul 2009, at http://
      en.wikipedia.org/wiki/Photovoltaics

197   "Global PV Market Perspective," *Solar&Energy*, June 1, 2009

198   "High Growth Reported for the Global Photovoltaic Industry,"
      Reuters Press Release, accessed July 11, 2009, http://www.reuters.
      com/article/pressRelease/idUS171170+03-Mar-2009+BW20090303

199   "High Growth Reported for the Global Photovoltaic Industry,"
      Reuters Press Release, accessed July 11, 2009, http://www.reuters.
      com/article/pressRelease/idUS171170+03-Mar-2009+BW20090303

200   PV Solar Electricity –A Future Major Technology," Dr.
      Winfried Hoffmann, presentation at Semicon 2007, July
      17th, 2007, San Francisco, accessed dom.semi.org/web/.../2-
      WinfriedHoffmannKeynote2007071.pdf

201   "Solar Generation — Solar Generation for Over One Billion People
      and Two Million Jobs by 2020," European Photovoltaics Association
      and Greenpeace, Sept 2006

202   "Bringing Sunlight Inside," *Science Daily*, May 1, 2007, Retrieved from
      http://www.sciencedaily.com/videos/2007/0507-bringing_sunlight_
      inside.htm

203   "Global PV Market Perspective," *Solar&Energy*, June 1, 2009

204   Nick Hodge, "Solar Energy Technology – Investing in BIPV
      Companies," SeekinAlpha.com, at http://seekingalpha.com/
      article/65138-solar-energy-technology-investing-in-bipv-companies

205 "Outside summer, inside winter: Indoor Dubai resort lets you ski when," *Deseret News* (Salt Lake City), July 23, 2009, at http://findarticles.com/p/articles/mi_qn4188/is_20090723/ai_n32182597/

206 "World air conditioner market continued to expand in 2006," *Refrige.com*, February 15, 2007, accessed July 31, 2009 at http://www.refrige.com/february-2007/world-air-conditioner-market-continued-to-expand-in-2006/menu-id-2637.html

207 "Central Air Conditioners: Full Report," ConsumerSearch.com, April 2008, http://www.consumersearch.com/central-air-conditioners/central-ac-pricing

208 "Facilities and energy management company reveals secrets of success at new trade show in Dubai," AMInfo, April 18, 2006, http://www.ameinfo.com/83347.html

209 "President Obama touts solar plant in Central Florida," *Miami Herald*, October 28, 2009, http://www.miamiherald.com/news/florida/story/1304127.html

210 "How long can you survive without water?," Survival Topics, at http://www.survivaltopics.com/survival/how-long-can-you-survive-without-water/

211 "Ogallala Aquifer." Wikipedia, accessed 13 Apr 2009 http://en.wikipedia.org/w/index.php?title=Ogallala_Aquifer&oldid=282311646

212 "Water," Appalachian Center for the Economy and the Environment, http://www.appalachian-center.org/issues/water/index.html

213 "China Water Crisis," (2009, August 7). In Wikipedia, retrieved from http://en.wikipedia.org/wiki/China_water_crisis#World_Bank_forecasts

214 "Ogallala Aquifer." Wikipedia, accessed 13 Apr 2009 http://en.wikipedia.org/w/index.php?title=Ogallala_Aquifer&oldid=282311646

215 *Scientific American*, October 2008 Special Issue, "Energy versus Water: Solving Both Crises Together," http://www.sciam.com/article.cfm?id=the-future-of-fuel

216 "California's Water – Energy Relationship," California Energy Commission, Final Staff Report, CEC-700-2005-011-SF, November 2005

217 Smarter Water Use on Your Farm or Ranch," Sustainable Agriculture Research and Education, http://www.sare.org/publications/water/index.htm

218   "Atacama Desert," (2009, May 12). In Wikipedia, accessed 20:32, May
      13, 2009, from http://en.wikipedia.org/w/index.php?title=Atacama_
      Desert&oldid=289463540

219   Laurie Stone, "Clean Water from the Sun," 1993, at http://www.
      ibiblio.org/london/renewable-energy/solar/general-info/msg00383.
      html

220   Peter Gleick, *The World's Water 2008-2009 – The Biennial Report on
      Freshwater Resources*, Data-Table 22, Island Press, 2009

221   "Australia Rice Production Hits 80-year low," May 23, 2008, *Oryza*,
      http://oryza.com/Asia-Pacific/Australia-Market/8561.html

222   "Australia's Dry Run," *National Geographic*, April 2009

223   Arjen Hoekstra, "A Comprehensive Introduction to Water Footprints,"
      Water Footprint Network, at http://www.waterfootprint.org

224   "Sucking California Dry," *The Science Monitor*, March 7, 2003, at
      http://www.encyclopedia.com/doc/1G1-98541298.html

225   "California Rice Statistics and Related National and International
      Data," Statistical Report, California Rice Commission, Oct 2, 2007

226   "California's Contaminated Groundwater: Is the State minding the
      Store?," Natural Resources Defense Council, retrieved June 28, 2009,
      from http://www.nrdc.org/water/pollution/ccg/execsum.asp

227   "Desalination Plant is Approved," *The New York Times*, May 14, 2009,
      http://www.nytimes.com/2009/05/14/science/earth/14aquifer.html?_
      r=1&scp=3&sq=desalination&st=cse

228   World Bank, "Seawater and Brackish Water Desalination in the Middle
      East North Africa and Central Asia," Final Report, December 2004

229   Union of Concerned Scientists, http://www.ucsusa.org/clean_energy/
      coalvswind/c02d.html

230   Franz Trieb et al, "AQUA-CSP - Concentrating Solar Power for Water
      Desalination," Final Report, German Aerospace Center, DLR, Institute
      of Technical Thermodynamics, Stuttgart, Germany, November 2007

231   "Perth Metropolitan Desalination Proposal – Water Quality
      Management, Change to Implementation Conditions." Environmental
      Protection Authority, Perth, Western Australia Report 1327 May 2009

232   "Tapping The Oceans," *The Economist Technology Quarterly*, June 7,
      2008

233   Al Shindagah, "Modernity and Tradition in Dubain Architecture,"
      Luiza Karim, Sept 1999, from http://www.alshindagah.com/
      september99/architecture.htm

234 "Dubai demand increase outstrips desalination supply.," *Desalination and Water ReUse*, March 31, 2009, http://www.desalination.biz/news/news_story.asp?id=4806

235 Dubai 2008 Report, Oxford Business Group, http://www.oxfordbusinessgroup.com/publication.asp?country=16

236 World Bank, "Seawater and Brackish Water Desalination in the Middle East North Africa and Central Asia," Final Report, December 2004

237 Franz Trieb et al, "AQUA-CSP - Concentrating Solar Power for Water Desalination," Final Report, German Aerospace Center, DLR, Institute of Technical Thermodynamics, Stuttgart, Germany, November 2007

238 "How much water is there on earth?," How Stuff Works, at http://science.howstuffworks.com/question157.htm

239 International Water Management Institute, Annual Report 2006/2007, http://www.iwmi.cgiar.org/About_IWMI/Strategic_Documents/Annual_Reports/2006_2007/theme1.html

240 Franz Trieb et al, "AQUA-CSP - Concentrating Solar Power for Water Desalination," Final Report, German Aerospace Center, DLR, Institute of Technical Thermodynamics, Stuttgart, Germany, November 2007

241 "Seawater Desalination with the power of CSP," CSP Today, May 20, 2009, http://social.csptoday.com/content/depth-seawater-desalination-within-power-csp

242 "Thermal Energy Conversion of Nuclear Fuels," U.S. Energy Information Administration (EIA), http://www.eia.doe.gov/cneaf/nuclear/page/uran_enrich_fuel/convert.html

243 "Coal to Electricity Energy Transfer," U.S. Department of Energy, Ask A Scientist ©, Environmental Earth Science Archive, at http://www.newton.dep.anl.gov/askasci/eng99/eng99187.htm

244 "The Connection: Water and Energy Security," Institute for the Analysis of Energy Security, http://www.iags.org/n0813043.htm, accessed July 6th, 2009

245 "The World Water Crisis," World Water Day 2009, http://www.worldwaterday.net/index.cfm?objectid=E39A970B-F1F6-6035-B9F75093B863ED13, accessed June 4th, 2009

246 "The World Water Crisis," World Water Day 2009, http://www.worldwaterday.net/index.cfm?objectid=E39A970B-F1F6-6035-B9F75093B863ED13, accessed June 4th, 2009

247 "CNN Innovators – Susan Murcott," MIT Tech TV , at http://techtv.mit.edu/collections/h2o-1b/videos/469-cnn-innovators---susan-murcott , accessed June 4th, 2009

248   "Ultraviolet Germicidal Irradiation," Wikipedia, http://
      en.wikipedia.org/w/index.php?title=Ultraviolet_Germicidal_
      Irradiation&oldid=75437165, accessed June 4, 2009

249   "Ultraviolet Germicidal Irradiation," Wikipedia, http://
      en.wikipedia.org/w/index.php?title=Ultraviolet_Germicidal_
      Irradiation&oldid=75437165, accessed June 4, 2009

250   Source: Solvatten website: http://www.solvatten.se/SOLVATTEN/
      Start.html (Copyright Solvatten).

251   "Sana'a." Wikipedia, retrieved July 28, 2009, at http://en.wikipedia.
      org/wiki/Sana'a

252   "Water for Sana'a and Taiz'z from Solar Desalination at the Red Sea,"
      prepared by the Trans-Mediterranean Renewable Energy Cooperation
      (TREC), Sana'a/Hamburg, November 20th, 2006

253   "China Faces a Water Crisis," *Business Week*, April 15, 2009,
      http://www.businessweek.com/globalbiz/content/apr2009/
      gb20090415_032220.htm

254   "China Water Crisis" Wikipedia, retrieved from http://en.wikipedia.
      org/wiki/China_water_crisis#World_Bank_forecasts

255   "Concentrating Solar Power for Water Desalination," Franz Trieb,
      German Aerospace Center DLR, Stuttgart, Germany

256   "Israel's Desalination Plants Make Up Water Shortages," *Israel New
      Tech*, accessed Aug 6, 2009, http://www.israelnewtech.gov.il/?Categor
      yID=166&ArticleID=31&sng=1

257   "El Sistema Eléctrico Español – Avance del Informe 2008," Red
      Eléctrica de España, December 19, 2008

258   "El Sistema Eléctrico Español – Avance del Informe 2008," Red
      Eléctrica de España, December 19, 2008 (p.4)

259   "Today's Outlook," California Independent Systems Operator, http://
      www.caiso.com/outlook/outlook.html retrieved June 21, 2009.
      Copyright California ISO @2009.

260   Tennesse Valley Authority, Hydro-electric Power, http://www.tva.gov/
      power/pumpstorart.htm , accessed June 4, 2009

261   "Pumped Storage Hydroelectricity," Wikipedia, http://en.wikipedia.
      org/wiki/Pumped_storage, accessed June 4, 2009

262   "Pumped Storage Hydroelectricity," Wikipedia, http://en.wikipedia.
      org/wiki/Pumped_storage, accessed June 4, 2009

263   U.S. Energy Information Agency, *Annual Energy Review*, 2007, p. 226

264   "10 Years, 430 Dams," *The New York Times*—Editorial, July 7, 2009,
      http://www.nytimes.com/2009/07/04/opinion/04sat3.html

265   The Solar Project, Wikipedia, , http://en.wikipedia.org/wiki/Solar_
      Two

266   "Solar Power and Salt Batteries," *Energy Matters*, December 29, 2008,
      http://www.energymatters.com.au/index.php?main_page=news_
      article&article_id=263

267   Potassium Nitrate, Wikipedia, http://en.wikipedia.org/wiki/
      Potassium_nitrate , retrieved June 21, 2009

268   Photo from Wikipedia: http://en.wikipedia.org/wiki/The_Solar_
      Project#Solar_One

269   Ignacio Ortega et al, "Central Receiver System (CRS) Solar Power
      Plant Using Molten Salt as Heat Transfer Fluid." in *The Journal of Solar
      Energy Engineering*, May 2008, http://scitation.aip.org/getabs/servlet/
      GetabsServlet?prog=normal&id=JSEEDO000130000002024501000
      001&idtype=cvips&gifs=yes

270   "Wind Turbine Design Cost and Scaling Model," National Renewable
      Energy Laboratory, Technical Report, NREL/TP-500-40566,
      December 2006

271   "Best Buy to Sell Green Vehicles," *The Wall Street Journal*, July 6,
      2009.

272   "The Truth about Cars," *Market Share*, June 2008, http://www.
      thetruthaboutcars.com/june-2008-market-share/

273   "Grid 2030 – A National Vision for Electricity's Second 100 Years,"
      U.S. Department of Energy – Office of Electric Transmission and
      Distribution, July 2003

274   "For a Smart Grid Look to Smart States," Jesse Berst, *Solar Today*, May
      2009.

275   "Grid 2030 – A National Vision for Electricity's Second 100 years,"
      U.S. Department of Energy – Office of Electric Transmission and
      Distribution, July 2003

276   "Detroitosaurus Wreck – The Decline and Fall of GM," *The Economist*,
      June 4, 2009, at http://www.economist.com/opinion/displaystory.
      cfm?story_id=13783014 , accessed on June 6, 2009

277   "King Coal losing its power" in *China Daily*, http://www2.chinadaily.
      com.cn/bizchina/2009-02/16/content_7478767.htm , accessed June
      6, 2009

278   Energy Information Administration – Official Statistics for the United
      States Government – Data for 2007 at http://tonto.eia.doe.gov/ask/
      electricity_faqs.asp

279   "Tesla Roadster," Wikipedia, The Free Encyclopedia, http://
      en.wikipedia.org/wiki/Tesla_Roadster

280   "How it Works: The Drivetrain," *Popular Mechanics*, December 2004, at http://www.popularmechanics.com/automotive/new_cars/1302716.html?page=1

281   "Quels seront les carburants de demain pour nos voitures?," *NaturaVox.com*, February 9, 2009, at http://www.naturavox.fr/Quels-seront-les-carburants-de-demain-pour-nos-voitures,5568.html

282   "ElectricVehicle," Wikpedia, http://en.wikipedia.org/wiki/Electric_vehicle

283   "Developing World's Energy Needs Set Stage for Fight," *The Washington Post*, Sept 8, 2009, at http://www.washingtonpost.com/wp-dyn/content/article/2009/09/08/AR2009090804019.html?hpid=topnews

284   "Rolling Blackout," Wikipedia, http://en.wikipedia.org/wiki/Rolling_blackout#India

285   Powershop website: http://www.powershop.co.nz

286   "Mobile Phones," Wikipedia, http://en.wikipedia.org/wiki/Mobile_phone retrieved June 21, 2009

287   "The Smart Grid – An Introduction," prepared for the U.S. Department of Energy by Litos Strategic Communication under contract No. DE-AC26-04NT41817, Subtask 560.01.04

288   Automobile. (2008, December 16). In Wikipedia, Retrieved 02:19, December 16, 2008, from http://en.wikipedia.org/w/index.php?title=Automobile&oldid=258241770

289   "George B. Selden.," in Wikipedia, http://en.wikipedia.org/wiki/George_Baldwin_Selden , December 15, 2008

290   "IBM Working on Battery Breakthrough," ComputerWorld, June 23, 2009, http://www.computerworld.com/action/article.do?command=viewArticleBasic&articleId=9134731

291   "The Smart Grid – An Emerging Option," Joe Miller, Modern Grid Team, Funded by Department of Energy, Conducted by National Energy Technology Laboratory, Dec 10, 2008

292   "The 2003 Northeast Blackout—Five Years Later," *Scientific American*, August 13, 2008, accessed at http://www.sciam.com/article.cfm?id=2003-blackout-five-years-later

293   *The Green Grid: Energy Savings and Carbon Emissions Reductions Enabled by a Smart Grid.* EPRI, Palo Alto, CA: 2008. 1016905

294   "Understanding the Smart Grid," Joe Miller, Modern Grid Team, Funded by Department of Energy, Conducted by National Energy Technology Laboratory, July 15, 2008

295   "Grid 2030 – A National Vision for Electricity's Second 100 years,"
      U.S. Department of Energy – Office of Electric Transmission and
      Distribution, July 2003

296   "What's Wrong with the Electric Grid," *The Industrial Physicist*,
      October/November 2003, at http://www.aip.org/tip/INPHFA/vol-9/
      iss-5/p8.html

297   "Utility investment in grid remains strong," Utlilities Online, July 7th,
      2009, http://uaelp.pennnet.com/display_article/365971/22/ARTCL/
      none/none/1/Study:-Utility-investment-in-smart-grid-remains-strong/

298   "The Electricity Economy—New Opportunities from the
      Transformation of the Electric Power Sector," Global Environment
      Fund, August 2008

299   "Options Choices Decision – Understanding The Options for Making
      Decisions about New Zealand's Electricity Future," Meridian Energy,
      Strategy Directorate

300   "Trans-Mediterranean Interconnection for Concentrating Solar
      Power" Final Report, German Aerospace Center (DLR), Institute of
      Technical Thermodynamics, Section Systems Analysis and Technology
      Assessment, April 2006

301   "Trans-Mediterranean Interconnection for Concentrating Solar
      Power" Final Report, German Aerospace Center (DLR), Institute of
      Technical Thermodynamics, Section Systems Analysis and Technology
      Assessment, April 2006

302   Trans-Mediterranean Interconnection for Concentrating Solar
      Power" Final Report, German Aerospace Center (DLR), Institute of
      Technical Thermodynamics, Section Systems Analysis and Technology
      Assessment, April 2006

303   "FPL, Miami-Dade County Announce $200M Smart Grid
      Project," *Environmental Leader*, http://www.environmentalleader.
      com/2009/04/21/fpl-miami-dade-county-announce-200m-smart-grid-
      project/

304   "BGE proposes smart grid initiative," *The Baltimore Sun*, July 13, 2009,
      accessed July 13th 2009, http://www.baltimoresun.com/business/bal-
      bge0713,0,1976055.story

305   David Leeds, "The Smart Grid in 2010: Market Segments,
      Applications, and Industry Players," July 13, 2009, *Greentech Media*, at
      http://www.gtmresearch.com/report/smart-grid-in-2010

306   "Miami Smart-Grid Project Powers Expectations For Clean Energy,"
      CNBC.com, April 20, 2009, http://www.cnbc.com/id/30307227

307   "GE Sees $4B Potential in Smart Grids," *Environmental Leader*, April
      28, 2009, http://www.environmentalleader.com/2009/04/28/ge-sees-
      4b-potential-in-smart-grids/

308   "Miami Smart-Grid Project Powers Expectations For Clean Energy,"
      CNBC.com, April 20, 2009, http://www.cnbc.com/id/30307227

309   "Cisco Adding Brains to Power System's Brawn," Cisco 'Feature Story'
      and Q&A, May 18, 2009, http://newsroom.cisco.com/dlls/2009/
      ts_051809.html

310   "The Smart Grid – An Emerging Option," Joe Miller, Modern Grid
      Team, Funded by Department of Energy, Conducted by National
      Energy Technology Laboratory, Dec 10, 2008

311   "Grid 2030 – A National Vision for Electricity's second 100 years,"
      U.S. Department of Energy – Office of Electric Transmission and
      Distribution," July 2003

312   "DOE Issues Rules for $3.9B in Smart Grid Stimulus Grants,"
      Greentech Media, June 25, 2009, http://www.greentechmedia.com/
      articles/read/doe-issues-rules-for-3.9b-in-smart-grid-stimulus-grants/

313   Greg Kolb et al, "Heliostat Cost Reduction Study," Sandia National
      Laboratories, Report SAND2007-3293, June 2007, p. 24

314   "Assessment of Parabolic Trough and Power Tower Technology and
      Performance Forecasts," Sargent & Lundy, 2003

315   Greg Kolb et al, "Heliostat Cost Reduction Study," Sandia National
      Laboratories, Report SAND2007-3293, June 2007, p. 24

316   Wikipedia, http://en.wikipedia.org/wiki/Heliostat, Dec 6, 2008.

317   Photo from Wikipedia: http://en.wikipedia.org/wiki/The_Solar_
      Project#Solar_One

318   "How LPT Works," from Brightsource Energy's website at http://
      www.brightsourceenergy.com/technology/how_lpt_works#heliostats

319   "Harnessing the Sun" in Walter Hines Page et al., *The World's Work
      – A History of Our Time*, Volume I, November 1900 – April 1901,
      Doubleday, Page, and Company, New York

320   "Harnessing the Sun" in Walter Hines Page et al., *The World's Work
      – A History of Our Time*, Volume I, November 1900 – April 1901,
      Doubleday, Page, and Company, New York

321   Travis Bradford, *Solar Revolution – The Economic Transformation of the
      Global Energy Industry*, The MIT Press, 2006

322   Travis Bradford, Solar Revolution – *The Economic Transformation of the
      Global Energy Industry*, The MIT Press, 2006

323   James Pacheco et al, "Summary of Solar Two Test Evaluation Programs," Sandia National Laboratories, Albuquerque, NM, February 2000

324   Greg Kolb et al, "Heliostat Cost Reduction Study," Sandia National Laboratories, Report SAND2007-3293, June 2007

325   Rebecca Henderson and Kim B. Clark, "Architectural Innovation: The Reconfiguration Of Existing Product Technologies and the Failure of Established Firms," *Administrative Science Quarterly*, Mar 1990

326   eSolar website: http://www.esolar.com/solution.html

327   "Radian," Wikipedia, http://en.wikipedia.org/wiki/Radian

328   BMW Website: http://www.bmw.com/com/en/newvehicles/7series/sedan/2008/allfacts/design/exterieur.html

INDEX

Made in the USA
Charleston, SC
29 March 2012